WHAT IT MEANS TO

D0454734

WHAT IT MEANS TO BE DADDY

Fatherhood for Black Men Living
Away from Their Children

Jennifer Hamer

COLUMBIA UNIVERSITY PRESS
NEW YORK

COLUMBIA UNIVERSITY PRESS

Publishers Since 1893

New York   Chichester, West Sussex

Copyright © 2001 Columbia University Press

All rights reserved

Library of Congress Cataloging-in-Publication Data

Hamer, Jennifer.

What it means to be daddy : fatherhood for Black men living away from their children /
Jennifer Hamer.

p. cm.

Includes bibliographical references and index.

ISBN 0–231–11554–7 (cloth : alk. paper) — ISBN 0–231–11555–5 (pbk. : alk. paper)

1. Afro-American fathers. 2. Afro-American fathers—Psychology. 3. Absentee fathers—
United States. 4. Afro-American families. 5. Afro-American families—History. 6. Fatherless
families—United States. 7. Fatherhood—Social aspects—United States. 8. Afro-Americans—
Social conditions—1975– I. Title.

E185.86 .H28 2001

306.874'2—dc21

00–064546

Designed by Lisa Hamm

c 10 9 8 7 6 5 4 3 2 1

p 10 9 8 7 6 5 4 3 2 1

To my son, Nile

CONTENTS

Acknowledgments
ix

Introduction:
Fathers' Lives in Context
1

PART 1: THE WORLD IN WHICH BLACK FATHERS LIVE
1. "There's No Such Thing as a Good Black Father":
Standards of Fatherhood
17
2. Slavery, Civil War, and Reconstruction:
Creating a Context for Black Live-Away Fatherhood
33
3. "Times Are Just Going to Get Worse . . .":
Fathers Chasing the American Dream
53

PART 2: EXPECTATIONS OF OTHERS
4. "Just Be There for the Baby":
What Fathers Say Others Expect
77
5. "Black Men Can Do Better":
What Mothers Say Fathers Do for Their Children
102

PART 3: BEING FATHERS

6. What Fathers Say They Do as Daddies

131

7. Live-Away, but Absent?

151

8. "Ain't Nothing Like Trying to be a Father and
Trying to be a Man": Barriers to Being Daddy

176

Conclusion: "Got to Make Fatherhood Work for Us"—The Meaning
of Fatherhood for Black Men Who Do Not Live with Their Children

199

Notes

221

Bibliography

235

Index

247

ACKNOWLEDGMENTS

I would like to thank everyone who provided assistance and support. First of all, a thank you to my dissertation committee, Norval Glenn, Ruth McRoy, Ronald Angel, and Christine Williams, for reviewing and commenting on the earliest versions of this manuscript. Norval Glenn in particular was a part of the writing process from its inception. His thought-provoking questions and distinct objectivity made my arguments sharper, and his efforts went far beyond what I ever expected. More importantly, his words were constant reminders of the importance of this work for families and family studies. This completed project is undoubtedly a product of his tutelage and his faith in my abilities. Steve Hansen and Hugh Barlow, both senior faculty at Southern Illinois University at Edwardsville, encouraged me to develop my dissertation into a book and then guided me through the process of learning to successfully balance the requirements of teaching and scholarship. The Department of Sociology at Southern Illinois University collectively developed a teaching schedule that enabled me to devote a maximum amount of time to the project. Tenured faculty in the department are expressly committed to the success of junior colleagues and have created an inviting, mentoring environment that encouraged me to pursue and complete this and other projects with full endorsement and in my own time. Linda Markowitz, a friend and colleague, also read early drafts of the manuscript and related funding proposals. Helen Neville, professor of psychology, University of Missouri, Columbia, provided a careful critique of portions of the manuscript that clarified and sharpened its theoretical assumptions. Herbert Lomax's insight as a parent and social work professional contributed greatly to the development of my survey instruments. A special thank you to Delores Lang Patton (my mother-in-law), whose understanding of the single-parent experience challenged me to reassess my interpretations of custodial mother and noncustodial father relationships. My graduate assistants Kate Marchioro and Faith Berry Barnes offered invaluable assistance by reviewing literature, collecting data, editing, and always being available at the last minute. Juliet E. K. Walker, Professor of History, University of Illinois-Urbana, provided sound advice about publishing that guided me throughout the writing process. Venessa Brown's friendship has always provided me with inspiration and social support. Our discussions always reminded me of the relationship between theory and application, and between sociology and social work, and keeps much of my work on the fence, contributing to both disciplines.

Thanks also to my editor John Michel of Columbia University Press for his interest in this study, for holding my hand throughout, and for warmly relaxing the deadlines. Thanks as well to his assistants Alexander Thorp and Karen Brissette, and to Roy Thomas, who guided the book through production. Joan McQuary, also of Columbia University Press, with an eye for detail thoroughly edited the manuscript and did a tremendous job of adding necessary clarity and consistency to the work. Also, thanks to Robert Staples for a partial review of the manuscript and for comments that encouraged me to be more critical of my own work. The ideas and comments of all those above are reflected all through the book. I hope I have lived up to their standards and expectations.

This project also received financial support. Partial collection of the data for this book was made possible by a 1997 Southern Illinois University Summer Research Fellowship. Additionally, Rudy Wilson and the Office of Cultural Diversity at Southern Illinois University provided funding for the final stages of data analysis and writing.

Certainly this study would not have been possible without the fathers and mothers who gave me their time and shared their life stories and experiences. I have attempted to maintain their anonymity by removing, modifying, and/or transposing all identifying information. However, I hope they will feel that I have captured the essence of what they were trying to convey. Moreover, I hope their words will help others in similar circumstances to better understand their own lives.

In many ways this book has been a family project. My grandmother Frieda Lewis, my parents Johnnie and Elsie Hamer, my sisters Frieda and Stephanie, and my brothers Mark and Lawrence and their partners Khadeja and Sonnie, respectively, all contributed in one way or another. They provided loving care to my son Nile on weekends and during weeks in the summer when I needed to focus my energies on writing and deadlines. As I drafted these acknowledgments, I began to reflect upon all the sacrifices incurred by myself and my family while I worked on this book. Weeks and weekends of collecting and analyzing data led me to miss many family birthdays and holidays—events at which we traditionally come together, celebrate, and reinforce our commitment and love for one another. I missed my niece Rabha's graduation. I have missed my parents' anniversary for the past three years and my nephew Regge's first track meet. I have never seen my niece Brianna tap dance or perform ballet. I was hundreds of miles away when my brother witnessed the birth of his firstborn child Lily, named after our paternal grandmother. Even though I have found great joy in this work, I regret each and every one of those special days that I chose to spend time on work, instead of with family. Yet everyone respected these decisions and encouraged me to work on the manuscript even though it sadly meant my absence. I cannot thank them enough for their patience, love, and understanding. What I know about families begins and ends with them.

This latter sentiment also applies to my partner in life, Clarence Lang. He has my deepest gratitude. He reviewed several drafts of each chapter as well as edited and offered extensive comments. His crystalline and constructive criticisms helped me to sharpen my understanding of class, gender, and race as they each relate to analyses of family life. He did all of this while managing his own work, sharing household responsibilities, and parenting. Most important, I would like to thank him for constant warm encouragement, emotional support, companionship, caring, and love.

Last but not least, thank you to my son Nile, for wanting to learn more about "what daddies do" and for being patient while I sought to find the answers.

WHAT IT MEANS TO BE DADDY

INTRODUCTION
Fathers' Lives in Context

*T*his book is about low-income black fathers in America who, for one reason or another, live separate and away from their children. These men are a notorious group. They are often publicly portrayed as unemployed, uneducated, and unwilling to provide or take responsibility for the children they are thought to heedlessly produce. As Hall suggests, "they are considered somewhat like phantoms or villains and alleged to have demonstrated little or no real feelings for their families' well-being" (Hall 1981:159). Yet, much of what the public assumes about the attitudes and behaviors of black fathers is predicated on a tangle of myth and nonempirical lore. Furthermore, this common wisdom tends to be grounded on the perceptions of social workers, custodial mothers, and social scientific interpretations of the words and experiences they offer.

The past two decades have witnessed a growing interest in manhood and fatherhood studies. Additionally, recent dramatic changes in welfare policy require noncustodial fathers to be more accountable for the children they produce. Yet despite these emphases, the parenthood experiences of adult black, never-married fathers who do not live with their children remain a neglected area of study in family research. *What It Means to Be Daddy* fills this void. This is a book constructed on the words of black fathers. Chapters and categories emanate from the rich descriptions men generously provided about their fatherhood. It is their thoughts about parenthood, work, relationships, and everyday life that are the foundation of all discussion. Resolute and poignant, they tell us that African American live-away fathers are not as paternally callous as popular notions insinuate. Nor is their manhood and fatherhood as unidimensional as it may publicly appear. Indeed, learning about these men's lives is somewhat analogous to a journey through a Walter Mosley novel. The black male characters are complex and the life decisions they make are compounded by the range of human emotions they demonstrate. These fathers experience feelings of anger and love. They exhibit parental steadiness and devotion. They feel excitement and frustration. They are sensitive to pain and rejection. They express feelings of sorrow and joy. And most possess a desire to be good fathers to their children.[1]

Still, there is more to this story. The emotions, attitudes, and behaviors of black men can be understood and described only in relation to the broader meaning of fatherhood they mediate for themselves within their respective circumstances. This negotiation occurs as they interact with their children, others, and institutions in often hostile, hazy, and uncertain social and economic realms. Relative to other groups, African American men experience some of the nation's highest rates of physical illness, homicide, suicide, substance abuse, incarceration, unemployment, and underemployment. Meanwhile, over 40 percent of black children live below official poverty levels, a figure that has changed little in the past three decades. In essence, then, the obstacles and weighty dilemmas of life for black men are produced and sustained primarily by the structure of American society itself.[2]

It is this cognition that provides a general guideline for subsequent chapters of my book on African American live-away fatherhood. Each element of the story is an attempt to clarify and elucidate low-income black men's experiences, to place them in context of the world that surrounds them, and to provide a means by which family researchers, policy makers, and the general public can listen and learn from black fathers themselves. In turning the pages of this narrative one is likely to discover that the account of black live-away fatherhood is less a study of black men and poor families than a disquisition on the relationships between the economy, social relationships, and conjoining cultural ideals that make up the very fabric of our daily world.

THEORETICAL EXPLANATIONS OF
AFRICAN AMERICAN FAMILIAL EXPERIENCES

What do black live-away fathers "do" as fathers and how do we explain their behavior? This question and our concerns about African American families are not new. Since the turn of the century, black live-away fathers have often been crudely linked to and blamed for the disproportionate level of poverty and relative poor quality of life for African American women and their children. Indeed, statistics seem to confirm this assumption. Currently, 70.4 percent of all African American births are out of wedlock—the highest proportion ever recorded. Relative to other demographic groups, African American children in fatherless homes are currently the poorest of all. Since the mid 1970s approximately 50 percent of African American fatherless families have been poor. The well-being of African American children and their relation to fathers creates more alarm when we consider that if current trends continue, over 85 percent of African American children will spend some portion of their childhood "fatherless."[3]

Researchers, policy makers, and the general public commonly assume that the full-time presence of the fathers in the lives of black children will break the cycle of poverty and mediate the detrimental effects of single-parent households. Thus, for decades upon decades many have attempted to explain poverty by showing its relation to "fatherlessness." Social scientists have traditionally poked and prodded in black communities in an attempt to understand and explain the psyches and behaviors of men and women in live-away father, custodial mother family forms.

Sites of study, sample population sizes, race and gender of the researchers, among other variables, have all varied over time. However, queries and studies of the values, attitudes, behaviors, and familial forms of black American family life have tended to take one of three perspectives. One of the earliest developed perspectives assumes that black family experiences are due to customs and behaviors that can be directly linked to their African cultural heritage. In other words, to explain contemporary familial attitudes and familial behaviors one must look to past and present West African societies. The work of W. E. B. DuBois, Melville Herskovitz, Niara Sudarkasa, Wade Nobles, and Andrew Billingsley, among others, provide support for this interpretation of African American family life. From their perspective, black family structure, customs, attitudes, and values are unique from other demographic groups. Moreover, they are vestiges of an African past adapted to historical racial hostility and discrimination experienced in the United States. In recent years, Antonio McDaniel has carried on this traditional approach by examining the historical living arrangements of children and concluding that while it and family structure are influenced by the socioeconomic past, black Americans, due to a culture rooted in Africa, are predisposed to certain familial forms over others.[4]

As a counter to this perspective, other researchers argue that familial Africanisms were destroyed in slavery. Thus, no direct link exists between African familial patterns and those born and raised on American soil. With emancipation, black family life underwent further destruction as ex-slaves no longer had the paternalistic structure and stability slavery afforded them. According to E. Franklin Frazier (1939), racial discrimination placed them at a severe economic disadvantage following slavery. Consequently, most of them ill-adapted to life after slavery. Black men were unable to meet the economic needs of their families. Relatively high rates of single-mother headed households, out-of-wedlock births, and absent fatherhood were outcomes. These characteristics resulted in the self-perpetuating pathological, dysfunctional, disorganized, and deviant black familial systems. Frazier's analysis suggested that families would become more stable with economic improvement. Following the Race Relations Model developed by his mentor, Robert E. Park, Frazier concluded that lower-income African American families must assimilate into the dominant middle-class, European-American lifestyle if they hope to produce well-functioning, success-oriented children and adults. For Frazier, low-income black familial disorganization and pathology was a transition that with economic improvement would eventually bring black families to emulate the middle-class lifestyles, values, and behaviors of European-Americans and the small black middle-class of the period. Though he linked experiences of poor black families with racial oppression he implicitly attributed their economic deprivation to cultural characteristics. His conclusions buttressed the 1965 report on the Negro family authored by Daniel P. Moynihan. Here an even more negative interpretation of black family structure was put forth. The report argued that, rather than experiencing a class transition, black families lived within a never-ending "tangle of pathology." Moynihan argues that female-dominated, matriarchal households were inherently dysfunctional, disorganized, unstable family structures that were the source of economic deprivation among low-income black Americans rather than the contrary position presented by Frazier. This cycle inhibited their ability to think and act in ways that would lead to strong familial systems and economic success, and led to a steady decline in the black family system.[5]

Still additional social scientists offered a third view. In the 1970s Furstenberg, Hershberg, and Modell, and Engerman and others, argued that the experiences of black families were primarily due to their socioeconomic position, rather than a primacy of cultural components. Their explanations suggested that if black families were not disproportionately poor, their familial values, attitudes, behaviors, and structures would be similar to those of mainstream middle-class European-Americans. John Scanzoni (1971), Joyce Ladner (1971), and others theorize that the form and content of black families are adaptations to poor social and economic circumstances. Both the form and the content of low-income black families are rational alternatives to these conditions.[6]

Are contemporary paternal attitudes and behaviors of black men vestiges of their African heritage adapted to racism and other forms of discrimination? Are they a reflection of black men's and families' inability to escape the remnants of slavery, adapt and transition into middle-class normative familial values and customs? Are they simply a direct response to consistent economic inequities that historically place black men, women, and children on the economy's lowest hierarchical rungs? The answers remain a matter of debate and are not intended to be answered in the scope of this book. What we do know however, is that fatherhood and family do not exist in a vacuum. A complete and holistic study must include an assessment of the role of culture, history, and economics. Sociologist C. Wright Mills explained, "Neither the life of an individual, nor the history of a society, can be understood without understanding both" (1959:3). In the end, the task is to examine how black families and fathers themselves interpret their past and present, particularly as it relates to their parenting options and decisions. The overriding purpose of *What It Means to Be Daddy* is to do just that. Here, how black live-away fathers define and act within their paternal role; and how significant others, communities, institutions, and the general public enhance or inhibit the part they play in their children's lives are explored. The roles of intimate others, work conditions, education, as well as the choices of men themselves, play a part in the development and maintenance of contemporary paternal behavior.

CONSIDERING THE PAST AND PRESENT: AN ECOLOGICAL APPROACH

Thus, our investigation of black live-away fatherhood requires us to use an ecological framework to understand family life, obligations, and decisions in terms of the dynamic social, cultural, political, and economic environments within which they were developed and are presently embedded. The work of Urie Bronfenbrenner provides a theoretical framework for understanding the role each of these elements play in the everyday lives of black families. He theorized that these multiple environments are best conceptualized as four spheres, or "four concentric circles, each contained within the next" (Bronfenbrenner 1979). The smallest of these structures and the smallest setting in which men engaged as live-away fathers is the microsystem—for example, the dyadic relationship between fathers and their children. Interaction between microsystems, father-child relationship—child's household, or father's work—child's household form the mesosystem. These elements are housed within the boundaries of the exosystem; large entities such as economic and political institutions in which the father may not actively participate but nevertheless may affect or be affected. Finally, each of these smaller bodies occur within what may be called the macrosystem, the largest ecological sphere. In this study, these are historical and contemporary Western ideals of family and public popular images of fatherhood that are consistently demonstrated through varying media and other institutional outlets (Bronfenbrenner 1979). They also undergird the content and form of family life for never-married, black, low-income parents and their children.

FATHERS AND CHILDREN: MICROSYSTEMS

In technical terminology, a microsystem is the pattern of activities, roles, and interpersonal relations experienced by the individual in a given setting. It is an environment in which fathers directly participate, and it consists of persons with whom he interacts on a face-to-face basis (e.g., children, close relatives and friends, and coworkers), their connection with other persons in the setting, the nature of these links, and their indirect influence on the individual. Ecological theory assumes that individual behavior and motivations cannot be understood solely from the objective properties of one particular setting without reference to its meaning for the people in the setting.

For our purposes, the relationship between live-away fathers and their children is the primary microsystem of concern in this study. It also explores their experiences in other microsettings, such as their places of employment and their own households. This study is concerned not only with the objective element of a father's fatherhood in the father-child and other microsystems, but also with the way in which their respective properties, such as functions, roles, and meaning are each perceived by the fathers themselves. However, we cannot understand what occurs in this small setting without first exploring the elements that surround it. Thus prior to studying how men define their fatherhood and analyzing their descriptions of paternal behavior we must understand the external contexts within which they mediate their parenthood.

FRIENDS AND OTHER FAMILY: THE MESOSYSTEM

The world of live-away fathers goes beyond the primary links that exists between themselves and their children. The links between this and other microsystems may affect what men do as parent. For example, fathers have varying types of relationships with their children's mothers that may serve to hinder or encourage their parental involvement. Additionally, their environment is extended whenever they move into a new setting, such as a marriage, remarriage, or intimate relationship, a new place of work, or enrollments in classes to improve their skills and education. Interconnections and interactions between the father/child and other settings may assume various forms. Fathers also interact with their own parents, siblings, and other kin internal or external to their household. Additionally, formal and informal communication may occur among settings, and knowledge and attitudes may exist in one setting about another. Like the microsystem, the mesosystem too exists within a surrounding body. These elements make up a father's "exosystem" and influence his daily life on both the micro- and mesosystem levels (Bronfenbrenner 1979).

SURROUNDING INSTITUTIONS: THE EXOSYSTEM

An exosystem is comprised of one or more settings that live-away fathers may never enter but in which events occur that affect what happens in their immediate environment. It extends beyond the immediate setting directly affecting live-away fathers. More specifically, it is the character and content of surrounding activities occurring in past and present economic, political, and social institutions (Bronfenbrenner 1979).

The pressures of the economy influence men's experiences in the labor market, the educational system, and ultimately the familial arrangements and activities of working family members. Live-away black fatherhood as a familial form has been developed, sustained, and established within our economic, social, and cultural institutions. That is, what fathers do is in part a consequence of live-away fatherhood as it has been abetted by the state through law and social policy. Their paternal activities have also become convention in communities as men and women have mediated the paternal role in context of their socioeconomic and political environments.

IDEAL FATHERHOOD AND AMERICAN CULTURE: THE MACROSYSTEM

Micro-, meso-, and exosystems all interact with one another to influence fathers' paternal attitudes and behavior. Intimate relationships, family systems, work and friendship networks (microsystems); the interaction between them (mesosystems), economic, educational, and political institutions (exosystems)—all interlink to create a complex interplay between fathers and their environments. A macrosystem "refers to consistencies, in the form and content of lower-order systems (micro-, meso-, and exo-) that exist, or could exist, at the subculture or the culture as a whole, along with any belief systems or ideology underlying such consistencies" (Bronfenbrenner 1979:26). Put simply, there exists laws, policies, dominant customs and values that encourage or discourage certain family forms over others. Belief systems, ideology, and culture mostly justify and perpetuate the conditions of each environment. It helps institutionalize notions and ideals about fatherhood and family that exist. In practice, these may vary for demographic groups by race or ethnicity, class, sexual orientation, and various other social and economic factors. For example, poor and working-class African Americans experience work conditions that are often qualitatively different from those holding white-collar occupations earning middle and upper-middle class incomes. Consequently, their recreational environments and activities may also differ, as well as their attitudes, concerns, and behaviors with regard to family and households. Regardless of racial or economic differences, however, all groups are expected to assimilate and adapt the values, attitudes, and behaviors of the dominant, European-American middle-class group. They are considered deviant if they do not appear to live up to this standard.

Overall, ecological theory allows for the observation of African American live-away fatherhood in the historical and cultural environment in which it occurs. It also allows for the analysis of their paternal ideals and attitudes according to the value system of their indigenous culture or subculture—thus providing a more balanced picture of the perceptions, roles, functions, and behaviors of this category of men than found in past research. Ecological theory is intended to provide a general framework for my study. Other than this, alternative theories were not explicitly used to guide the research. In effect, the result was essentially a grounded theory—generated through the use of original categories and relationships that were derived from the collected data.[7]

THE FATHERS: WHERE THEY ARE FROM, WHO THEY ARE, AND HOW TO MAKE CONTACT WITH THEM

Inevitably, when people inquire about a work on live-away African American fathers, one of the first questions asked is: "Where did you find them?"—almost as if they were an invisible group. True, black men in general are a notoriously difficult group to access. Qualitative research conducted by Cannon and others (1988) suggest that recruiting black respondents generally requires labor-intensive strategies involving personal contact—usually verbal, face-to-face contact with an African American researcher. The findings of these and other researchers also suggest that when recruiting noncustodial fathers, word of mouth or a snowball technique is a more sufficient technique than traditional social science recruitment strategies, such as letters to those known to fit the study criteria and announcements in the public media. I utilized as many of these strategies as possible—particularly local newspapers, appropriate newsletters and bulletin boards, African American radio stations, word-of-mouth, and face-to-face contact with prospective respondents. Public and posted announcements in various media, organizations, and church bulletin boards in towns and cities met with little to virtually no success. Reliance was placed most heavily on those strategies and settings in which a prospective respondent and myself had face-to-face contact. Visits were made to local malls, auto part stores, government housing developments, local African American events, and major retail stores such as Walmart, Target, and others. Consequently, the respondents in the study tended to be drawn from areas in my proximity—the south and midwest regions of the United States. They primarily resided in one of five states—Texas, Oklahoma, Illinois, Missouri, and Michigan. A few fathers lived in southern states such as North Carolina and Arkansas. Interviews lasted from forty-five minutes to two hours. Fifty-three fathers participated in multiple interviews; data was collected at varying periods from 1994 to 1997.

TRUST AND COMMUNICATION

Establishing trust and communicating the importance of their help in a study of black men, children, and families was the basis of all recruitment strategies and communication with respondents. I made an effort to be honest with potential respondents regarding my identity as a researcher as well as describing the purpose of the study. However, I experienced very little difficulty in locating men interested in participating in the study. I chose to go where black families and men tended to visit, which fortunately were places that were often part of my everyday or weekly activities. These were, for example, major discount retail stores, low-income neighborhoods and communities, and the various gymnasiums, recreational centers, and auto parts stores within them. Bus stops, popular public walkways, and the parking lots of various mom-and-pop type stores in predominantly African American communities were also frequent hangouts. In the end, many fathers expressed gratitude for being afforded the opportunity to talk about their parenting and their children. They also explained that the interviews encouraged them to reflect, according to one father, "on my good and bad habits of being a father."

THE FATHERS: WHO THEY ARE

The eighty-eight men who participated in this study ranged in age from 19 to 54. Similar to the 19- to 54-year-old African American population as a whole, the highest percentage of men in the study were under the age of 35. About half (48 percent) were age 25 to 34; 23 percent were age 35 to 44 and 19 percent were age 19 to 24. They had become fathers at various stages of their lives. However the majority (56 percent) had done so prior to age 23. In total, fathers reported living separate from 153 children. Nine percent (8 fathers) reported court-set visitation arrangements with children. Twenty-five percent had fathered children with multiple mothers.

Their levels of education, too, were reflective of national averages. While half of the men had completed high school, 15 percent had less than a twelfth-grade education; 31 percent had some level of college or technical training in such areas as computer skills, truck driving, restaurant management, and business administration. Regardless of training and education, most fathers (86 percent) earned annual incomes of less than $20,000. Over 38 percent of all fathers earned less than $10,000 in the twelve months prior to their participation in the study. Those reporting incomes higher than $20,000 (14 percent) generally did not do so through a single employer. Rather they tended to work at more than one job and/or participated in the underground economy. However, regardless of income level, several men earned some money through underground activity, such as selling goods (electronics, drugs, and clothing) and services (haircuts, lawn care, home repair, automobile repair, and vendor food items). In terms of legal employment, the highest percentage of fathers (38 percent) were employed in various types of service work. They worked as physical and mental rehabilitation technicians, sales clerks, retail store and supermarket stockers, and as food service helpers. A large percentage (16) were also employed in the protective service field as security guards, drivers, and/or nightclub bouncers. An equal percentage were employed in the construction trade as laborers for roofers, carpenters, and other building fields. Ten percent of these men worked in transportation, and 16 percent were officially unemployed. At the time of their participation in the study, none of these men had ever legally married the mothers of their noncustodial children.

OTHER PERSPECTIVES

It was my general intent to focus on the perceptions and voice of black, never-married, noncustodial fathers. However, the voices of other African Americans are also included. Thirty-three of the mothers of these fathers' children also participated in the study. They too were low-income, and all had received some form of welfare assistance since the birth of their children. Interviews with adult children of noncustodial fathers (n=21) of generations past were also collected. Both the mothers of children and adult children were asked to describe their expectations and ideals of fatherhood. They were also asked to describe their experiences with the fathers of their children and their fathers, respectively. The information they shared simultaneously enriched and confounded that presented by the fathers I interviewed. Some of their experiences supported those offered by fathers. Others were quite contradictory. Nonetheless, utilizing the perspectives of these other black demographic groups certainly enhanced the quality and validity of the data collected solely from fathers.[8]

DEFINING LIVE-AWAY FATHERS

Men experience fatherhood in various forms. Some fathers visit there children often, some not at all. Many provide consistent economic support, others have little to offer in this regard. Still, many provide care and nurturance to their children, while others show little if any affection. Various terms have been utilized to define specific types of fatherhood. Noncustodial fathers, absent fathers, deadbeat dads, visiting fathers, sperm fathers— none seemed to capture a true description of the reality of all fathers who, for whatever reason, do not reside with their children on a full-time basis. Each is fairly specific and none encompass the scope and varying forms of fatherhood that exists in black America.

"Noncustodial" or "nonresident" fathers appear to be the preferred terms among contemporary social scientists. It is generally defined as those who do not provide daily emotional support or care to their children. Generally, these children reside with their mother on a full-time basis.

"Absent fathers" is another popular term used to describe the fathers of children who live in single-parent mother-headed households. Generally, the definition implies that the father has no formal or informal presence in the home. Its use is, perhaps, slightly more popular among media agents than the villainous "deadbeat dad"— a very specific description of "bad" fathers who fail to pay child support. Both the absent father and the deadbeat dad may have, at one time, resided in the home with their children as full-time fathers, contrary to the "sperm father" who, with the biological act of ejaculation, completed his fatherhood prior to the birth of child.

Visiting fathers are those that remember birthdays, holidays, pay child support, and come by to visit on a regular basis. As David Blankenhorn suggests, "a reformed Deadbeat Dad can aspire to become a Visiting Father" (1994:148). Regardless of how many presents he brings or visits, the visiting father remains somewhat distant and separate from that which is the origin of his fatherhood.

The point of origin for a "father"—that is, the basis for his existence as a father—is that point in time at which his child is born. At this point he becomes a father and their exists some attachment between himself and the child—whether it is an emotional bond or simple genetics. The fathers of this study are all situated, in some form or manner, away from their point of origin—their child—the single essence of their fatherhood. They are, in essence, distal fathers. Webster's Dictionary (1993) defines the term: "distal": situated away from the point of origin or attachment . . .

Noncustodial fathers, absent fathers, deadbeat dads—none of these terms reflect the general reality of African American fatherhood for those who do not live with their children. A father's existence precludes his total absence. Moreover, no father lives without some attachment to his child— whether he is present physically, emotionally, part-time, full-time, or at no time. And, regardless of the form of fatherhood, no child is "fatherless"— each and every child has, at least, a biological father. Although the term "distal" comes closest to capturing the essence of fatherhood, its appropriateness for describing the parental attitudes and behaviors for African American fathers is problematic. It is commonly utilized as a medical term and does not fully capture the positive emotional and social aspects of parenting. Equally important, it does not fully describe the range of experiences fathers reported in this study.[9]

The search for *the* defining term remains elusive and reflects the ambiguity of the parental role men seem to play in their children's lives. However, each of these fathers reported that they lived away from their children. They did not use terms such as deadbeat, absent, or noncustodial to describe their status in their children's lives. Rather, many of these fathers reported that their formal "live-away" status was the only element that separated them from other fatherhood forms. Needless to say, fathers who do not reside with their children on a full-time basis are different than those that do. Their position is somewhat remote, separate—regardless of how much money or time and attention they do or do not provide to their children. As a group, they are not necessarily noncustodial—because many do provide consistent care and nurturance to their children. They are not necessarily absent—because many are consistently present in the daily lives of their children. They are not necessarily "deadbeats"—because, as we shall see, many fathers provide some form of economic or subsistence support to their children on an informal and often inconsistent basis. Live-away fathers, though, may or may not be noncustodial, may or may not be absent, may or may not be deadbeat dads, visiting fathers, or sperm fathers. The term encompasses a multitude of father-child relationships and provides a general and more accurate description of such a father's place in the lives of his children. Terminology aside, this study is concerned with black fathers who, for one reason or another, are not full-time, live-in dads. Formally, they are "live-away" fathers, leading and living lives separate and away from their children.

TELLING THE STORY

We actually begin our story of black live-away fatherhood by examining the macro or cultural elements that encompass men's daily lives. The images and ideals of fatherhood are interconnected with, and enshroud, the exo-, meso-, and microsystems. Thus, part 1 examines the larger forces that define the social world of fathers. Chapter 1 explores Western notions of father-hood and masculinity that have historically set standards by which to judge the parental attitudes and behaviors of black men. The apparent behaviors and attitudes of black men have traditionally been viewed as opposite to those of good family men. More importantly, we find that the noncustodial father family form lacks the formal institutional support that may serve to sustain strong paternal bonds with children and healthy relationships with custodial mothers, although, as is explored in chapter 2, African American men have historically found it difficult to live up to Western notions of good fatherhood. Moreover, the noncustodial father/custodial mother family form was created and sustained by past economic, political, and social insti-tutions. Chapter 3 moves us closer to a more intimate understanding of contemporary fathers' daily lives. The world of work is examined. For low-income men in particular, the realm of employment, earnings, and sustenance is a harsh and nebulous environment. Their experiences here have consequences for the other elements that make up their daily lives, including their fatherhood.

Part 2 examines what fathers feel significant others expect of them as fathers and how they behave under these circumstances (Chapter Four). In chapter 5, the mothers of their children provide perspectives on what fathers actually do in their parental role, a view that sometimes contrasts with those of fathers and further illustrates the ambiguity of norms that govern interaction between mothers, fathers, and children.

In part 3 fathers' parenting roles and functions are examined more thoroughly. In chapter 6, they describe what they do for their children. However, not all fathers "do" for their offspring. Chapter 7 explores the parenting decisions and experiences of men who are quite literally "absent" from their children's lives. These are men who rarely if ever visit or have contact with their live-away offspring. Chapter 8 examines the various elements that present barriers to most fathers who live away from their children. In part 4, chapter 9 examines the implications of this study for improving the lives of black fathers, custodial mothers, and their children.

Overall, each chapter brings us closer to understanding how paternal behaviors evolve as a function of interplay between black fathers and their surrounding environments. Black men modify and impact the world in which they reside, while the spheres and the environment as a whole exert their influence on their fatherhood. Concretely, this all means that we must examine live-away fathers' attitudes and behaviors in the context of their relationships with significant others, their work conditions and experiences, and past and present contemporary cultural and ideological prescriptions for paternal behavior and involvement. We consider how each of these elements impact upon what fathers do and say as fathers.

Simultaneously, we consider how fathers act to direct and control their everyday paternal circumstances in the context of these surrounding factors. Ultimately, African American men and women create their maternal and paternal roles and functions. However, they do so within ever-evolving present conditions. In the following pages, contemporary black live-away fathers talk about their goals, walk us through their workplaces, allow us to meet their families and children, and enable us to view the world of parenthood through their eyes (Bronfenbrenner 1979; McAdoo 1993).

PART 1
The World in Which Black Fathers Live

In 1965 John Oliver Killens suggested that "the Problems and the Burden of black men are historical, economic, cultural, and [sic] social" (p. 44). His point was that, in essence, the problems and burdens of black men are produced and sustained by the structure of American society. The structure of American society has positioned black men on one of the lowest rungs of its hierarchical ladder. Black manhood and, in effect, black fatherhood are elements of life grown within this environment of social and economic inequities. Within slavery and throughout the twentieth century, black men have been faced with uneven and inconsistent opportunities with which to negotiate life circumstances for themselves and their children. Moreover, the condition of their lives as black men have had repercussions for the roles and functions as fathers.

Part 1 discusses the macro- and exosystems that frame the conditions of life for black men in both past and present America. While working-class and low-income black males in general must negotiate their livelihood in a grim political economy, live-away fathers do so as black men and as parents. Chapter 1 provides a brief review and analysis of how traditional Western ideals of fatherhood, issues of black masculinity, and popular culture publicly define fatherhood for lower income never-married black men. In this chapter fathers discuss their public image and social status in a society where their parenting is, as the thirty-year-old live-away father of two insists, "trapped in a system hostile to the self-respect of black men . . . especially black fathers trying to do right by their children." Chapter 2 describes the historical precedent of black live-away fatherhood and how economics, politics, and social systems buttressed and sustained a live-away parental status for black low-income fathers. Chapter 3 is an overview of contemporary economic conditions and how these fathers attempt to negotiate their work and education within the current environment. In this chapter black fathers talk about their experiences in the labor market and higher education.

1

"THERE'S NO SUCH THING AS A GOOD BLACK FATHER"
Standards of Fatherhood

*A*ny discussion of live-away fatherhood should begin with the cultural elements encompassing men's worlds. These are the belief systems, ideologies, and traditions that define normative paternal behavior in a given society. Public ideals and images, entrenched within varying mediums, tell men what they ought to look like, how they ought to talk, how they ought to relate, and how they ought to behave as fathers. These standards are not transhistorical, but rather have reflected the experiences, events, and circumstances of a moment in time. From the turn of the century to the 1970s, "ideal" fathers were primarily perceived as warmhearted providers on whom all family members could depend for counsel and support. In general, men measured their success as men in terms of their breadwinning role and the standard of living they were able to provide for themselves and their families.

Increasing numbers of white middle-class women in the paid workforce, and a decline in family wage occupations for men, are just two factors that have modified the paternal ideal in the latter decades of the twentieth century. We no longer assume that all households are male-headed. Nevertheless, men continue to idealize themselves as a family's primary breadwinner. They are also expected to spend more quality time with their children, and participate more in their daily upbringing. These popular standards tend to apply across race and class, despite the variance that may occur within these categories. No extensive research is necessary to get a sense of how black men, in particular, are perceived with regard to meeting the criteria of fatherhood. One need only turn the pages of a newspaper, visit a local movie theater, or tune in to prime time television. The messages are irrefutably negative.

This chapter is a brief overview of popular ideals and images of family, fatherhood, and black men. As Earl Ofari Hutchinson (1996) asserts, popular ideals and images suggest that black men fall short on publicly prescribed paternal tasks, and lack normative masculine characteristics.

According to Hutchinson, black men are America's universal bogeyman. In his recent work, *The Assassination of the Black Male Image*, with chapters titled, "The Fine Art of Black Male Bashing" and "The Negro. . . . A Beast or in the Image of God?" he takes readers on a tour of contemporary popular representations of African American men. His book and other works demonstrate that negative images of black males permeate not only today's media but most historical and contemporary cultural channels. Music, classic and award-winning literature and film, popular books and magazines from the past and the present provide a warped and sensational view of black men as men, and as fathers.

STANDARDS OF FATHERHOOD

In the United States, the "nuclear" family, consisting of a husband, wife, and children, tends to emerge above most others as the "ideal" form. Conventional wisdom holds that it provides "family members with guidelines for proper behavior in everyday family life," and "presumably, these guidelines contribute to the unity and stability of families" (Cherlin 1978:634). The biological "nuclear" family form predominates in Western industrial countries generally, and has traditionally been the dominant family structure among European Americans for many economic classes. Its structure has been institutionalized in tradition, policy, and law as the appropriate familial guide for parents, children, and communities. Hence, the rituals, habits, practices, and values that make up this familial structure receive significant state sanctions and economic and ideological support.

There are many examples of this. Marriages between men and women are legalized by the state, publicly celebrated and announced. Folks outside of the marriage expect that marital partners be committed to one another sexually and emotionally. Thus, they are not available for dating. With marriage, each partner acquires recognized kin, mothers- and fathers-in-law, as well as brothers- and sisters-in-law. Such marriages bring with them certain benefits and privileges, like lower rates of federal income tax and automobile insurance. The state protects a spouse from testifying against a marital partner in a court of law. Other invisible boundaries exist around the marital partners and their shared offspring. Parents are allowed to spank their children. On their own accord, they may also pick them up from school early and enroll them in extracurricular activities. As parents, married couples have customary motherhood and fatherhood guidelines. They are expected to coordinate discipline practices and control their children's behavior. Together they are expected to make major decisions regarding their children's health and well-being.

For men, the nuclear family structure seems the widely accepted guide defining the primary roles and functions of their fatherhood. Among other social scientists and commentators, T. Tripp-Reissman and S. E. Wilson (1990) provide a summary of model fatherhood that has traditionally dominated Western culture. They suggest that fatherhood can be described in terms of men's interactional social responsibilities and functions.

First and foremost is the legal and genetic endowment a father provides to his offspring: in addition to providing his children with hair and eye color, a father may also provide them with his surname, a lawful relation to a kinship network, and a legal right to inheritance.

Second, fathers may provide sustenance to family members, usually in the form of housing and food. With industrialization, the "adequate provision for children through work and wages won outside the home" was the primary function and role assigned to fathers (Stearn 1991:42). "Good" fathers also provide economic allowances and support in children's pursuit of happiness, careers, and academic fulfillment.

The third primary function of fathers is to protect their children from physical harm, as well as demonstrate a genuine concern for their well-being.

Fourth, fathers may participate in the indirect and direct daily care of their children—participating in childbirth classes, changing and washing diapers, preparing school lunches, reading stories, and other forms of affective involvement.

Finally, Tripp-Reissman and Wilson (1990) suggest "formation function" as another paternal function. This is defined as fathers' distinct contribution to the formation of children's character and personality.

Although the image has changed slightly in recent years, all of these functions, correctly packaged, constitute the makings of a good family man or a "good father" in the European-American/Western view. For David Blankenhorn, and others who accept and aspire to this ideal, a good father is first and foremost a provider. The "male income" is perceived synonymously with the "male image." For the ideal father, the two fit together. His ability to provide economically for his family is concomitant to his being a father. Blankenhorn explains:

A good father is one who is married. He stays around. He is a father on the premises. His children need him and he strives to give them what they need, every day. He knows that nothing can substitute for him. Either he is a father or his children are fatherless. He would never consider himself "not that important" to his children. (1995:201)

The "ideal" good father does not live separate from his children. Nor does he contemplate child support, visitation, or divorce. Blankenhorn states:

It would never occur to him—or to his children or to his wife—to make distinctions between "biological" and "social" fathering. For him, these two identities are tightly fused. . . . Consequently, he seldom ponders issues such as child support, visitation, paternity identification, fathers' rights, better divorce, joint custody, dating, or blended families. (1995:201)

Yet, not all men share this paradigm of masculinity and fatherhood. Blankenhorn himself suggests there are varying levels of fatherhood both inside and outside the home.

Regardless, there are social commentators and social scientists who argue that a present lack of marital ties and legal father/child bonds contribute to the lack of commitment noncustodial black fathers appear to demonstrate toward their children. Without such formal and legal connections, there exist no rules to govern or control fathers' paternal behavior (Popenoe 1998). Nor is there any means to curb their natural irresponsibility, "tame" their desire to "hang out with their boys," or encourage monogamous intimate relationships. Thus, good paternal behavior as a nonmarital, live-away status is not impossible, but at a minimum is extremely difficult to attain. The argument appears to support the popular assumption that most black men continue to produce children they care little, if anything, about. Relative to most other demographic groups, black men are less likely to appear on children's birth certificates. Additionally, in 1994, single-parenting women accounted for 60 percent of all African American family groups with children present (Shinagawa and Jang 1998). If trends continue, almost all African American children will be spending some portion of their lives without a father's presence in the home. If one is to accept traditional and popular standards for good fatherhood, black children more than any other demographic group are doomed to a harrowing life.

In October 1995 an estimated one million African American men participated in the Million Man March in Washington D.C. Implicitly embracing the Western view of fatherhood, the march's Mission Statement called for African American men to "stand up" and "take responsibility," be more accountable and dependable, and assume familial obligations and duties. While certainly laudable, this view uncritically adopted the traditional ideal of fatherhood and much of the conservative rhetoric espoused by politicians and policy makers, particularly the assumption of black male irresponsibility to their families and children. In their recent work titled *Black Man Emerging*, Joseph White and James Cones III contest that one of the two primary conclusions that could be drawn from the March "is that Black men are willing to take responsibility for initiating interventions that will transform themselves and the Black community." However, they also point out that "no amount of individual or group transformation will change the economic and social obstacles with which Black men are confronted in a racist society" (1999:8).[1]

Economic class further complicates the issue of men's paternal attitudes and behaviors. What tends to be left out of public discussions are studies indicating that middle- and working-class African American men may assent to the importance of the economic provider role and the paternal accountability one. Which one is viewed as most important may be influenced by socioeconomic status. In Cazenave's (1979) study, working-class men perceived their provider role as primary. This was followed by husband, father, and worker, respectively. In a subsequent study, Cazenave (1984) found that among white-collar workers, aggressiveness, success at work, and competitiveness were used to define the essential characteristics of the "ideal man." Still, other research suggests that as they age, black men's views of manhood begin to diverge from those of whites and are less likely to reflect traditional notions. These findings indicate that overall, different groups may have varying notions about fatherhood, and variances may occur due to race and ethnicity, class, and/or age.[2]

Majors and Billson, in *Cool Pose: The Dilemmas of Black Manhood in America* (1992), also accept much of the popular discourse. Specifically, they argue that live-away fathers' laxity is part of a "cool pose." From this perspective, they argue that black men adapt to limited opportunity and attempt to maintain some control over their manhood by acting aloof and cool toward women and the children for whom they cannot provide. Thus time and again, black men maintain this composure in order to maintain some control over their manhood. This demeanor well fits what William

Julius Wilson suggests is pathological behavior and "ghetto specific culture." Majors and Billson contend that black fathers accept traditional Western ideals of masculinity and fatherhood, each striving to be a "good provider for self and family." However, political, educational, and economic systems thwart attempts to fulfill this dream (a point discussed at length in later chapters). This, in turn, inhibits their ability to fulfill expected roles in family systems and to be present and supportive fathers. The authors cite Robert K. Merton, who theorized that individuals shut out of sanctioned means to success may actually be motivated to adopt deviant behavior to achieve some prestige and social standing. Still, rather than marshaling empirical evidence, the authors' work rests primarily on anecdotal evidence and general assumptions—a fact not missed by critics. Yet, this has not prevented the work from aiding in the persistent images of black men and fathers.[3]

ARE WE NOT MEN?
POPULAR PERCEPTIONS OF BLACK MEN IN AMERICA

Popular perceptions of African American men historically have represented extremes. Characterizations have ranged from hypersexual to emasculated; from dangerous to less than intelligent, comic, or lazy. Each stereotype has appeared at an appropriate place and time to justify racial proscription. One example is the popular 1915 film *Birth of a Nation*. Here, a fictional black man's "savage" and brutal sexual assault of a virtuous white woman was accepted by much of the film's audience as an accurate description of black males' animal character. Adapted from the play *The Clansman*, the drama was privately screened by Woodrow Wilson in the White House during his presidency. Even today, the American Film Institute ranks it as one of the top fifty greatest American movies ever made. The film was one of several that attempted to justify the fierce social control of black men through publicly sanctioned lynchings, beatings, and incarceration. Such racial media tactics were successfully repeated almost seventy years later when, as a political ploy to woo white middle and working-class voters, George Bush's 1988 presidential campaign aired the infamous Willie Horton ad. The broadcast vividly depicted a black male parolee's brutal rape of a white woman. If they are not brutal savages from whom the public needs protection, they are lazy, inept, cowardly buffoons with childlike tendencies. From *Amos 'n' Andy* in the 1950s (which began as a radio show in 1928) to *Sanford and Son, Good*

Times, and *The Jeffersons* in the 1970s, black men have been more likely to perform as ignorant jesters than as dramatic leading actors.[4]

This trend has continued into the 1980s and 1990s with primetime programs like *The Jamie Foxx Show, The Wayans Brothers, Martin,* and *Family Matters.* In each of these, the leading characters sustain a tradition of clownish and often slapstick black performances. While *The Hughleys* and *The Cosby Show* offer leading men with successful careers and strong, healthy familial relationships, these characters' primary objective has been to make the audiences laugh. This is not to suggest that black men have not received dramatic roles. One may consider as evidence *I Spy, Police Story, Hill Street Blues, ER, Chicago Hope, NYPD Blue, Homicide: Life on the Streets, New York Undercover,* and *Law and Order.* But even on these programs, strong supportive characters are often countered by a procession of black stock characters—junkies, woman abusers, and hoodlums. Overall, stereotypes emphasize the divergence of black men from their white counterparts; each has, at some point in history, been accepted as a contribution to the definitive reality of African American men. In the age of television and film, they have rarely been portrayed as strong, independent, successful, or completely competent as men or as fathers.[5]

In a 1993 study examining how television commercials portray men of color, Cheryl Johnson found that of 264 ads only three portrayed black men working, and these were in low-skill service occupations. Black female fiction writers also participate in decimating black men's character by offering a rash of popular literature in which men are shiftless, cheating, and simply no good. Stella, in Terry McMillan's novel and successful screenplay, *How Stella Got Her Groove Back,* had to leave the borders of the United States to find a decent man to help her "get her groove back." In an earlier, more successful work, *Waiting to Exhale,* four female friends find respite with one another from poor relationships with black men.

Even in black popular journals, stereotypes persist. In the November 1998 issue of *Essence,* a feature column discussed how African American men "relate to their penises," which dictates much of their behavior. If advertisements and popular literature are to be believed, black men spend all their money on cars and all of their leisure time playing basketball. They are more likely to grace news headlines as carjackers, homicidal gang members, and petty thieves than as successful, compassionate, industrious workers. In the same way, they are less redeemable in their paternal roles, choosing thuggery, wine, and a bevy of women over traditional fatherly responsibilities.[6]

Negative fatherhood images have inundated even contemporary African American cinema. From filmmaker John Singleton's *Boys N the Hood* (1991) to Spike Lee's *He Got Game* (1998), black male characters are mostly absent or peripheral members of family units. An exception is Singleton's Furious Stiles, a character played by Laurence Fishburne in *Boys N the Hood*. Stiles is a single father who triumphantly raises his son Trey, despite the vicissitudes and dangers present in their urban ghetto. A member of the working class, he gives his son a steady home life and male guidance that his son's mother is unable to provide. This contrasts with the upbringing of Trey's friends, Ricky and Doughboy. Raised by their single mother, one becomes an unwed teen father, the other a neighborhood drug dealer. The movie's primary thesis is that fathers are the only ones able to provide black male youth with the stability and tutelage necessary for them to survive and live meaningful adult lives. Singleton suggests that for fathers to accomplish this, they should do as Stiles—reside with their children and take charge of their upbringing. While this film celebrated Stiles's paternal role, it simultaneously denigrated black single mothers and live-away fathers. The flipside of the film's message is that fathers who maintain live-away status are not doing what they are supposed to do as fathers; consequently, their offspring are producing children out of wedlock and falling victim to ghetto street crime.

The movie's theme seemed to reaffirm the same conventional wisdom that has proved durable since the 1960s and was advocated in a 1980 public television special titled *The Vanishing Father*. Host Bill Moyers blamed supposedly absent noncaring fathers for everything from drug use in black communities and trash-ridden neighborhoods to children's gang activity and poor academic performance. A *U.S. News & World Report* cover story (February 27, 1995) again supported Moyers's conclusions, by focusing on two black youths charged with murder after they dropped another child from a highrise apartment window in Chicago. This behavior, the journalist argued, should have come as no surprise to middle-class America, given the lack of paternal care and positive male role models available to children in black communities.

More recently, ABC's *20/20* kicked off its 1998 season with a segment titled "Sad Children of the NBA." Here, correspondents make unsubstantiated claims about current NBA superstars who, they say, have "fathered hundreds of illegitimate children," refuse to pay child support, and spend little if any time with their offspring. All but one of the fathers featured was black. While her father earned millions of dollars a year, one four-year-old girl lived in abject poverty, sleeping on a sofa with her sister and mother "in a one-bedroom house shared by five people." Another, nine-year-old Dominique Maxwell, begged his father—Vernon Maxwell of the San Antonio Spurs—to phone or visit. Maxwell had only done so twice in the child's lifetime.

Of course, if valid and reliable, these stories are tragic, particularly for the children and their mothers. However, such one-sided journalistic accounts do not reliably explain the perceived options, circumstances, or feelings of all black children, their mothers, or the fathers themselves, not even most of those in the NBA. A fifteen-minute television segment did not capture the diversity or the patterns of paternal behavior that may occur between NBA fathers and the mothers of their children with whom they negotiate their parenting roles. Nevertheless, 20/20 reporters and commentators, puzzled and outraged by the audacity of NBA stars, turned to David Blankenhorn and similar social commentators for popular narrations explaining absentee fatherhood as a whole. Blankenhorn suggested that the NBA, which is 80 percent black, simply reflects the "staggering reality—70 percent of black children in America grow up without fathers." Further, fatherhood activist Bill Stephney clarified, many of these superstars themselves are "victims" of "fatherlessness." Harking back to the arguments of Moynihan and Frazier, he explained that their poor paternal behavior is part of a vicious circle of fatherlessness that subsists in black America.

Certainly, this book is not an attempt to defend those fathers who unabashedly abandon and refuse to take responsibility for their children, or even to suggest that they do not exist. However, public accounts of negative live-away fatherhood are generally founded on little or no empirical evidence, and yet often generalize about black live-away fathers as a whole. Consequently, they do much to create and maintain stereotypical images of black men as fathers. Their popularly reported instability, promiscuity, aloofness, and abandonment of paternal responsibilities make them culpable for the myriad circumstances that disproportionately impact African American children: high school incompletion, teen pregnancy and childbirth, poverty, membership and violent activities in gangs, and the use and sale of drugs. Black men are even less redeemable as fathers. According to the 1995 issue of *U.S. News & World Report* cited earlier, "The absence of fathers is linked to most social nightmares—from boys with guns to girls with babies . . . a missing father is a better predictor of criminal activity than race or poverty [and] growing up with both parents turns out to be a better antidote to teen pregnancy than handing out condoms." Although statistically supported, such reports fail to describe and explain the many healthy and stable black children parented in the noncustodial father family form. Nor do they capture the attitudes and experiences of many live-away fathers who do not abandon their children.

MANAGING THE STEREOTYPES

While commentators, journalists, advertisers, and social researchers hash out the reality of black masculinity and fatherhood, poor and working-class black men live in the wake of public sentiment. African American men are well aware of their popular image.

In the words of Russell Franklin, a live-away father of one, and a participant in this study, there exists a public notion that black fathers are "simply no good." His girlfriend Stephanie, present during the interview, likewise observed, "If you believe what you see on the TV, then it's a miracle that any children get raised."

Russell continued: "Anyone who knows me knows that I'm a good father to my daughter. There can be no doubt about that. People see me taking her to the store with me. I take her to McDonald's a couple of times a month. I take her to her cousin's. Just about everywhere I go, if I can't take her with me then I don't go."

Stephanie, listening to Russell's description, confirmed his paternal activities. "He goes and gets her almost every weekend at least," she said. "He's a good father . . . He does more than what most men do for their kids."

At the time of the study, Russell had been a father for eight years. His daughter, Tonya, was conceived when he and her mother had an "exclusive" relationship (dating only one another for almost two years prior to the pregnancy). At age 34, Russell placed fatherhood as the essential part of his life. But such fatherhood behaviors are considered an anomaly in black communities. "We are like the lowest of the low," Russell explained with some expression of frustration. "People see all of these bad stereotypes about black fathers leaving their children, not taking care of them, and they think all men are like that. . . . That's simply not true. Some of us are good fathers, and some of us can do better, and some of us are just plain fucked-up parents. But instead of seeing it like this, the public generally puts *all* of us in the 'plain fucked-up' category."

According to another live-away father: "Regardless of what they actually do as fathers, black men will always come up short in the public eye."

Another father expressed a similar sentiment: "The whole world thinks there is no such thing as a good black father . . . We just don't exist." As a whole, these fathers were troubled and hurt by the negative images of black fathers popularly portrayed in various media. However, they seemed more hurt than troubled. Many expressed an understanding that these portrayals were, both in the past and the present, "part of everyday life." Although they necessarily coped with the pervasiveness of the stereotypes, many felt it important to correct them and refute these unfavorable conventional ideas by describing their own lives and experiences with fatherhood, all of which, one father said, "undermines the humanity of black men as a whole." As Gibbs (1994) has argued, "from a very early age, Black males daily receive subtle and overt messages that they are expected to be unsocial, unmotivated and, undisciplined" (p. 135). Their self-esteem, competence, and dignity as black men is consistently placed under assault by the negative interactions that often occur in everyday circumstances.

Twenty-two-year-old Derik Bennett explained that there have been many instances that have left him feeling "like half a man." He described an incident that occurred while he was "doing like other fathers do and was shopping for a present for my son's birthday." Upon their entrance into the mall foyer, it seemed that he and his friends were immediately marked by security guards. "They follow us around," he contended, "from this store to that." This was not the first time he had had such an experience; in fact he said this occurs each time he goes to the mall. According to Derik, the security guards have a "bad perception" of black men. "They didn't care that I was trying to shop for my son . . . they just waiting, expecting, and hoping that you're gonna step outta line . . . that's the way they perceives us black men. Like we can't never do nothing right."

Derik was not alone in the experiences he described. Most fathers had similar reports of interaction in public places. Theo Harris, a middle-aged, tall, slender, and lightly bearded live-away father of four described how he felt he was viewed by others in common spaces such as shopping centers, walkways, and parks. He said that white women in particular were quite hostile toward him.

"If they don't know me, they think I'm a thug, a rapist, or something." He based this assessment on the fearful way "they look[ed] or act[ed]" when they noted his presence. Theo says that when he was younger, such behavior by whites, male and female, would anger him. He laughingly recalled how he would "get an attitude" and pretend he did not notice their rejecting behavior and deliberately walk in a path that would force them to walk around him. Theo's mood became more somber when he recalled the stress "of feeling not good enough" whenever such incidents occurred. "The thing is," he continued, "I dress better and I'm more polite than most white men out there . . . but for some reason they see me as an animal. . . It's that simple. Dark skin, plus man, equal animal."

Even within seemingly racially tolerant communities, color prejudice influences behavior toward black males. In Elijah Anderson's *Streetwise*, an ethnographic study of two neighborhoods in an urban setting, "an overwhelming number of young black males . . . are committed to civility and law-abiding behavior." However, this fact is lost on passers-by and neighbors both black and white. Anderson (1990) explains that black men have a hard time convincing others that they are nonthreatening human beings "because of the stigma attached to their skin color, age, gender, appearance, and general style of self-presentation. Criminality, incivility, toughness, and street smartness are often attributed to the unknown black male."

These fathers' analyses of how they are perceived and treated in public are echoed in the final report authored by President Cllnton's *Advisory Board to the Initiative on Race* (1998). In general, much of the report was a reiteration of the Kerner Commission's finding some thirty years prior (1968). Most African Americans and whites live in two separate worlds. They have different friendship groups, attend different churches, shop in different stores, watch different television programs, and live in different neighborhoods. African Americans continue to encounter racism and discrimination at the work place, in stores and restaurants, and recreational facilities. Consequently, they endure considerable stress when they are in predominantly white settings, whether they are playing the role of worker, shopper, or father. Offering some support to Majors and Billson's argument, these African American live-away fathers did feel the need to act "cool," particularly in public places, in an attempt to maintain dignity and self-worth. As one father explained, "When someone is racist towards you, and if he or she doesn't want to treat you like everybody else you just have to be cool—show them no emotion. Otherwise, you always going to feel bad about it." According to another father, appearing cold and uncaring was one means of "protecting your manhood," he explained. "This way you don't end up committing suicide or something." But it seems their apparent coolness was meant not only to protect their manhood but their children as well.[7]

With their children present, fathers were particularly aware of their status and treatment in public places. One father described how he felt when he and his son were grocery shopping under the "watchful eyes" of two security guards.

"It makes you feel like you doing something wrong by just being there," he said, incensed. "It makes you mad, especially when my boy is with me." He explained that he is never quite certain how to react to these incidents when his son is present. "In fact," he said, "sometimes I end up hollering at him instead of at the store owner or guard."

When this happened, he explained, he could feel himself "icing up" and trying to control all emotion. At one level he wanted to let his son know that "this is the way it is for us black men," but simultaneously he did not want his child to see the ugliness or pervasiveness of the prejudice directed toward African Americans. "It's my job to protect him," he said, "but I know I got to prepare him, too."

Yet overall, when they were with their children, admiration often replaced the lack of respect African American live-away fathers felt they received in everyday interactions. Store clerks were more courteous and seemed less cautious. Unemployment officers were more helpful. And women, white and black, were more friendly and tended to initiate conversations.

One father summed up the feelings of others with the following explanation: "When I have my boy with me, then I don't be worrying about how I'm going be treated in that store there or that one over here." From his experiences, he said, "it don't matter if it's a man or a woman [salesperson], white or black, they always treat you right when you got your child."

This was particularly true, according to fathers, if they were alone with their children and no other accompanying adult was present. The same father explained how it felt to walk into a store or restaurant under these conditions. "It's like another world done opened up," he said, "a whole 'nother world."

Another father made similar observations:

"Well, it's like, if you're by yourself you're just another nigga going out seeing what you can get or trying to get over—that's how they think—that you're up to no good. But that changes like that [snaps his fingers] when you're holding your children. Then you're a man; you get service; you get respect . . . and you feel it, too. It feels good—you say—'So this is what it's like.' And you're really proud because your children are there."

Elijah Anderson's findings suggest that different demographic groups are more readily accepted than others. Specifically, his findings suggest that "children readily pass inspection, white women and white men do so more slowly, black women, black men, and black male teenagers most slowly of all." In their 1995 study, St. John and Tamara Heald-Moore's findings indicate whites fear encounters with black strangers almost regardless of other characteristics such as age, gender, and setting of the encounter. Still their research suggested whites were most fearful of black male adolescents and young adults. The experiences of these fathers suggest that their master "black male" status is somewhat softened when in the company of small children for whom they are the obvious caretaker. The courteous treatment they receive when with their children may be result of racist notions of most black men as fathers. Ironically, this courteous treatment reinforces black men's feeling of honor in being fathers.

Despite how they were perceived and treated in their daily public interactions, these fathers expressed a confidence with themselves as men and as fathers. Several fathers commented:

"You always hear about the big bad black man. He's on the news, he's in the movies, he's everywhere. See, those things they be doing in the media—robbing and killing—that don't leave a brother nothing to be proud of. I've been a part of that life and I'll tell you, I like this life a lot better. I wouldn't trade it for the world. It's not glamorous—no fancy cars, no shopping sprees—but it's respectable."

"I don't make much money and in this world sometimes it seem like a man ain't nothing unless he makes some money. I'm hear to tell you that's a myth. It ain't about money. It's about how you treat your kids, your mama, and yourself. That's all that matters in the end."

"You've got to look at yourself in the mirror every morning. If you don't like what you see then ain't nobody else gonna like it either . . . I do right by my kids and by myself because I want to feel good about myself everyday . . . can't nobody take away your self-respect."

Although the public tends to define them otherwise, these black live-away fathers, regardless of the time they spend with children, view themselves in a manner sharply divergent with that of the public. When asked to provide five responses to the question, "Who Am I?" 31 percent listed "intelligent," or "smart." Almost half listed "Black Male," and 28 percent of these did so as a first response. About 73 percent described themselves with one or more of the following terms: "friendly," "nice," "caring," "loving," "good," "worthwhile," "patient" and "thoughtful."

Black fathers who do not live with their children are publicly perceived to place little to no meaning in their "fatherhood." The experiences of fathers in this study do little to uphold that assumption. Rather, their attitudes and behavior indicated the opposite. Being a father and spending time in public with their children lifted the social status of these men, both intrinsically and extrinsically. Their father status provided them with a modicum of dignity and respect they felt poor and working-class black men would not otherwise receive.

Some might argue that little progress has been made with regard to how black men are compared to their white counterparts and/or represented in the media. In 1999, Kweisi Mfume, president and CEO of the National Association for the Advancement of Colored People (NAACP) castigated major television networks for their lack of diversity on primetime television. While African Americans watch more television than most other demographic groups, of the twenty-six shows scheduled to begin in the 1999 fall season, none had a minority in a leading or starring role. A study commissioned by the NAACP (1999) found that over 60 percent of African Americans felt their demographic group was misrepresented on television.[8]

Not only are black fathers disappearing from our television screens, but according to a statement issued by the Morehouse Conference on African American Fathers (1999), "All across the United States, fathers are quietly disappearing from the lives of children" (p. 6). This, it reports, is a trend driven by "growing rates of out-of-wedlock births, separation, and divorce" (p. 6). The joint statement issued by Morehouse Research Institute and the

Institute for American Values acknowledged that the trend toward non-marital births among African Americans is a complex one. Research suggests that black families have traditionally provided their children with sufficient social and emotional support. And black men have historically had a presence of some sort in their children's familial systems. Research also indicates that African American women are less likely than other demographic groups to be awarded or to receive child support payments. An ongoing study by Sara McLanahan and Irwin Garfinkel, titled "The Fragile Families and Child Well-being Study," indicates that many fathers live with the mothers of their children at the time of birth. It and other studies suggest that men are also involved in the daily care of their children for at least a brief time following the onset of their parental status. As the numbers of black children in poverty escalates, fathers are being pressed more and more to provide what seems to matter most to policy makers.[9]

Fathers are well aware of how they are publicly perceived as men and as fathers. Choices and decisions about interactions and parenting are made in this context. Most significant, they are made under publicly ambiguous ideals about the quantity and quality time and the type of roles and functions live-away fathers should play in their children's lives. That is, low-income African American families have an ideal of fatherhood and what men are supposed to do in this capacity that does not quite mesh with popular Western notions. Despite misrepresentations and the lack of positive representations, findings from fathers and custodial mothers in this study distinctly reveal that they are a category of men who are setting their own standards with which to measure their parenting.

2

SLAVERY, CIVIL WAR, AND RECONSTRUCTION
Creating a Context for Black Live-Away Fatherhood

Slavery, the Civil War, and Reconstruction all served to sustain live-away fatherhood as a family form among African Americans. Within each, informal rules, formal policies and laws were developed that contributed to how and when fathers played paternal roles. Their fatherhood was negotiated within social, economic, and political institutions that were guided not by a social contract, but by systems attempting to sustain black people as a cheap labor source. Consequently, even after emancipation, noncustodial fatherhood as a family form was a significant part of black family life.

FATHERHOOD IN SLAVERY

For African American men, "live-away" and elements of noncustodial fatherhood are elements that were established centuries ago in the institution of slavery. "Noncustodial" fathers with whom the child does not primarily reside and who have an obligation established by an administrative judicial order to pay child support on the child's behalf. From both a historical and contemporary Western perspective, men are perceived as having "natural" rights to their biological offspring. Such rights assume custody as fathers are expected to reside with their children and provide for some measure of their well-being. Yet, as much past literature and documentation indicates, these rights and responsibilities did not exist under the system of slavery.

Unlike other demographic groups, bonded fathers were denied both legal rights to their children, and legal responsibility for them. While informally many black men were co-parents, sharing the daily care of their children with the children's mother, all slave fathers were formally noncustodial, having no legal attachment to their children whatsoever. Most records of slave births listed the name of the child and mother, while excluding the names of fathers. Furthermore, the lack of legal bonds and legal recourse enabled slave owners to remove black men from their families and homes at will, selling and trading them to maximize profits and minimize debts of Southern planters and early industrialists.[1]

The absence of black fathers' "natural" rights and responsibilities, as maintained by the system of slavery, served as a means of establishing black noncustodial fatherhood in this early period of black American history. It was an economic and social system that forced blacks into servitude and provided them with little and inconsistent control over the most fundamental aspects of their daily existence. A lack of formal bonds between enslaved fathers and children, the terms of marriages among bondsmen and women, and the conditions of childbearing all contributed to the live-away aspects of many bondsmen's fatherhood. Moreover, the conditions of family under this system were a precursor for what is often referred to as our modern day family tragedy. That is, almost 90 percent of all black children today will at some point prior to their eighteenth birthday live in a home in which their father does not reside.

THE TERMS OF MARRIAGE
IN THE AMERICAN SYSTEM OF SLAVERY

As a system, slavery developed to ensure the Southern economy maintained an expansive source of controlled cheap labor. Laws established to protect, encourage, and reinforce the nuclear family structure of the free white population did not apply to bondspeople. Marriage among slaves, for example, had no legal sanction. This is not to say that marital unions did not occur; to the contrary, enslaved men and women commonly joined as "husband" and "wife." Despite the absence of legalities, marriage was generally a solemn vow made between men and women before God. Slave owners, black preachers and, at times, white ministers presided over ceremonies. However, husbands and wives had no bond that was recognized or protected by law.[2]

Slave owners understood that permitting and encouraging marital unions produced slave offspring, which subsequently augmented their supply of cheap labor and increased their property values. Owners also recognized that marital unions tended to produce a more stable and contented slave community. Such communities, particularly those with historically long kinship lines, tended to be more economically productive than those less stable. White planters also recognized that, like relationships within the free society, the postponement of marriage to a later age assured the maturity of the couple and further encouraged stability. Thus, they and many bonded parents discouraged young slaves from marrying, until after the boy and girl were at least twenty years of age.

Overall, slaves tended to enter marriage by one of two means—involuntarily and voluntarily. Involuntary unions were those in which one or both partners was forced to marry the other. Such marital unions quite often sprang from the slave owner's greed. Women of child-bearing age were often forced to marry or live with a male slave of their owner's choice. Such marriages were often filled with discontent and presented a source of instability for the owner and the slave community as a whole. Such marriages, too, were more likely than others to end in separation, divorce, and live-away fatherhood prior to and after emancipation. The circumstances of Rufus and Rose provide an example. Their owner insisted that because the two were healthy and "portly" they should come together to produce children. They were forced to live together as husband and wife. However, the arrangement was staunchly against the wishes of Rose, who threatened Rufus with bodily harm when he attempted to consummate the "marriage." Eventually, Rose consented but upon emancipation she "quit" her husband, although they had two children together (*American Slave* 1972).

Voluntary marriages sometimes occurred for pragmatic reasons but extensive past research suggests they were often borne of love and affection between bonded men and women. Relationships between slave men and women tended to follow their natural course when an equitable marriage pool existed on plantations and farms. Slave owners generally permitted and encouraged men and women to seek and marry partners with whom they felt a reciprocal attraction. The love, affection, and emotional bond that developed would often lead to voluntary, long-lasting, fruitful marriages. Of such marriages one slave commented: "[y]oung folks took their time and went together a long time and [when] they married they stayed married" (Escott 1979:49).

EQUALITY IN MARRIAGE AND THE NECESSARY
SELF-RELIANCE OF SLAVE WOMEN

Whether marriages were voluntary or involuntary, short or long-lasting, neither the father's role nor the father's sense of masculinity tended to be defined in terms of the traditional Western or European American standard. While blacks seemed aware of the emphasis white society placed on proper "masculine" and "feminine" behavior within the family, these were generally not used to judge "proper behavior" among themselves. Unlike many marriages in free society, particularly among the well-to-do, those in slave communities did not have the same concrete set of husband/father or wife/mother duties on which masculine and feminine roles were based. Yet, there is some evidence to suggest that some salve owners attempted to encourage European-American division of labor on the slave community. Women were expected to labor in the home after a day's work in the field— sweeping, cooking, laundering, sewing, and other "women's work." Men were often encouraged by owners to hunt, trap, and fish to supplement the family paltry diet (Genovese 1972).[3]

Still, evidence indicates that to some extent men often shared women's work tasks with their mates. Likewise, women participated in most if not all tasks traditionally performed by men. While research suggests the majority of slave owners provided their slaves with enough food to eat, meals were often coarse and monotonous. Consequently, malnutrition existed, and would have been much worse if meals had not been supplemented with freshly picked fruits and vegetables from slave gardens, and game they had acquired. There is little doubt that slave families fared better with a male in the household. "Black women fell victims to white lust, but many escaped because the whites knew they had black men who would rather die than stand idly by."[4]

Nevertheless, bonded women typically had no choice but to learn to fend for themselves. They tended to engage in all activities that would insure the survival of themselves and their children. Fathers, brothers, and particularly husbands were in a tenuous situation—each could be "sold away" or otherwise separated from the family without a moment's notice. Equality in unions and marriages was a necessity for survival in the system of slavery, its manifest function being to make certain that women could take care of themselves and their children with or without the presence of the children's father. Nancy Boudry, an ex-slave interviewed during the Federal Works Project, recalled the live-away status of her husband and what this meant for her and her children.

My husband didn' live on de same plantation where I was, de Jerrell place in Columbia County. He never did have nuthin' to give me 'cause he never got nuthin.' I had to work hard, plow and go and split wood jus' like a man.[5]

"ABROAD" MARRIAGES

Generally, two types of marriages occurred among slaves—those between men and women living on the same property or plantation, and those occurring "abroad" between slaves from different plantations. Men marrying abroad were, essentially, live-away fathers in that they could not live with their wives and children on a full-time basis. Jasper Battle, an ex-slave at the age of 80, spoke of his family's structure:

> Mammy b'longed to Marse Henry. She was Harriet Jones. Daddy was Simon Battle and his owner was Marse Billie Battle. De Battle's plantation was off down der nigh de Jones' place. When my Mammy and Daddy got married Marse Henry wouldn't sell Mammy, and Marse Billie wouldn't sell Daddy, so dey didn't git to see one another but twice a week—dat was on Wednesday and Sadday nights.[6]

Another ex-slave confirmed the experiences of many: "If a man married abroad it meant that he wouldn't see his wife [but] only about once a week."[7] Other reports, like Battle's, indicate that approved visits generally occurred once or twice a week, on Wednesdays, Saturdays, and holidays. Additionally, it was not uncommon for men to have more than one bonded wife and two sets of children. Fathering was often a role that was assumed part time, at best. And, as Deborah White (1985) and others explain, many men preferred the separation to witnessing the daily degradation experienced by their families. In this way, they could avoid the pain of seeing their wives and children suffer under the torturous elements of slavery, particularly since they themselves were often helpless to defend them (Genovese 1972; White 1985).

DIVORCE AND SEPARATION

What distinguished slave marriages from those of the free society was not the occurrence of divorce, separation, and out-of-wedlock births. These elements were part of white society as well, though to a much lesser degree. Rather, it was the conditions of each that served to institute and sustain live-away fatherhood both during and after slavery. Fathers were often separated from their children's household through separation or informal divorce. They were also forcibly parted from their families by sale and or by their children being born out of short-term unions.

Unlike white women during this period, slave women were not legally or economically tied to their husbands. Nor were they dependent on husbands for goods and services. Food, clothing, shelter were all provided for by slave owners. And, as discussed, women supplemented family diets with gardens and hunting, and produced clothing and such by their own hand. Relative to free women, they could separate or "divorce" from husbands and remove their children's father from the household with comparative ease and, apparently, with little social constraint. The status of mother superseded that of wife and fathers, who had no legal claims on either.

The bonded child's physical welfare came from slave owners, whether or not the father resided in the household. Slave owners were not concerned with how a marital disruption might affect the emotional well-being of children present in the household. Similarly, the child's emotional well-being was probably not of great concern to the father or mother, particularly if the father lived on the property and could still be an active part of the child's life. Eugene Genovese suggests that "their easy attitude towards divorce was strongly reinforced by the knowledge that the blow to the children would be greatly softened in a community in which all looked after all and the master had to feed all" (1972:471). However, if a father lived abroad and a divorce were granted, he would possibly lose the visiting privileges offered by his wife's owner, given that an acknowledged and sexual and "fruitful" relationship between the two would no longer exist.

In determining divorce actions, slave owners were, again, primarily concerned with potential pregnancies and resulting births. The potential for the women to bear future slaves was the central element in the slave owner's consideration of a divorce between those who were bonded. They tended to discourage divorce only when there was a shortage of men and/or the women was of childbearing age. If she were beyond childbearing age, there was probably no objection at all. Once granted, a divorce served to remove the father from his children's household, though he still might remain in the slave community.[8]

"SOLD AWAY" AND SEPARATED FROM CHILDREN

In addition to divorce, fathers were often separated from their children when one, or the other, was "sold away" to a slave trader or another owner. Historical records and slave narratives suggest that slave fathers and children were quite often separated in this manner. It was more likely that children and fathers, rather than children and mothers, would be separated by sale or other various means, at least when the children were young. According to laws regarding slavery, a "slave family" consisted of a mother and her children. Recognizing the emotional bond between young children and their mothers, and the psychological harm that may ensue when separating the two, some states made it illegal for slave owners and traders to separate children under age ten from their mothers. However, it seems that only the state of Louisiana was successful in maintaining this lawful bond. Regardless, no such law recognized or protected the relationship and bond between a slave father and his children.

Yet, it is certain that slave owners knew such bonds existed between fathers and their children. In one account, a bonded father, quite visibly shaken, cut off his hand with an ax when his son was sold away from him. Still another broke down in uncontrollable sobs when his children were sold away. An owner's whim, death, disability, or financial problems could at any time lead to the sale and separation of a slave father from his children. With this knowledge, fathers often charged a trusted male friend with the responsibility of looking after their children.[9]

Physical separation did not prevent slave fathers from remembering and caring for their children. Many went to great efforts, and overcame many obstacles, to remain a part of their children's lives. Hannah Chapman, a voice from the Federal Writers Project of the Works Progress Administration (WPA) provided an example:

> My father wuz sold 'way from us when I wuz small. Dat wuz a sad time fer us. Mars wouldn't see de mudders' way from der chillun so us lived on wid her wid out de fear ob bein' sold. My pa sho' did hate ter leave us. He missed us and us longed fer him. He would often slip back ter us' cottage at night. Us would gather 'round him an' crawl up I his lap, tickled slap to death, but he give us dese pleasures at a painful risk. When his Mars missed him he would beat him all de way home. Us could track him de nex' day by de blood stains.[10]

When Nettie Henry's owner gave her, her siblings, and her mother away to a relative, Nettie's father refused to accept the breakup of his family. For five years he traveled across the state line to visit them. Later, after being moved to Texas and following emancipation, he returned to set up a farm for his loved ones.[11]

OUT-OF-WEDLOCK BIRTHS

Premarital sex and out-of-wedlock births were an integral and acceptable aspect of slave communities. There appeared to be relatively few, if any, social impediments to either element. According to Genovese "slaves did not separate marriage or sex itself from love . . . they held the theory that good Christians did not sin by sleeping together out of wedlock, for they were pure and could not defile each other (1972:471). Men often had children with women out-of-wedlock. However, there was little social pressure for them to marry the mother of their children. Bonded single mothers might eventually marry. However, the partner chosen was not necessarily the father of her offspring, though this was often the case. Herbert Gutman's (1976) description of slave relationships and union suggest it was also quite likely that she would choose to marry and raise her children with a man other than her children's natural father.

Regardless of the type of marriage, bonded men were generally not in the position to provide either wives or children with the traditional benefits of marriage and fatherhood—protection, discipline, shelter, food, or clothing. They could not protect their wives or children from varying forms of physical and emotional abuse, including sexual exploitation that occurred at the hands of slave owners as well as from other slaves. Thus, they could not use the provision of protection or subsistence to establish or maintain authority in the family, although there is some evidence to suggest that some fathers asserted their familial authority as much as they could. Martha Spence Bunton recalled that following the death of her mother, her father performed all parental functions for herself and her siblings, managing the household as well as the discipline:

> I remembah ho on Sunday mawnin's when we didn't have nothin' to do, he'd git out ob bed in our log cabin, make a big fire, and tell us: "Jimminy-cripes! Yo' chillun stay in yo' beds. I'll make de biscuits." He would too. I still laugh when I think about dem big rye biscuits dat was so laghe, dat we called 'em "nigger Heels". . . Oh, fathaw was good to us. Ob course, he whooped us when we needed it.[12]

Overall, the roles and functions black fathers played in the lives of their children is somewhat vague and has historically been a matter of scholarly debate. Yet, it appears that many fathers were forced to play a less than full-time role in regards to the care of their children. Martha Spence Bunton's father was a live-away father until the death of his owner and his subsequent purchase by the owner of his wife and children. Some early researchers of the slave family argue that because marriages were not legally sanctioned, the father's role was peripheral and that he was not expected or encouraged to participate in the socialization of his children. For example, C. H. Nichols (1972) argues that enslavement prevented African American fathers from protecting or disciplining their children and often from residing with them. The law did not recognize slave fathers as head-of-household or grant him the authority that the title entails. Rather, rewards and punishments, and the provider role were performed by slave owners. As a result, he and others argue, parental obligations were often abandoned.

While there is much evidence to support the paterfamilias role assumed by slave owners over slave families there also exists evidence pointing to the ability of slave fathers to "father" their children despite the hardships and obstacles of slave-time-fatherhood. To repeat, many contemporary interpretations suggest that slave owners often permitted and encouraged slaves to live as a family unit. Based on records and narratives from those formerly enslaved, this view maintains that fathers played an essential role in the lives of their children. The father often imposed his authority over the family—unfortunately, at times, by force. He disciplined his children, entertained his children with songs and stories, and supplemented the family diet by hunting and trapping small game.[13]

THE CIVIL WAR AND THE MAINTENANCE OF LIVE-AWAY FATHERHOOD

While the system of slavery ensured that many fathers would never reside with or be able to fully provide for their children, the Civil War served to reinforce the live-away experiences of African American families. At the start of the war many bondsmen, women, and children fled the plantations, farms, and owners to whom they were bonded. In search of freedom and protection, they set up small shanty communities near and around Union army encampments. These "refugee settlements" served as recruiting posts for the Union army, which sought to draft the strongest and healthiest black men into its regiments. Fourteen percent of the black male population, approximately a quarter of a million men between the ages of eighteen and forty-five, served the Union war effort in some formal capacity. They served as soldiers, laborers, teamsters, craftsmen, and servants. While black men wanted freedom for their families, not all of those who joined the Union army did so voluntarily. Many were literally "wrenched" from their families, causing great resentment and sadness among wives and children who, for all that was known to them, would never see their husbands and fathers again.[14]

Regardless of how these men entered the Union army, the well-being of their children and wives remained a constant source of anxiety. Yet, whether their wives and children had remained in the plantation or had settled in refugee camps, soldier-fathers from Confederate states were unable to secure safe conditions for their families. Slave owners often took their anger over the war out on the bonded children and women who remained on the plantations. As one bondswoman wrote to the soldier father of her child: "They are treating me worse and worse everyday. Our child cries for you" (Berlin and Rowland 1997:98).

Such pleas were agonizing for black soldier fathers who could do little to ease their families' woes. Although they were supposed to be paid for their service, fathers generally had no means of consistently meeting their families' economic needs. Pay from the Union Army quartermaster was a notoriously slow and unpredictable process, and families suffered immensely as a result.[15] Rosanna Henson, the wife of a black soldier, made a written plea to President Lincoln:

> Sir, my husband, who is in Co. K. 22nd Reg't U.S. Col'd Troops (and now in the Macon Hospital at Portmouth with a wound in his arm) has not received any pay since last May and then only thirteen dollars. I write to you because I have been told you would see to it. I have four children to support and I find this a great struggle. A hard life this! I being a cold woman do not get any State pay. Yet my husband is fighting for the country. (Berlin and Rowland 1997:85–86).

Their lack of pay and pleas from their families prompted many soldiers to petition for a military discharge in an attempt to better provide for their children and other relatives. John Turner, a northern black soldier made the following request to a state military agent:

> My circumstances and the circumstances of my family are such that I feel it my duty to ask for my discharge. I enlisted on the 5th October last— and never have received a cent since I have been in service. My family are sick and absolutely naked, having no clothes to wear. They are also threatened with being turned into the street. Now I respectfully ask for my discharge that I may be able to attend to the wants of my family—or

if I cannot obtain my discharge I earnestly petition for my pay. (Berlin
and Rowland 1997:101)

Women with children who set up settlements near their husbands' military camps were treated like prostitutes and "vagrants" by white Union soldiers and officials. Thus, married women and children who had spouses and
fathers in the military were essentially no better off than those who had no
relations in the military. Whether were separated from their fathers via the
military or by mothers and extended family systems consisting primarily of
women, mothers generally assumed the well-being and care of children.
According to the findings of historian J. Jones:

> Although many women had no choice but to seek food and safety from
> northern troops . . . others managed to attain relative freedom from
> white interference . . . in areas where whites had fled and large number
> of black men had marched—or been marched off—with the Union
> army, wives, mother, daughters, and sisters often grew crops and cared
> for each other. (J. Jones 1985:50)

As on the plantation, the organization and the processes of the military
system assured that women necessarily continued to manage themselves
and their children without the full or consistent participation of fathers.
Regardless of black men's intentions, they hardly outweighed the cavalier
attitude the Union Army seemed to have toward helping black soldier-
fathers care for their children. It appears that while black live-away fatherhood was built into the system of slavery, it was perpetuated by the very war
that eventually brought an end to this system of bondage.

AN ENDURING FAMILY FORM

It appears that noncustodial fatherhood was often not the relationship
black fathers preferred to have with their children. Yet, despite their freedom, black men could not escape the wrath the conditions of enslavement
continued to impart on their fatherhood. Following emancipation, many
black men who had been separated from their families by slavery and war
sought to relocate and return to their children and "wives." Additionally,
after the Civil War many freed fathers left the plantation of their former
owners to live with their abroad wife and children. However, slave-time

practices, such as the practice of selling and reselling of slaves, the inauthenticity of slave marriages, and the practice of encouraging adult men and women to have sexual relationships without wedlock meant that even with freedom, live-away fatherhood would remain a prominent and steadfast form of black family life.[16] While many fathers successfully located families after emancipation, others were destined to fail. As a means of identifying one's birthplace and kin it was customary for slaves to take the name of their slave owner. Through this means of identification, father's sought to trace the whereabouts of their children to a particular location. Unfortunately, many children were sold away and resold time and time again, leaving many fathers to search in vain. Under such circumstances, noncustodial fatherhood was the only type of relationship many fathers could ever hope to have with their missing children. Nevertheless, the often inevitable futility of searching for children did not deter many from the attempt. For more than a decade after emancipation, black publications printed "Information Wanted" advertisements from freedmen-seeking information about children and relatives from whom they had been separated by slavery and war.[17]

NONLEGAL MARITAL UNIONS

Since marriages were not legal under slavery, men and women divorced and remarried without legal ramifications and without the knowledge of the original spouse. Men who were sold away or fought in the Union Army were forced to leave behind wives, lovers, and children. Many men returned to their old homes to find their wives "married" to someone else. Narratives and accounts from former slaves suggest that while many women remained faithful to their men, others set up households with other men, often legally marrying them.

Harrison Smith, like many fathers, was determined to reestablish bonds with the child he and his wife conceived under the system of slavery. Following the war, Smith learned that shortly after he had joined the Union Army his wife of eight years began "keeping the house" of another man. His concern for his noncustodial child's welfare prompted him to seek custody of his son. Because he was stationed in a state distant from his child, he requested that his sister-in-law, Minty, retain temporary custody until his return. He wrote:

> Minty I ask of you in this letter to go and take my boy from my wif as sh
> is not doeing write by him take him and keep him until I com home if sh

is not willing to gave him up go to the fried mands bury [Freedman's Bureau] and shoe this letter it is my recust for you to have him I doe not want her to have my child with an another man she is not living writ to rase children . . . I will be hom next fall if I live asholder stand abad chanc but if god spars me I will be home.[18]

Narratives and accounts by former slaves also reveal the emphasis slave owners placed on reproducing the slave population. Such emphasis made noncustodial fatherhood after slavery an inevitable reality for many black men. Maggie Sternhouse, a former slave, explained: "Durin' slavery there were stockmen. . . They were weighed and tested. A man would rent the stockman and put him in a room with some young women he wanted to raise children from" (Escott 1979:45).

This practice not only separated many bonded fathers from the children with whom they had once shared a household but, in many cases, also separated the bearing of children from fatherhood itself. This researcher's interview with eighty-five-year-old Lilly Booth encouraged her to recount a story her mother told about Lilly's grandfather: "Not only was he what they call a stud during slavery—having all kinds of children but then he went and got married at least twice, as I was told, and had more children."

Such fathers were noncustodial during slavery and, following emancipation, necessarily continued in this vein. Even if Lewis Jones's father had chosen to marry her mother, he would still have been a noncustodial father to his other thirty-eight children conceived with various women. According to the diary of Thomas Wentworth Higginson, Union colonel of a black regiment: "It was not uncommon for men to have two or three wives in different plantations—the second, or remoter, partner being called a 'broad wife,'–i.e., wife abroad" (Higginson 1970:258). Marital predicaments like these could only encumber the experiences of children living without fathers, and fathers living away from their children.

While these slavery practices enabled noncustodial fatherhood to be perpetuated in freedom, they can only account for experiences up to the late nineteenth century. By this time, all children born under the conditions of slavery would have reached adulthood and begun building families of their own. No matter, the economic, political, and social conditions of life in twentieth-century America created conditions that sustained a live-away family form among many black low-income families.

INSTITUTING FORMAL MARRIAGE

With freedom, men and women took great pride in legitimizing those intimate bonds which, under slavery, had no authority. Emphasis was placed on
the marriage ceremony, on the marital institution itself, and on raising children within these marriages. In the late nineteenth and early twentieth centuries, marital ceremonies were particularly large and extravagant family
events, particularly among "society" blacks and others earning relatively
comfortable incomes. Such events often mirrored the pomp and circumstance of those of their white counterparts. Engagements were relatively
long and publicly announced. Photographs of the intended brides and
grooms and a lengthy description of their social backgrounds could often
be viewed in the weekly editions of black community newspapers and journals, a tradition that continues to this day.

Most blacks, though, could ill afford the costs of such pageantry. Nor did
they have the time to devote to lengthy engagements or extravagant wed-
ding preparations. For the most part, black weddings occurred on a much
smaller scale. Couples often chose to marry through a justice of the peace
who performed an efficient and simple ceremony. Others married in small
church gatherings with family, friends, and a feast consumed by all after the
ceremony.

Emancipation appeared to release the black family from the detrimental demands of slavery. Men's participation in the Civil War, the end of slavery, and progressive southern state constitutions which were developed
between 1867 and 1869, provided impetus for black males to seek and gain
patriarchal privileges. Many of these constitutions abolished property
qualifications which had previously prohibited black men from holding
office and voting. During the period of Radical Reconstruction, blacks
served in Southern state legislatures as representatives and senators. Additionally, as sociologist Donna Franklin (1997) explained, they demanded to
be afforded the same patriarchal privileges provided white males. These
demands were steeled by many state constitutions and Freedman's Bureau
policies, which designated black men as heads of households, made them
responsible for children and wives, and gave them legal rights to sign con-
tracts for the entire family. Simultaneously, violent white organizations
developed to maintain "white supremacy" and to keep blacks "in their
place." Moreover, by the end of the nineteenth century much of the progressive legislation had been repealed. Black men were effectively disen-

franchised and neither their patriarchal authority or economic security became firmly established.[19]

Additionally, sharecropping and tenant farming arrangements enabled plantation owners to remain steadfast in their attempt to maintain a cheap labor source. Black Codes and Vagrancy Laws were designed to control blacks' labor and where they lived. Additionally, there exist many accounts of children being forcibly separated from mothers and fathers through Southern apprenticeship laws during the period of Reconstruction. Such laws enabled whites to keep custody of black children despite parental objection and an end to slavery. In such cases fathers and mothers often sought the return of children through the established court system, or stealthily took their children from the premises of the former slave owners.[20]

Regardless of continued struggles, historical interpretations of the black family praise the strength of marital bonds within slavery and in the hundred years following. During this period, legal divorce and children raised in one-parent households were relatively uncommon among African American families. Indeed, for the century following the end of slavery, the majority of families with children were two-parent households. This family form seemingly remained stable among African Americans from 1890 to the mid-twentieth century. In fact, there is evidence to suggest that Southern ex-slaves were more likely than Northern free blacks to maintain two-parent households. Contrary to the Frazier thesis, chaos and disorganization did not consume black families. However, many men and children continued to experience fatherhood in residences away from one another. The theses espoused by Frazier and Moynihan have consistently been refuted by those emphasizing high rates of two-parent households among blacks during this period. However, they do not emphasize the experiences of reconstituted families and live-away fathers, and other established, viable, and legitimate family forms.[21]

IS THAT YOUR "REAL" DADDY?

Despite the dramatic change in social conditions, the terms of fatherhood continued to be subject to the American class and caste system, which placed blacks at the bottom of the social and economic hierarchies. While the majority of families with children consisted of dual parents, the extent to which these marital unions were reconstituted or "blended" is virtually unknown. Although the term was not utilized as such during this period, "blended families" were those marriages or remarriages in which at least one partner brought a child from a previous relationship into the new marital union. Following separations, divorce, and out-of-wedlock births, most African American children tended to remain with their birth mothers—an aspect of the past that remains in contemporary black family life. Marriages and remarriages in which children were involved likely consisted of a mother, her children, and a stepfather.

In 1864–1866 marriage records for Vicksburg, Mississippi, 57 percent of 2,053 black men who were remarrying reported having at least one child from a previous marriage. Ruth Reed, in her 1926 study *Illegitimacy in New York City*, reported that single-parenting mothers and noncustodial fathers were not uncommon among black Americans. And Borchert's 1980 study of turn-of-the-century "Alley Life" in Washington, D.C., demonstrated that live-away fatherhood was an ordinary occurrence. Young unmarried mothers often stayed in their parents' homes and children often lived within an extended family structure. The same was reported in a study of a small Georgia town during the same period, where of 44 women participating in the study, 21 had one or more children before marriage. Moreover, the proportion of out-of-wedlock births increased by over 100 percent (106.3) from the mid 1900s to 1962.[22]

Census data collected in the early decades of this century do not reliably reflect the proportion of children residing without their biological fathers. In 1940 alone, approximately 25 percent of all births among the rural non-white population and 11.6 percent of urban births missed being recorded, and it is likely that an even greater proportion of out-of-wedlock births went unregistered. In 1950, the missed births among rural blacks (then two-fifths of the black population) were reduced by half, but this still left over 11 percent of black births unreported (Bernard 1966).

Nor does data from the nineteenth and the early part of this century provide us with information sufficient enough to ascertain the full extent to which children of dual-parent families were actually living with a stepfather rather than their birth father. U.S. Census data on whether parents were living with their "own" children did not become available until 1960. Yet even then there was virtually no means to account for stepfathers or stepchildren. The 1960 census defined "own" child as "a single (never married) son, daughter, adopted, or stepchild." Nor do we have consistent census data revealing the extent of live-away fatherhood—the proportions of black single men who had fathered children, or the proportion of married or remarried men who had biological children that were not a part of their current household. Other evidence, however, indicates that the noncustodial father family form endured throughout the nineteenth and twentieth centuries. The question, then, is not whether they existed; such family forms are a historical reality. A more detailed analysis of the extent of their existence is probably best left to social historians or at least a separate study. Rather, the present problem is uncovering the experiences of those within such family forms, and particularly roles men played as fathers to their live-away children.

There is an indication that some live-away fathers were an integral part of their children's daily lives. In turn-of-the-century alley housing in Washington D.C. it was not uncommon to find poor and working-class men (whether they lived in the home or not) caring for children while mothers were at work. Although they tended to earn more income per day than women, their employment was less consistent. Also, there is evidence that some men legally claimed their children and paid regular child support. An example can be found in Borchert's (1980) study of this period. A man named Hutchinson headed a household in the same community as that which his former common-law wife and shared offspring resided. Through the Juvenile Court he paid for the support of his children. Evidence also suggests that black fathers, as in slavery, were likely to participate in many aspects of parenthood, not just economic ones. Hutchinson performed expressive roles, and was described as being quite domestic—sitting for hours in the doorway with his son Joe in his lap. It did not appear that his live-away father status was looked down upon. Indeed, it was reported that he was a steady worker and well-respected by most in his community.

Other evidence suggests that some live-away fathers were not as paternal in their behavior as Hutchinson. In 1920s New York, for example, thousands of unmarried mothers sought assistance from varying social service agencies in an attempt, among other things, to "discover the whereabouts of the lover who had disappeared and failed to fulfill his promises of marriage or financial aid; or because they wish advice as to means of forcing him to meet his obligations in the support of the child" (Reed 1926:73).[23] While this suggests that many mothers expected fathers to provide at least some economic support, interviews with a sample of African Americans born between 1910 and 1920 in the Midwest suggest something to the contrary. Several elderly African Americans participated in this study. According to those who came of age in the 1920s and '30s, children born out of wedlock during that period were considered "fatherless." As one respondent explained:

"There was Essie S., now I know she didn't have a Daddy. She was illegitimate. See, it used to be that if your mother and father weren't married you couldn't put the father's name on the birth certificate. Of course, now when I was coming up we didn't even have birth certificates. So if your momma wasn't married then you just didn't have a daddy! Even though everybody might know who he really was."

Other respondents' reports suggest that fathers were not expected to provide economic or social support for their children, particularly when they did not have dependable, well-paying employment:

"Back then illegitimate children were just absorbed by the mother's family. They helped her raise them probably better than having the man around would. At least then they [the custodial mothers] know there's always help from her mother and her father. I mean financial help and just raising the children. Men weren't expected to be responsible for their illegitimate children."

"All I know about my father is that he moved from one job to another and from one woman to another. He was known for that. He was a ladies man who mostly lived on his good looks. Everybody knew it. My mother just got swayed by him. He never intended on marrying her. I was raised by John Bennett. He's the only daddy that has ever done for me."

"My mother said she never asked him [his father] for anything because he didn't have much, and he never gave. That's just the way it was then."

Despite the memories recalled above, many live-away black fathers, particularly those with regular employment, did provide for their children. Eighty-seven year old Millicent, whose father worked "steady delivering ice" and 89-year-old Nancy, whose father was a coal miner, told of their live-away fathers:

"I always knew who my father was. I knew he was married and had kids. He recognized me as his daughter, though. Sometimes he would take me downtown, buy me little girl things, sing to me. Sometimes he would visit me and my mother. He was always in a clean shirt. Very neat. I guess that's where I get it from.

"See, I don't really know about their relationship because I wasn't told anything and adults have certain conversations in front of kids. I barely remember what he [my father] looked like. I really have to concentrate to imagine him because it has been so many years. But he was handsome . . . Worked in the coal mines for awhile, took sick and stopped working. Started doing some piddlin' around. He was from Tennessee. I mean his kin was, and for awhile he went back there. He was loving and kind, gentle for a man.

"When I was about 9 or 10 my mother got married and we moved to another town where my stepdaddy could get work. After that I never saw my father again until I was grown—at a family reunion. He recognized me right off."

Nancy's parents were never legally married but she recalled that her father spent "a couple of days a week" at her and her mother's home, though she saw him "only an hour or so" on those visiting days—mostly due to the long hours he kept at work. Holidays were generally spent visiting her maternal grandmother, and her father would often accompany them on these special occasions. "He was just part of the family," she offered.

She could not recall what eventually ended the relationship between her mother and father except "my stepdaddy was moving to Chicago and I guess she knew that was the only way she'd get there." Visits with her father were abruptly halted once the move occurred. Letter exchanges between the two were few and far between; although Nancy completed the eighth grade, her father could neither read not write. In adulthood, she was able to communicate with him via telephone on a somewhat regular basis. However, she said they were never able to "recapture the time that had passed" and each sorely regretted the circumstances that prevented a stronger father-daughter bond.

Economic, social, and political institutions provide a basic context for the development of live-away fatherhood among African Americans. Each in some way influences the roles and functions fathers serve in their children's lives. In slavery, the Civil War, and Reconstruction black men negotiated their manhood and fatherhood roles despite formal and informal sanctions and work schedules that discouraged traditional paternal behavior. Despite continuing academic debates, it seems that throughout American history, black men attempted to parent their children. However, work, proximity, and new relationships often served as hindrances.

But what we also find is that despite its historical precedent, the noncustodial parent family form continues to have a nebulous definition that provides little guidance for fathers' parental behavior. Whether they visit with their children once a week, once a year, or not at all, what fathers do for children seems to be influenced by what they do for a living—the type of work they do, the hours they must put in, the skill level of the occupation, the potential hazards and hardships of the occupation, and the amount of pay they receive for what they produce. This inexorable reality seems to hold true whether one reflects on black families in the past or present.

3

"TIMES ARE JUST GOING TO GET WORSE . . ."
Fathers Chasing the American Dream

*I*t is increasingly difficult for low-income, low-skilled American black men to be economically responsible for their children. Relative to those who marry, never-married fathers tend to be poorer, have less education, and fewer job skills. Yet, as was discussed earlier, our society continues to define noncustodial fatherhood in primarily economic terms. Black live-away fathers today then, like those in the past, must negotiate ideal parenting under obscure circumstances. Fathers in this study demonstrate an understanding of this predicament for themselves and others in similar economic circumstances. In this chapter they discuss their livelihood and their attempts to improve the quality of life for themselves and their children. We begin with Justin Banks, interviewed in his home in Houston, Texas.

Justin Banks lay his sleeping ten-month-old nephew in the middle of Justin's mother's wood-frame bed. The child seemed to stir slightly and I watched, waiting for him to cry. Eyes closed, he simply repositioned himself on his grandmother's taut pink sheets. They were tucked neatly and tightly in military fashion.

"During the day, I usually make a pallet for him on the living room floor," said Justin. "Then I take a nap with him. But, the dog done tracked mud all in here this morning," he said rather whimsically. He later told me how the baby had leaned against the unlatched screen door and enabled Chester and his four muddy paws to trample throughout the house—much to the child's amusement. The only room left unscathed was the bathroom, and that was only because the door was always kept shut. Justin picked up toys from the floor and placed them in the cardboard box at the end of his mother's bed. I scanned the room, noting the assortment of perfumes, faux jewelry, and hair combs organized on top of a dresser. My eyes rested on the many photos that were neatly taped to the dresser mirror: "Are these yours?" I asked, pointing to a photo of three children, posing handsomely against a sky-blue professional photographers background.

"Naw, those are my sister's. They live across the street, probably be over here in a little bit . . . These are mine," he said, motioning toward another photo of three children. The group was kneeling in front of a Christmas tree. "Christmas Eve last year at their mama's house," Justin stated, as if reading the question from my mind. With a tissue, he wiped a small smudge from the mirror. He gently covered the child with a light, worn, green baby blanket, and then we both exited the room.

Directly adjacent to his mother's room was the living room. Justin offered me a seat on the somewhat tattered, mauve-colored sofa. It sat opposite a console television and a ten-gallon fish aquarium. The pump on the aquarium hummed softly and the breeze from a window fan made the room quite comfortable. Other than the muddy dog prints, the home appeared quite tidy, in stark contrast to the littered and pot-holed streets that surrounded it. The aroma from the pot of hamhocks and beans simmering on the kitchen stove made for a homey atmosphere.

Justin sat in an old rocker and began folding laundry from a plastic basket that sat at his feet. He looked easily at home, comfortable, doing what is often considered "women's work." He laughed when I commented on this. "Well, it's true . . . I'm like uh, uh, what's that, uh Mr. Mom. Always doing something around the house and always have kids trailing behind me when I go somewhere, but," he continued, "it's important that I keep busy since my working isn't always too steady." He continued folding the laundry, an assortment of men's, women's, and mostly children's clothing. I ask him about his work.

"Well . . . " he put down the laundry and rested his arms on the squeaking chair. He turned his eyes away from mine and toward the black television screen, and there was silence for a few moments, "Right now I work for a construction contractor. But like, now, his business is slow so he don't need my help everyday." He explains that his work situation varies little from that of other men in his neighborhood. "In fact," he states with a hint of certainty, "it's likely a heap a lot better."

This was true, I thought. The employment situation for black men in general, was bleak. However, it was particularly acute in Justin's neighborhood, the primarily black, impoverished, and run-down area of Homestead in Houston, Texas. Justin lived here, with his mother and nephew, in a two-bedroom, one bath, wood frame house. Paint was peeling on the outside, the roof leaked in places, and two broken windows had been cleverly patched with layers of masking tape and plastic. Justin's three children, ranging in age from 6 to 10, lived with their mother in one of Houston's several distressed wards. They spent most weekends and all summer living with him. Since it was Saturday, the kids were staying with Justin and had been told to play with their cousins across the street for the duration of Justin's interview.

Since the age of 18, Justin had worked for a local major construction company. After the birth of their first child, Justin and his girlfriend began living together. The relationship produced three children. His work paid well and offered partial health care coverage for the children. His girlfriend worked as a nurse's assistant. Justin says, "Back then, we was working steady . . . a paycheck every week, either from mine or her job, so there wasn't a week go by when somebody didn't get paid . . . We were doing all right, financially."

Like many others, his steady employment was abruptly halted when the Texas economy experienced a major slump in the 1980s. "Construction work just dried up," he said. "You could go around and see jobs, buildings, malls half finished or finished but standing empty . . . For a black man like me, well, at least I finished high school, but it don't matter much because I was still laid off . . . Now I'm still looking for steady work half the time and doing this and that the other half."

Since his layoff he has only been able to find temporary full-time employment, working for contractors here and there. He became despondent and began to drink heavily for a while. His family was able to rely on him less often than they had in the past. It was after his layoff that his girlfriend applied for and began receiving Aid to Families with Dependent Children, food stamps, and sexual advances from her white male boss. According to Justin, her boss offered to buy her things and take her out— things he could not afford to provide. The increasingly intimate relationship with her employer lasted for about three months—long enough for her and Justin's long-standing relationship to abruptly end. "I left," he stated sharply, "but I left her, not the kids. They always the most important thing to me—whether I'm working none or sixty hours in a week."

The baby began crying and Justin quickly excused himself to go check on him. From my position on the sofa I could see the baby's tiny head of black curls resting secure on Justin's shoulder. He was gently rocking the child to sleep. While waiting, I began to think about Justin's words and his economic situation.

His story, I thought to myself, could have been told by his father, his grandfather, or his great-grandfather. Black men have worked in Houston since its foundation in 1836. Along with Mexican laborers, black slaves were forced to clear the land for the city site. In the decades following emancipation they continued to the Sunbelt city finding work as unskilled laborers and on the city's docks. In the middle of the century job opportunities continued to expand in Houston. During the 1970s, the city was the leader in the creation of new jobs. Yet, racism was a persistent factor influencing the labor market experiences of black men. In 1980 blacks were three times as likely as whites to experience unemployment and underemployment. They were less likely to own their own homes and businesses. And, even in 1980, there remained a stark gap in income between whites and blacks in Houston. The median income was $15,442 and $25,669 for black and white Houstonians, respectively. And blacks were nearly 3.5 times as likely to live below the poverty level. These gaps widened during the recessions that hit the city in the 1980s. During times of economic sluggishness, blacks were often the last hired and first fired. As Robert Bullard summarizes, "Blacks have been troubled with double-digit unemployment" in Houston since this period.[1]

Hundreds of miles east in the smaller city of Greenville, North Carolina, Wesley Johnson lived a life similar to that of Justin Banks. At the time of our interview in 1998, he had recently been laid off from his job as assistant supervisor of janitorial services at a major retail store. This was an occupation he had worked at since his junior year in high school. Following graduation, he completed several courses on housekeeping services at a local junior college and after four years with the company he was promoted to the position of "assistant."

Soon after his layoff, he found steady employment as a technician in a nearby substance rehabilitation center. The work differed drastically from that which had occupied him for his entire adult life. It required shift work and the ability to physically manage often out-of-control clients who were recovering from various substance abuse addictions. The pay was slightly above minimum so he was compelled to seek a job as a part-time stock clerk at the grocery store near his home.

"I was embarrassed to let my sons know I was out of work. So I literally took the first decent job that was offered to me. It wasn't so much that I needed the income . . . I was getting unemployment so I was getting by . . . See, I didn't want my sons to see me whipped. I didn't want them to see me down and beat down because of a job. I've seen that happen to too many brothers when they get laid off. A man can't let anything control his life like that."

Despite his layoff, Wesley was able to "keep a little money in the bank" and make steady payments on the small two-bedroom house he purchased three years prior. Compared to other working-class live-away fathers in the area, he felt fortunate.

In late 1990s, the city of Greenville had a poverty rate of approximately 24 percent. Nearly half the population earned annual incomes of less than

$24,000. The city was 50 percent black, yet this demographic group earned significantly lower incomes than their white counterparts and were more likely to rent than own the relatively poor housing available to them.[2]

According to Wesley, men should take pride in themselves and their work—regardless of their occupation. Most importantly, he added, they should be able to "leave a legacy" for their children. He explained:

"It's not that its demeaning work. I just thought by now I'd have something more substantial to show. By now I should have had my own retail business, trucks with my company emblem painted on them, a house, and money to take my kids on vacation once a year. As it is, I don't have those things to show . . . I have self-respect though. That's something a man has to work for, to get it and to keep it. This is the legacy I have to offer my boys . . . how to maintain your dignity."

Wesley's and Justin's stories were not unlike those of many black fathers, many of whom experienced the emotional and physical toll of declining economic and occupational opportunities, and a simultaneous rise in educational demands. Tenuous economic and social conditions are and have been the state of affairs for generations of black American men born and raised in the Sunbelt city of Houston, and the southeastern community of Greenville. But they are also the experiences of those from Chicago, Baltimore, Detroit, Huntsville, Texas, and most any other city in the United States—past and present.

Recent reports from President Clinton and various political officials celebrate general declines in unemployment, increases in job creations, and rises in college enrollment. However, these reports are misleading and paint a rosier picture of economic conditions than those generally experienced by low-income black live-away fathers. Contrary to political public announcements, these men are encountering staggering high rates of unemployment, underemployment, incarceration, and low academic achievement. More jolting are trends indicating that the circumstances for this demographic group are becoming increasingly acute. "Black men have spent generations chasing the American dream," said one live-away father interviewed, "but the dream is more like a steady nightmare . . . times just keep getting worse and worse."

EDUCATION, OCCUPATIONS, AND SOCIAL MOBILITY

Contemporary concerns have continuity with triumphs and tragedies of past eras of black history. In 1868, during the period of Reconstruction, the Fourteenth Amendment provided all blacks with United States citizenship. This was soon followed by the Fifteenth Amendment, which, in 1870, gave black men the right to vote. In the decade following emancipation black men were elected to public office, black southern churches began in earnest to educate black citizens, and men and women legally married. Despite these constitutional strides forward, racial barriers—legally sanctioned by the courts and state and federal governments—continued to prevent black men from practicing rights afforded the European-American majority. In effect, argues Carnoy (1994), black men and women were denationalized as U.S. citizens. Their freedom did not translate into a status equal to the majority group.

Osofsky's examination of the making of a ghetto in Harlem during the years of 1890–1930 provides a similar interpretation of blacks' early experiences as free people. Whether in the north or south, blacks were essentially second-class citizens. They were allocated to the same type of work they performed as slaves, mostly in the service industries. They were consigned to the most demeaning labor and offered only the lowest wages. Their families lived in the most dilapidated housing in the poorest sections of towns and cities. Educational and health facilities and supplies, when available, were often substandard. Black men, women, and their children generally experienced lower academic achievement, higher rates of morbidity, and shorter life spans than American-born and foreign-born European Americans.

During the period of Reconstruction, black men across the nation shifted from a life of enslavement into a caste system in which they were at the bottom of the social, economic, and political hierarchies. Although substantial legal gains had been attained during this period, their rights as free men were subsequently and consistently taken away and were not wholly granted until the 1960s (Carnoy 1994; Osofsky 1963).

In the hundred years following emancipation, black men experienced considerable mobility in the labor market. Most occurred in the decades between 1940 and 1970. They experienced rapid gains particularly in the 1940s, with the massive employment of blacks in major manufacturing industries. Prior to this, beginning with the New Deal in the 1930s, the public sector had been a primary source of black advancement enabling many black men and their families to begin their ascent into stabler areas of the American working class.

Nonetheless, in every decade since slavery, black men experienced higher rates of unemployment, underemployment, and lower wages than their white counterparts. From the Civil War until World War I, for example, the largest proportion of black male workers were engaged in low-paying service occupation. In 1910, 48 percent of all waiters were African American. Due to social and economic prejudice and discrimination, they were literally shut out of major manufacturing and mechanical pursuits. Employers preferred homogeneous work forces and aimed to secure employees by hiring the foreign-born and the friends and relatives of these immigrants (Katzman 1975; Trotter 1990).

Katzman observed that nationally: "Of the 36,598 men in the 1900 census to have been engaged in manufacturing and mechanical pursuits, only 139 were Negro, and of these, forty-seven were in the building industry. In 1910 only twenty-five Afro-Americans were recorded among the 10,000 mostly foreign-born, semiskilled operatives and laborers who worked in Detroit's automotive factories (1975:105). Southeastern European ethnic immigrants soon displaced even the economically successful northern blacks, who had previously established themselves as self-employed caterers, barbers, and other service providers.

Still, the service industries remained the most prominent employer for black men and women for early decades of the twentieth century. Yet, as in slavery, employment in service occupations required immense "emotional labor." Emotional labor, a phrase coined by sociologist Arlie Hochschild, is the commercialization of human feelings. Black men as waiters, bellhops, janitors, and other service workers, for example, are expected to act as instruments. On cue they are to smile, act kind and courteous, regardless of illness, anger, or inner frustration. Such job requirements were not only belittling to black men but also increased stress and lowered overall health and well-being. In the early twentieth century, black men were expected to behave in a servile manner and again, according to Katzman, "they served many masters; they had to please customers, head waiters, and proprietors" (Katzman 1975:111), all for some of the lowest pay for men in the service industries.[3]

In addition to service, other industries courted the employment of black men. However, such industries generally offered danger and hazard for substantially little pay and/or inconsistent employment. In Detroit, and other port cities, black men were sometimes hired as dock workers, generally on an hourly basis, by a discriminating boss or stevedore. Arduous labor, dock work was not conducive to family life or men's health. Those fortunate enough to be chosen would load and unload incoming and outgoing cargoes, and acquire severely knarled hands in the process. Those not hired would generally await the next tenuous employment opportunity in one of the many bars or houses of prostitution that peppered the docks (Katzman 1975).

Coal mines in the Virginias and the Midwest heavily recruited black male workers and, argues Joe William Trotter (1990), enabled blacks to establish a working-class status by offering them substantially higher pay and stability than was afforded in southern rural life. However, these benefits were not without their cost. Coal mines were notoriously unsafe and a physical threat to those who worked within them. Black men, relative to whites, were employed in the most dangerous aspects of the industry.

When the depression hit, black families, more so than most other demographic groups, were fired or laid off from even the most menial occupations. In visiting a homeless shelter in 1931 Pittsburgh, H. A. Lett estimated that over 40 percent of the 2,000 men present and standing in the breadline were black. A laid-off carpenter, with two stepchildren and a wife, who had worked for one of the city's most reputable contractors, had for months been searching for work. Another, with four children, was recently provided with a permit to sell apples as a street vendor. Neighborhoods with the highest concentrations of black families tended to have the highest unemployment and poverty rates (Lett 1931).

Despite labor force challenges, many black men and their families inched their way into meaningful wage work. Yet, even their substantial advancement in the public sector in the late 1930s and '40s was overshadowed by the persistence of stark inequities between themselves and whites. With the advent of World War II, black men began to experience dramatic advances in the manufacturing labor market, particularly in the automobile industry in the 1940s. Opportunities began to diminish shortly thereafter. Industries began leaving the central cities. Postwar highway construction, spurred by state and local expressway initiatives in the 1940s and federally funded highway construction after 1956, made central industrial location less necessary by facilitating the distributions of goods over longer distances.

Automation increased as owners attempted to limit the cost of labor and decrease the power of workers on the shop floors. In the major midwestern and northeastern major manufacturing cities, staggering job losses occurred not only within automotive plants, but also among supplier industries, which were forced to go out of business. Due to steadily improved technology and automation, their products were no longer in demand by car manufacturers. Auto manufacturers were also fleeing the high taxes and cost of union labor in central cities. They moved to less urban areas where they were able to negotiate lower taxes and have more control over city governments. Manufacturers often relocated senior employees to new plants, a selection process that tended to exclude blacks who were likely the last hired. Additionally, housing segregation and discrimination kept many blacks from relocating to areas where new plants and occupational opportunities were developing. Throughout the 1960s and into the '70s, most black men were limited almost entirely to manual or lower nonmanual occupations, while white males tended to advance upward into better paying middle-income managerial positions (Pomer 1986).

Once legal rights were gained in the 1950s and '60s, many who fought for social justice assumed that a fair system was created. William Julius Wilson and others argue that race has been replaced by class as the primary determinant of one's quality of life. However, deindustrialization devastated job opportunities and potential economic mobility of urban working-class black men and their families more so than other demographic groups. From "1973 to 1986 the proportion of Black men eighteen to twenty-nine employed in manufacturing declined by 43 percent" and "between 1970 and 1980, nearly a half million low-skill jobs left the cities of Boston, Chicago, Cleveland, Detroit, New York, and Philadelphia" (Kasarda 1989:159). All of which produced an inadequate demand for black male labor and long-term unemployment. A growing schism that continued to widen even in the 1990s was occurring among blacks themselves between middle-class "haves" and those working-class and poor who had little.[4]

In essence, the civil rights era promises of equality in opportunity have not translated into equality of condition for all segments of the African American population. Many political and economic gains experienced in the middle decades of this century were short-lived and reversed in the 1970s, '80s, and '90s as a conservative backlash swept the nation. Slashes in social welfare programs, the introduction of Temporary Assistance to Needy Families (TANF), the loss of manufacturing occupations, and significant court rulings against Affirmative Action disproportionately and negatively affected the conditions of life for the lowest skilled and poorest black Americans. Former President George Bush's (1988–1992) veto of the Civil Rights Bill reflected the increasingly negative attitudes and lack of patience the public majority held toward blacks and other minority groups. Black males as a group disproportionately suffered from the reversal in trends. As a group they experienced increased rates of homicide, delinquency, suicide, involvement in criminal activities, incarceration, unemployment, underemployment, and a decline in rates of college enrollment.[5]

Blacks, more than most other demographic groups, continue to experience social, economic, and political subjugation, making black progress, in sociologist Alphonso Pinkney's words, "a myth." While a loss of manufacturing occupations has had an impact across male demographic groups, black men have experienced greater tolls. In 1975, 30 percent of employed black men worked in manufacturing. By 1993 this proportion had dwindled to less than 20 percent. Earnings of black males have subsequently declined. From the mid 1970s to the early 1990s, median weekly earnings of full-time wage and salaried black male workers declined from $445 to $392 in constant 1993 dollars. This situation has left them earning 77 percent and 74 percent of wages earned by white males in 1975 and 1993, respectively. Throughout the 1970s and '80s, the labor force participation of black men steadily declined. In 1984, approximately 60 percent of all 16- to 24-year-old black men had no work experience at all. Black males were 5 percent of the labor force in 1986, and yet were 12 percent of the unemployed.[6]

Today their official unemployment rate is approximately 8 percent, more than double that of white males. The unemployment rate is even higher for those ages 20–24, rising to about 16 percent. However, official unemployment statistics do not capture the entire available workforce. Seventeen percent of black men of childrearing and working age (20–54) who are not employed are not counted. These are men who are marginally attached to the workforce or who have stopped looking for work altogether, because of a perceived lack of job opportunities. This reflects lethargic economic growth in the United States—low-skill workers' incomes are stagnant and or declining. And, as the nation's working class and poor whites experience an income decline, the gap between white and black incomes is closing. From 1989 to 1996 the poor and middle-class real incomes dropped about 3 percent; while the richest Americans experienced a 15 percent increase. Black men are disproportionately experiencing the effects of deindustrialization, the continuing rise of the service economy, corporate downsizing, mass layoffs, and mergermania. But as alluded to above, black men's economic experiences may be impacted by more than just their class. Their employment continues to be aggravated by racial discrimination. Survey data from a national sample of black Americans analyzed by Phillip Bowman (1991), indicated that "33 percent of active job seekers and 18 percent of the hidden unemployed responded yes to the question: Have you ever not been hired on a job because you were black?"[7]

IN PURSUIT OF HIGHER EDUCATION

Poor experiences in the labor market can often be linked to those in education. Despite an increase in education levels that were enhanced by the 1960s' social welfare programs, black men have consistently lagged behind white males in this regard. In 1998, approximately 70 percent of black men aged 25 and older had completed high school compared to about 80 percent of white males and 71 percent of black women. With regard to high school completion, black men and women have nearly reached parity with their white counterparts. However, they continue to lag significantly behind in obtaining higher levels of education. Relative to white men throughout the 1970s, '80s, and '90s, proportionately fewer black men have obtained a college degree. Moreover, the difference between the two groups has increased from about 10 percent in 1970 to almost 14 percent in 1993. Recent statistics reveal that more black men are spending time in prison than on college campuses. The high school dropout rate for black males in major cities is higher than that for most other gender-ethnic groups and 2.5 times greater than that of black females. Additionally, relative to other demographic groups, black males are more likely to be enrolled below the modal grade for their age group. Many, then, are ill-prepared for employment in the private or public sectors, nor are they able to advance into secondary education, take advantage of the few and declining Affirmative Action programs, or obtain steady employment providing living wages.[8]

Again, this is not to say there have not been increased educational opportunities. Recently, the United Negro College Fund's Frederick D. Patterson Research Institute reported that black male and female undergraduate and graduate enrollments are growing at a rate that exceeds that of whites. Those age 25 and older who had earned a four-year college degree increased from 3 percent in 1960 to 13 percent in 1995. Black students represented 11 percent of all undergraduates in 1996, up from 9.6 percent 1990. However, black students continue to be underrepresented among traditional age college students

(Asch 1998). The proportion completing four-year degrees are two times lower than the rate of whites. Nontraditional students often attend school part time and are unable to take advantage of campus life or put maximum effort into their studies. Of black men enrolled in two-year colleges, 40 percent work full-time; of black males enrolled in four-year colleges, 15 percent work full-time. Seventy percent of part-time black male students enrolled in four-year colleges work full-time. Compared to whites, blacks take significantly longer to graduate and, black men in particular, experience notably lower levels of retention. Thirty percent of black males enrolled in college are on two-year campuses. Of these, less than one-half attend full time. Additionally, delayed enrollment, part-time attendance, working full time, having children, and bearing full responsibility for expenses are associated with leaving school for a period of time and/or stopping formal education completely.[9]

As this suggests, slight increases in college enrollment have generally not improved economic conditions for working-class and poor blacks and their families. A considerable wage gap continues to exist between black and white males in American society. In 1997, black men earned an average hourly wage of $12.92, far less than the $18.20 averaged by their white counterparts. Among those managing to attain a college education, there was a slight wage increase—with black men's wages growing twice as rapidly as whites. Black men with a bachelor's degree have a median income double that of those with only a high school diploma ($31,047 and $18,683, respectively). However, college-educated blacks continue to fare worse than whites, earning almost $5.00 an hour less. Overall, white male wages grew by 2.5 percent in the past five years, while black men's rose less than 1 percent (Malveaux 1998).[10]

Ample evidence indicates that many black men are motivated to continue and complete higher education. Michael Nettles, reporting from the United Negro Fund's Frederick D. Patterson Research Institute, argued that an increasing number of black high school students not only aspire, but expect, to attend college. The voices of these fathers support the Institute's findings. Yet, being a parent often presents encumbrances that make academic goals elusive and difficult to attain. Despite obstacles, however, many fathers are not deterred from seeking higher education. Franklin Webster, the live-away father of 8-year-old Brittany, asserted that, "education is the most important avenue to bettering your life and the life of your children." A truck driver for a regional trucking company, he attends his city's community college. "My plan is to get a degree in accounting," he explained. "So I'm taking courses here part-time, saving up some money. Then I plan to get a bachelor's at the University of Oklahoma."

Whether attending vocational or community colleges or universities, those who managed to enroll tended to echo the words of Roman Hayes, the live-away father of two young boys: "Individuals have to take advantage of the educational opportunities so their children can have a better life, less worries." However, he said, "it's definitely not easy—especially knowing that whatever education I receive it's not going to provide me with everything I want out of life." Evidence indicates that community college vocational training does little to improve black men's income levels, while private vocational training boosts their incomes in average of 12 percent. However, private institutes are costly to attend.

And, although they seek social mobility through higher education, the education they are able to obtain mostly provides them with lower income job opportunities. In *Schooling in Capitalist America*, Bowles and Gintis provide an analysis of how the educational system maintains the status of most students—particularly those of little means. Schools in lower income communities groom children for occupations in the low-paying service sector. In East St. Louis, Illinois, for example, home economic courses are taught so as to secure individuals for the housekeeping field—cleaning dishes at restaurants, changing sheets at hotels, and sweeping floors of the very universities reserved for those with middle- and upper middle-class economic backgrounds. The majority of black children attend schools in predominantly black, lower-income communities where college preparatory courses and state-of-the-art educational equipment are a rarity. A result is minimal preparation for higher education. This, combined with family commitments and work schedules, take a heavy toll on black fathers who are students, negatively affecting their grades and their ability to fully participate in academic environments.[11]

Even those who manage to maintain course work on a consistent basis have problems.

One father, Dewey Trimble, wakes up each weekday morning at 4:30 to catch the city bus at 5:15. He arrives at work at 7:30 where he is employed as a janitor for an elementary school. He completes work at 5:00 in the late afternoon, catches the 5:50 bus two blocks from his place of employment, and arrives at the city college 15 minutes late for his evening classes. Following classes, he waits 30 minutes for the bus and arrives home around 9:30 each night. He then eats dinner, showers, calls his children and his mother, sets his alarm clock, and studies until he falls asleep—usually around midnight. If his mother is ill or his children have an after-school activity, or if he must care for the children on a particular day (at least once a week), he will often skip classes for the evening.

Dewey explains why he, as yet, has been unable to complete an associates degree in computer science: "I chose the wrong path early in life—started having kids too early. Seems like every week or another something comes up with the kids, or work, or both ... it's hard to stay focused on your studies when you have too much on your plate. Kids are worrisome, even when they don't live with you."

Having children was generally not the only barrier to obtaining or completing education or for working more than one job. However, children were the primary reason given for wanting to pursue a particular trade or higher education. Fathers seemed less concerned with present wages than with what their future could bring. They intended to be able to earn enough in the future to send their children to college or trade school. They had tremendous hopes and dreams for their children's success.

Tilton Moore, a 27-year-old noncustodial father of three children and a full-time security guard, remarked with both hope and resignation: "I want to make my children's dreams come true. It's not going to happen now. It's probably not going to happen tomorrow. But, when they are as old as I am they are going to be living like they supposed to live ... That's what I'm here for, so that when they older like me they don't have to struggle."

Thirty-four-year-old Carl Evans echoed Tilton's feelings: "My son has potential. He can be whatever he wants. It just takes initiative and support, like from me. It's my place to make sure he gets the education he needs to make it in this world."

Such words of hope as Carl's are glimmers in an overall dismal scenario marked by a decrease in the proportion of black dual-working households, an increase in rates of divorce and separation, and high rates of out-of-wedlock births, single-mother households, poverty, and welfare dependency.

Undergirding these issues is the broader matter of economic insecurity. Quite often black fathers perceived their personal experiences as similar to those of other men, and explained their circumstances in the context of larger social, economic, historical, and contemporary trends. Many specifically compared their occupations and wages to those of their own fathers, uncles, or grandfathers.

Daniel James, a 36-year-old truck driver and father of two provided an example: "I'm doing better than my father in some ways because I was able to go to college and I went for a couple of years. He did the best that he could by finishing high school . . . but financially, we have probably done about the same."

Daniel explained that his father was a self-employed carpenter with six children. The family had a car, clothes on their backs, plenty of food, and extra spending money most of the time—at least when his father's work was steady.

"When business was bad everything was bad . . . Mama and Daddy would argue more, we'd have the same thing for dinner seven days of the week . . . I hated my dad sometimes—because kids just don't understand these things."

Daniel blamed his father's early death on hard work and poor health: "He never took the time from work to go to the doctor. He'd get up and go to work, 5:00 every morning, rain or shine, sick or not. Said he couldn't afford no doctor. But because of the type of work he did, no matter how hard he worked he was never going to get ahead."

Daniel concluded that black men in general work too hard for meager economic returns and that the "system" was not designed to benefit black men.

Many men voiced the same concern. The "system" was loosely defined as "the way society is structured." It consists of the "U.S. state and federal governments, the educational system, the media, and major corporations" that provide more privileges to white men than to any other group. The definition of privileges had both tangible and ethereal components: paid vacation time, a company car, high wages, job security, occupational mobility, and respect, which men felt played an important role in the choices they made as fathers. As one respondent put it, the system is:

Everything that black men struggle against to make a better life for themselves and their families. Your supervisor's a part of it when he only gives you a nickel raise. His supervisor is a part of it when he allows him to do this. The supermarket is part of it because you have no choice but to pay whatever they charge for a head of lettuce or some hamburger. So instead of taking your child to the Smithsonian, for example, you take him to McDonald's because you don't make very much money and it's the cheaper choice. You make the same types of choices every year because you always make the same amount of money. See, that's the system. It's like, all the major institutions that we are part of, our place, black men's place, has been deemed to stay in the lowest part.

Many fathers explained that they had not always felt so pessimistic about their economic success. Rather, as young children and adolescents, they recalled expecting much more from their lives. Similar to the young black men in Jay MacLeod's *Ain't No Makin' It*, these fathers felt they were somewhat oblivious to oppressive structural conditions, or at the very least as one father states, "Me and my friends thought that nothing could stop us from being rich and entrepreneurial." This father, like many others over the age of 30, had past dreams of owning his own business or working for a major computer firm, marrying, and raising children in a two-parent household. However, with increasing age, significant economic mobility was something many fathers decreasingly expected for themselves. "I have been disappointed too many times, laid off too many times, and worked for minimum wage too many times to keep thinking that I can overcome the system." For some, leveled aspirations were expressed as a loss of faith in the beliefs imparted to them by their parents and other older relatives. Evan Pike explained:

"My father's father thought that all a black man needed to get ahead in life was a good trade. My father thought that all a black man needed was an education. From where I sit right now . . . I say they both was wrong . . . It seems like black men ain't never gonna get ahead."

A live-away father employed as a full-time East Texas correctional officer and part-time auto repair technician related a similar story:

"Times have changed for black men . . . Now, my stepfather, he had no education— I think he went up to 6th grade—and was a plumber. He took care of all of us— and there was eight kids . . . But me, even though I finished high school, took a couple a computer courses, I'm working two jobs to take care of myself and just three kids."

Despite their recognition of the macro forces and trends influencing employment and wages, black fathers looked to no external elements to improve the quality of life for themselves and their children. A 24-year-old live-away father—a part-time stock clerk, part-time car wash attendant, and a part-time college student provided an example:

"Right now, I know I can't get no good-paying job. I don't have the credentials . . . Black men have got to have their credentials . . . so I know I have to improve myself, not just for me but for my daughter. I want to give her a life that I didn't have when I was growing up . . . Because of work and school I don't get to see her as much as I want to, but, it's because of her that I do it."

Like most African American men, these live-away fathers tended to be employed in some form of service work. While a few held financially secure positions as correctional officers or low-level state workers, many more worked as security guards, food service workers, and health-care orderlies. Others worked as low-paid sales clerks, service station attendants, custodians, construction workers, or store stock clerks.

Yet, fathers tended not to discuss employment in terms of the financial support their earned wages could provide for their children. What many fathers earned was barely sufficient to support themselves. Whether they worked one or two jobs, most felt as if they were struggling to meet their own needs, much less those of their children. Fathers who worked for the state or various other government agencies were in a much better position than many others to provide financially for their children. However, they too found it difficult to make ends meet and not all provided a consistent source of economic support to their children.

For most fathers—particularly those in relatively low-paying occupations—employment was generally a means to support themselves. These fathers' wages were generally intended to provide monies for their own rent, food, clothing, and occasional entertainment or "going out." However, for most "going out" meant visiting a friend or going to a party. Rarely did it require that they spend great amounts. Many of these fathers said that when they were able they would provide some monies, clothing, gifts, or various necessities for their children. While many of their occupational activities occurred in the legitimate market, a few fathers earned part or all of their income through illegal activity.

"IT'S ILLEGAL, BUT I'M A FATHER": OTHER WAYS TO MAKE A LIVING

The above words were emphatically spoken by Oliver Watson, live-away father of two sons. His words were an exegesis on the necessity of illegally obtaining earnings. Offering only allusions to the specific underground activities in which he was engaged, he suggested that he was no different than many other black men.

"We make choices to get involved in certain things but that's partly us and partly the fault of society," he said. "What choices do they give black men, really?" Oliver argued that black men are often met with a dilemma, particularly when they become parents. "When I first found out I was going to be a father, I was ecstatic," he said. "I had this dream that I would go to college, marry [his son's] mother, move, buy a nice house, work a nine-to-five—you know the script . . . But at the same time I knew it was a dream—in this neighborhood dreams don't come true that easy."

Oliver grew up the baby of his family, raised in a midsize northeastern city. His oldest brother moved out of the home when he was in his mid teens and the other, two years older than he, makes his living in a similar manner. The two continue to reside in their mother's home, and she continues to work in the housekeeping department of a nearby hospital—a job she has held since Oliver was about 13. None of the brothers have ever married, and each except the eldest has at least one child.

Oliver completed high school and managed to take a few courses in basic computer skills after the birth of his second son. However, the courses did not pay off and the jobs he was able to secure were monotonous, offering little opportunity for advancement. "I'm not saying that working at McDonald's isn't a good job but it's hardly one that will pay your bills, you know what I mean. . . . by the time you get off work, you're tired, frustrated, and you still can't relax because bill collectors are calling, you see."

Although officially unemployed due to a work-related injury, Carter James managed to earn some income by working as a handyman—doing odd jobs around his neighborhood and by peddling small amounts of marijuana and various other illegal substances. Regardless of how his income is earned, Carter insists that he does what he does because "a man has to do what he can for his children."

Overall, fathers were generally quite reluctant to discuss their engagement in illicit business activities. However, when they did, it was generally qualified as a means of educating younger men about their mistakes and the difficulty of maintaining such criminal lifestyles.

In the past two years Derek Birch has been in and out of Chicago's local jails twice for selling stolen property. He does not break into people's homes, he says, but works as a "broker"—storing and selling the goods on commission for various others. It is a business, he says, that is relatively safe and keeps his young son, Malcolm, in decent clothes and shoes. This, he says, "is a part-time gig."

His full-time job is with a small downtown pizzeria. Here he works about twenty-eight hours weekly, bussing tables, washing dishes, and earning minimum wages. Admittedly, he prefers the illegal activity to that which is above board.

"That's because I have more control over things . . . I make as much in two days sometimes as I do in a week at my job," he said. "If I didn't have this outside gig I couldn't support myself or provide those things for my son that he needs." Jail and the prospect of prison, he says, are the only downsides. "I know that when they catch up with me next time I'll be going away for a while longer. I just hope my son understands, that's all. . . . But right now," he explains, "I don't know what else to do. There aren't too many places that hire someone with a record."

Derek and others in underground occupations insist that if they could, they would prefer to make their living from "regular" jobs or legal employment. However, such employment opportunities that pay living wages are rare in the context of their life circumstances.

Dramatic and consistent declines in legal, well-paying employment opportunities have increasingly pushed and pulled poor and working-class black males into an underground economy. Such circumstances make them more likely to be arrested and brought into the criminal justice system. Dramatic increases in incarceration rates reflect this decline in occupational alternatives, legislative efforts to take tougher positions on crime, and recent state and federal mandatory sentencing guidelines. While black men make up less than 7 percent of the U.S. population, have a 29 percent chance of serving time in prison at some point in their lives. "Racial profiling, targeting of urban areas, mandatory minimum sentencing, and the disparities in drug laws have made imprisonment a 'rite of passage' for young black men" (Cha-Jua and Lang 1999:9).[12]

The major victims of downsizing and deindustrialization, black communities have been left with few job opportunities or legitimate sources of social mobility. Many young black men are left jobless and prey to the drug trade and other illegal activities. As mentioned, more black men are housed in America's prisons than enrolled in postsecondary education. Moreover, over half of black males between the ages of 16 and 24 have little or no job experience. Consequently, more and more black live-away fathers are going to prison. In 1997 black men were incarcerated in prisons and jails at a rate of over 800 per 100,000. Furthermore, recent estimates indicate that approximately 3.5 million children, or 1 in 50, have a parent behind bars. While there exists recent programs developed to address the needs of fathers in prison and their children, such programs remain few in number. Moreover, even less have been evaluated to determine their effectiveness in helping imprisoned fathers to maintain paternal relationships.[13]

For some, fatherhood has meant not only negotiating grim economic circumstances, illegal activity, and the hardships of incarceration, but many have also had to wind their way through a labyrinth of drug and/or alcohol abuse.

In and out of jail since the age of 16, 29-year-old Dexter Bailey is the live-away father of a 9-year-old daughter. A product of a home consisting of two alcoholic parents, he recalled: "When I would come home from school my mother wouldn't know that I was there, she was drunk everyday." He managed to get odd jobs, mowing lawns, picking up trash around restaurants, and cleaning out apartments following evictions. However, he says "I have always been addicted to something."

He began drinking when he was about 9 or 10, and from there graduated to marijuana; he later used heroine for a while. He was recently released from a treatment center, where he battled his addiction to crack cocaine. "It's not that I don't want to work and get an education," he says. "I've tried both, tried to get my G.E.D. . . . and that's what I'm working on now. I'm trying to keep my head level, get my education, get a job, so I can take care of my daughter."

Expressing similar concerns for his child, Junior Woods explains that whenever he has money he sends as much as he can to his daughter's mother, a woman with whom he is still in love. However, his parenting decisions are often influenced by the addictive substances that persistently consume him. "When I'm straight I'm pretty cool," he says, "But when the drugs get into my system then I'm an ugly individual." All told he said, "In the past year I've given her about two thousand, twenty-five hundred dollars." He estimates that this is about one-third of what he earned, "hustling mostly."

Sometimes though, he has to make the decision to purchase something for his daughter, eat, or buy drugs. "Unfortunately," he said, "sometimes I choose the drugs over my daughter . . . I don't like to think about it like that but that's essentially what I'm doing."

Junior explained that he tends to get high following disappointments. For example, "When I have a job that's good then I don't use, I can stop it like that," he asserted snapping his fingers. "But when that falls through then I go back on, that's all. What else is there to do . . . It's a respite."

Said another father: "Not to make excuses but it seems that if I was straight—and I am more so today than I was three years ago—I still couldn't earn enough money to provide a decent life for me and my children . . . I'm not blaming nobody per se. I'm just saying that you can't expect me to provide a set amount of money every month when there ain't no jobs that pay me enough to do that."

The toll of substance use and abuse among black males, noted by social scientists since the earliest decades of this century, continues to waylay many men's struggle to effectively parent. Over a decade ago, Robert Staples explained that among black people, abuse of both drugs and alcohol are a product of an exploitative economy that offers minimum wages, little employment, and a lack of educational opportunities. Since then, the economy has become more distressing for working-class and poor black Americans, and these men's accounts seem to confirm Staples' analysis. For many black men, he argued, substance use and abuse "is a means of coping" and escaping from an abysmal social and economic life course. Such circumstances leave many vulnerable to the readily accessible products available in their communities. When compared to most other neighborhoods, predominantly black areas have disproportionately more liquor stores, and the sale of drugs is more likely to occur in public space. For example, East St. Louis, a city with a 90 percent black population, an unemployment rate over 26 percent, disproportionately high rates of drug and alcohol abuse and related mortalities, has more liquor stores than grocers and other retail-ers combined. Black men here and elsewhere in the United States are at twice the risk of developing cirrhosis and experiencing other substance abuse disorders and incidents than are white males.[14]

Drug abuse, incarceration, low wages, unemployment, underemployment, and low-level education—all have marked the daily life experiences of these and other low-income African American fathers. Education has historically been a primary means by which these groups moved into higher paying occupations and better housing. However, regardless of the difficulty of course work, many low-income, live-away fathers can ill afford the cost of a bachelor's degree. They often have little money to invest and little time. Consequently, for those who are able, a community college or technical school are often where they continue their education. Yet, even the pursuit of education on two-year campuses is often fraught with financial limita-tions and time constraints. Because of paternal obligations, fathers were often unable to attend classes regularly and/or were forced to drop out. Nev-ertheless, many fathers obtained a college education or technical school training, such as for computer, truck driving, security and criminal justice, or auto mechanic employment. However, higher education was not a guar-antee for well-paying jobs. Rather, rising educational demands and a lack of good jobs placed many fathers in tenuous occupations and forced several into the underground economy.

Recent federal policy reports and state-of-the-union addresses attest to nationally low rates of unemployment, increases in job creation, and gen-eral expansion of the economy. However, these positive accounts can be misleading. While downsizing and deindustrialization are creating more jobs, these occupations tend to be either highly technical and require four-year academic degrees, or low-paying service work. Decent paying, blue-collar employment opportunities, historically available to poor and work-ing-class men, are steadily declining. Consequently, as the live-away father of two stated, "For black men, times are just going to get worse . . . worse for us, and worse for our children."

PART 2
Expectations of Others

The world of live-away fathers goes beyond the primary links that exist between themselves and their children. Daily living leads fathers to interact with various individuals and groups, some of whom may directly or indirectly affect their fatherhood. Fathers may have intimate relationships with women other than their children's mother. They have friendships and work relationships that bind some of their leisure time and energy. They have kin networks from whom they may receive and provide guidance and different types of support. The nature and content of these many relationships and interactions may affect fathers' attitudes about parenting and what they actually do in this capacity. For example, a father's environment is extended whenever he moves into a new setting, such as a marriage, remarriage, or intimate relationship, a new place of work, or enrolls in classes to improve his skills and education. Interaction may take various forms, and others in these settings may participate in fathers' relationships with their children. Additionally, formal and informal communication may occur among settings, and knowledge and attitudes may exist in one setting about another.

The extent of men's day-to-day involvement with children, what they provide, and how often they interact must be understood in context of these interconnections. Whether or not a father visits his live-away children every Monday or Tuesday, or only once a month, is interconnected with his responsibilities, activities, and experiences in other aspects of his daily life. For example, fathers' balance of home life and live-away family, work schedules and type of occupation, dating patterns and recreational activities, all may impact upon what he does or does not do with his live-away children. All of this, too, is negotiated within a poor to working-class existence, where fathers must organize all of the above within significant financial and social constraints. The extent to which some live-away fathers visit with their children, attend their ball games or school plays, take them to the movies or to the doctor, or simply sit around and talk, must be balanced with other aspects of their daily lives. The number of hours they work, the degree of physical and emotional labor required on the job, physical distance from children, and financial constraints may impact how they negotiate their time as fathers .

Added to this possibility, research also suggests that within live-away fathers' worlds the attitudes and behaviors of their current partners affect *their fathering. Cohabitation and marriage—due to the complexity and constraints of balancing time between families—may decrease fathers' involvement with their children. Seltzer and Brandreth (1994) found that relative to fathers who remained single following divorce, those who remarried or cohabited discovered managing time for their children proved more difficult. Relative to those who did not live with children, remarried or cohabiting noncustodial fathers who lived with other biological children or stepchildren were more involved with their noncustodial children and more positive about their fatherhood. Though these findings are specific to divorced men, they may nevertheless offer some explanation for never-married fathers—particularly those who at one time resided with the mothers of their children.*

Most significant in influencing men's participation in their children's lives is their relationship with the mothers of their children. Kurdek (1983) found that relative to those with congenial relationships with the mothers of their children, fathers experiencing antagonistic relationships were likely to have little to no contact with their children. Noncustodial fathers maintaining a good relationship with the mother of their children were more likely to remain in contact with their children.

There is also some indication that custodial mothers may inhibit or enhance the role of fathers in the lives of their children. They may do this by monitoring the time men spend with their children and controlling children's availability and accessibility. In other words, they may act as "gatekeepers," regulating when fathers visit, choosing not to inform them of the dates and times of children's extracurricular activities, or insuring that the children are too busy to visit Dad. Regardless, many single parenting women say that live-away fathers do not spend enough time with their children and that they would like for their children's fathers to participate more in the everyday lives of their offspring.[1]

While the above studies tend to primarily focus on white middle-class divorced couples, black adolescent single mothers seem to share their sentiment. They, too, say fathers do not spend enough time with their children and would like to see them doing much more.

Part 2 explores the roles of significant others in contributing to men's paternal attitudes and behaviors. In chapter 4, men discuss what they think others, particularly the mothers of their children, expect of them as fathers. Chapter 5 explores how custodial mothers, and children of noncustodial fathers perceive paternal responsibilities.

4

"JUST BE THERE FOR THE BABY"
What Fathers Say Others Expect

*R*esearchers suggest that the transition to parenthood is one of the most dramatic life-cycle events experienced by most men and women. Both generally consider the bearing of children as major turning points in their lives. But overall, traditional Western norms on fatherhood provide few guides for live-away, never-married fathers. Social rules guiding and governing their paternal behavior are unclear and made more complicated by society's consistent emphasis on the inappropriateness of parenting out of wedlock. Additionally, the transition to parenthood often places new demands on fathers' time and routines, particularly if they intend to be significantly involved in child-care duties.

But what fathers are supposed to do in their paternal role has traditionally been defined within a marital context, wherein fathers negotiate their responsibilities within traditional male and female Western prescriptions. Mothers are generally the primary caregivers, while fathers as husbands generally have been expected to provide financial support. Research indicates that within these settings, even today, fathers are less involved with their children than mothers. Moreover, the extent of fathers' involvement has been found to be associated with their relationship with their marital partners. Like many fathers who do not live with their children, the men in this study were uncertain and hesitant about what was expected of them as fathers. Said one father, "There's no book that tells you what to do." Their perceptions of how others viewed their paternal behavior were elements that guided and contributed to how they behaved and thought about parenting. This chapter specifically describes what men think others—the mothers of their children, their own mothers, and their children—want them to do in their father role.[1]

FRIENDS, LOVERS, AND ENEMIES: THE MOTHERS OF THE CHILDREN

According to Lavette, she and Robert had maintained a "regular boyfriend-girlfriend relationship" for four years prior to the conception of their five-year-old son, Cedric. "We dated, went out, and things of that nature," she said. Both lived in their parents' homes. Robert worked as a full-time sales associate for a major retailer, and Lavette worked in the same store as a customer service clerk. When their schedules permitted, they generally spent two to three hours daily together. Sometimes they would go to the movies, visit with friends, or go for walks. They talked about marriage, sports, music, and day-to-day activities. However, Lavette could not recall the subject of children ever being discussed during that period.

They were each surprised when she became pregnant. "I was in between birth control . . . it just so happened that one time we didn't use no protection," she said. At the time, she was 19 and Robert 21. Both felt they were not ready to have a child; Robert urged her to get an abortion. Although she quickly rejected the notion, she simultaneously understood his preference for this option. "He was just scared . . . really scared about having a child," she explained. Upon wrestling with her consistent opposition to this alternative, he eventually relented and "pampered" Lavette throughout her pregnancy.

Despite Robert's indulgence toward Lavette, the couple's relationship did not progress through the pregnancy unencumbered. Problems began to arise. Most troublesome was her decision to discontinue their sexual relationship. "He thought I was crazy," she recalled, "because I told him we couldn't have sex no more." She maintained this position for about six months following Cedric's birth. "My main thinking was my child . . .he's the only thing I had time to think about," she said. She explained that she did not have time to engage in recreational activities, such as the movies and visits with friends as she once had.

In addition, the couple had little privacy; time they once had alone now included their son. Robert " didn't understand that," Lavette offered. The relationship was made more complicated by their struggle to negotiate their parenting roles. Robert attempted to take a very engaged role in the parenting of his infant son, something Lavette's mother and his own greatly encouraged. "He came over everyday, changed diapers, washed baby clothes, everything like a family," reported Lavette. They simultaneously began to bicker and argue about child-care duties. According to Robert, "I felt like I was a better parent . . . like I was better at taking care of him [Cedric]." Meanwhile, Lavette felt that Robert was overstepping his role as father and intruding and overshadowing her own parental activities. "He would come by and say 'I'm taking the baby to here or here . . . he never asked me if he could take him, he just did it," she said sharply.

She endeavored to maintain as much control over the baby's caretaking as possible. She felt that as Cedric's mother, he was her primary responsibility, not Robert's. She was reluctant to take child care advice from Robert and hesitant to encourage him to take Cedric on father-son outings. She recalled "people would say we were arguing over our child or fighting over him." The situation was not helped by the lack of privacy that existed because of their living arrangements. The couple rarely spent time alone together.

When Lavette and Robert were at work, a cousin was paid to take care of Cedric. Finding a baby-sitter to look after him during other times was not only difficult, but also quite costly. It was following a heated public argument that the two acknowledged that their relationship was in jeopardy and that their incessant quarreling could only be psychologically injurious to Cedric. They abruptly decided to break off their relationship for an indefinite period.

This lasted for about three days. Despite their disputes, the two remained fond of one another. Also, Robert was quite attached to Cedric and insisted on being a part of his son's daily life. His determination compelled the former couple to explicitly converse about their parenting roles, something they had not done heretofore. "I didn't understand that I was trying to keep him away from my child sometimes," Lavette recalled. "And he didn't think about how I was always tired and things . . . we just really found things out."

Although they continued to have disagreements, they became less hostile, and each felt the relationship improved after "we forced ourselves to talk about our problems." They agreed that each needed the other to provide the optimum care for their son. "It's like I know I can't be a good father unless she helps me to do that; and she know she say she can't be a good mother unless I'm there to help her with what she needs," Robert stated. Lavette reported that despite their differences, they remain good friends. She explained that Robert is a good father and often does more than she when it comes to Cedric's physical care. "I have never asked for child support because he gives him everything he needs . . . takes him to the doctor . . . takes him shopping . . . . He's always there for him," Lavette said.

Robert and Lavette conceived Cedric within a loving and committed relationship. Although it took time, the strength of their long-term relationship seemingly enabled them to communicate their parental and personal needs and expectations to one another to provide the best care for Cedric, and maintain a mutual respect and friendship.

As past research suggests about married couples, the type of relationship never-married men had with the mothers of their children also seemed to contribute to what they felt was expected of them as fathers. However, all fathers did not have healthy relationships and/or positive outcomes with the mothers of their children. These fathers had varying associations with the mothers of their children and these relationships ranged from one extreme to another. Overall, fathers' descriptions of their current relationships with the mothers of their children created three distinct categories; intimate, friendly, and antagonistic. Some fathers expressed feelings of hatred toward the mothers of their children; others professed love and affection. There were fathers who considered mothers as "just friends," while others considered the relationship much more intimate. Furthermore according to fathers, some relationships drastically changed following the birth of a couple's child.

INTIMATE RELATIONSHIPS

The birth of Jasmine seemed to strengthen the long-term bond between Scott and Ramona. Scott explained: "It was like she [Jasmine] made us complete. A child was the only thing that our relationship was missing."

The couple met while both were in high school; she was two years older than he. Their on-again, off-again romance blossomed once Scott completed high school. He managed to get some part-time work cutting lawns, while she continued to work as a home health aid. "We talked a lot about getting married," Scott said. "But we never went through with it," he continued, without explaining why. The two were "practically living together," sharing her room in her mother's apartment at the time Ramona became pregnant. "Well, we had an apartment of our own for a short time but the bills got too deep," offered Scott. They had managed to maintain their own apartment for about one full year after he graduated and began working.

They had been living with Ramona's mother for approximately six months when Jasmine was conceived. Her mother's presence had its advantages and disadvantages. She often agreed to baby-sit, which saved the couple quite a bit of money. However, the apartment was small and the young couple had little privacy. Nevertheless, the environment was a positive one for the new parents. Ramona's mother respected them as parents and "she wasn't always into our business," Scott said. And while Ramona and Scott sometimes argued over child care duties, routines, and various other elements, Scott reported that these disagreements were very minor and "just everyday stuff that people got to get off their shoulder." Since the child's birth three years earlier, their living arrangements had changed, much to the couple's chagrin. Scott spent most of the week at his parents' home, though not because he and Ramona had ended their relationship (actually it remained quite strong). Rather, his newest job at an auto glass company was closer to his parents' home, and staying there was much more convenient in terms of time and transportation costs. He prided himself on his commitment to Ramona and Jasmine. "They're my heart," he said placing his hand on his chest. "We always going to be together, make no mistake . . . I'm always going to be there for my child . . . That's what her mother mainly wants me to do."

Several fathers claimed to have intimate relationships with their children's mothers.[2] Of those reporting such information, eleven relationships could be placed in this category. For the father, "intimate" meant that he and the mother were far more than friends and had a consistent sexual relationship. However, this sexual relationship did not always mean that the couple was monogamous or that they intended to marry. According to one father, he and his son's mother had a relationship that was unique to that he shared with other women. "When I go to visit sometimes I spend the night and sometimes I don't . . . .Sometimes we sleep together and sometimes we don't." From his perspective, the two did not expect the relationship to be anything more than what it was already. That is, he did not expect that they would seek to expand or formalize a commitment to one another. "We don't expect nothing from each other, really . . . I don't think she expects anything from me," he said in closing.

Another father explained his relationship in the following way: "Right now I say that we are dating . . . but we go out with other people, too . . . She knows I go out with other women and I know that she's been out with at least one other man besides me." Overall, fathers in this category generally expressed having "deep affection" or "strong feelings" for the mothers of their children. Few used the word "love" with regard to the mothers of their children. And fathers seemed reluctant to say that they would one day marry their children's mothers. This was true even though all the fathers stated that they would prefer that their children be raised in a two-parent household.

Fathers in intimate relationships felt they had good relationships with their children. They enjoyed spending time with both the mothers and the children. This, it seems, was also what the mothers of their children expected from them. In the eyes of fathers, mothers expected fathers to spend time with them and the children simultaneously. One father summarized what he thought was expected of him:

"When I'm there she expects it to be like a family. We go to the park together, the grocery store. I watch the baby while she goes to her mother's or runs errands. All that. I'm there or she's here. We see each other most every day. We like a family, really. I been taking care of my daughter since she was born—changing diapers, reading stories. I put her to sleep most nights. I do everything a daddy do that married to the mama."

Contrary to fathers with "friend-mothers," fathers in intimate relationships perceived that they were expected to focus their attentions on both mother and child rather than primarily the child. When asked if they would have a continued intimate relationship if they had not had a child together, fathers responded with uncertainty.

"When we're all together it's like we're a family . . . and that's the way it really should be, for the children."

"Who can say . . . seems like sometime all men and women got in common is their kids."

Still, one father seemed to express a bit more confidence in the stability of his relationship with the mother of his children than did the others:

"My son didn't bring us together in the first place, but he has made our relationship stronger. Would I still want to marry her if we hadn't had him? Probably. Yeah, probably."

Whether they had intended to marry or not, several intimate relationships ended following pregnancy or the birth of the child. Some fathers, after intimate relationships had gone sour, tried even harder to be fathers to their children than they had consciously done in the past. One father explained why he felt his fathering improved following his "falling out" with the mother. "I want my little girls to have at least one good parent, one good role model . . . So I have hung in there even though their mother, the things she be doing, sometime turn my stomach."

Not all fathers expressed such disgust for the mothers of their children. However, most fathers reported that relationships with the mothers of their children ended during the pregnancy or subsequent to their children's birth. Following a break-up, some fathers were able to maintain good terms with their children's mothers and remain engaged in their sons and daughters lives; others found this quite a difficult task.

JUST FRIENDS

James Williams lived in an early nineteenth-century Victorian-style home. The original six-bedroom house had been transformed into separate apartment units with a communally shared kitchen, dining, and living room area. This was a halfway house where men with mental disabilities were transferred prior to their formal release from a state hospital. Tenants remained in the home for up to one year, learning and relearning basic everyday living skills to ease their transition to independence. James was one of two of the home's full-time live-in skills trainers. He lived on the premises for five days of the week and generally stayed with his mother on his nights off. Job compensation consisted of room, board, and $283 a month.

He had been working at his present job for approximately six years, getting raises here and there and increasingly receiving more and more responsibility. He started the job soon after high school, working as a part-time van driver. It was through his place of employment that he met Jesse. She worked at a nearby nursing home as a nurse's assistant. They began dating almost immediately. Seven months later, they conceived their son, Tarik. The child was born two months premature and remained in the hospital for several weeks before his mother took him home. Both mother and child lived with Jesse's mother and brother, and James recalled that his work schedule "really did not allow me to be around as much" as he had wanted, particularly during the time of her pregnancy. He felt disconnected from Jesse during this period and as time passed, he began to realize that his primary attraction to her was a physical one.

But the pregnancy and childbirth had moderated their intimate interaction, and James began to see and treat her more as a friend than a lover. "I just wasn't sexually attracted to her anymore," he stated blandly. He never explicitly explained his feelings to her, rather, he said, "I just stopped being affectionate . . . I'm really an affectionate person."

As his feelings changed, he perceived that she grew hostile toward him. "I think she expected that I was just there for the baby and not her . . . That wasn't all the way true though," he asserted. He admitted he cared for her but did not expect or intend for their relationship to lead to anything more than a friendship. Feeling confused about what to do about the relationship and his impending fatherhood, he decided to "talk things over" with his mother. His own mother, after talking with him about the relationship, firmly encouraged him to "treat her right . . . [because] . . . she's the mother of your child." He understood this to mean "don't abandon her . . . be there for her and the baby," something he aversely recalled his own father not doing.

According to Jesse, she will always love James and insisted that he visit despite his reluctance to continue the relationship. She recalled feeling hurt about his apparent attitudinal and behavioral changes toward her during her pregnancy. She noticed that he curtailed his frequent visits to her, dropping from daily contact to once or twice a week. However, she was certain that he had strong feelings for her and would eventually choose to reestablish his commitment and possibly ask her to marry him. Given this, she felt comfortable urging him to at least resume a more physically intimate association.

Thus, several months following the birth of Tarik, the former couple resumed sexual relations on occasion, but James said he made it clear to her that "we were just friends and he did not want a commitment." He explained that this was his attempt to pacify Jesse's desire to renew their relationship and remain in her good graces so that he could maintain contact with his son. At the time of the interview, seven years later, he still visited regularly with Tarik. He and Jesse continued to have an intimate relationship, but it was much more sporadic and generally occurred when he was "not seeing somebody else." He still considered Jesse a friend who expected him to "do what I can for Tarik."

Jesse admitted that she knew of James's continued reluctance to reestablish their relationship. Nevertheless, she perceived their relationship as a bit more complex. According to her, James "is a boyfriend and a friend and my child's father . . . he's all of those things." She continued, "Therefore, I expect that he needs to behave like that. . . . he should be there for me and my son." Speaking with confidence, she explained that, "no matter what woman he is involved with, he ain't going to leave what he's got here."

Unlike Jesse, James said he does not anticipate his feelings will change toward her and he expects that he will always be a visiting father. "I know she want more from me but . . . I also know she don't expect me to be anything more than what I am . . . I think . . . the most important thing she wants me to do is come over, play with Tarik . . . just be around for my son," he said in closing.

Regardless of the status of the relationship prior to or at conception, most relationships (66 percent) between fathers and the mothers of their children were presently friendly. Fathers considered mothers as "friends" for various reasons. These women were friends because they were the mothers of their children. They were friends because they were someone with whom fathers could talk about their children. Most importantly, these "friend-mothers" were someone fathers could count on to take good care of their children. Fathers felt as though their contributions were significant for the child and for the mother. Despite the expressed reason for the friendship, the relationship generally found its strength in the bond created by the children. Additionally, from fathers' descriptions, "friend-mothers" encouraged and supported their paternal engagement. Research suggests similar patterns occur among married couples. Fathers are more likely to engage in paternal activities when they are not discouraged or feel shut out by a child's mother.

Kenneth Bates, 25-year-old live-away father of a 3-year-old son, made the following statement: "We didn't really know each other until after she got pregnant and had the baby. Really not 'til after she had the baby . . . We became good friends after that." Kenneth explained that at first he was uncertain of what was expected of him as a father. He recalled wondering whether he "should offer to baby-sit or just give her money and buy diapers." He said that he thinks that he and his son's mother became friends because she perceived that he was genuinely concerned for her and their child. "Therefore," he says, "it was okay for me to make some mistakes."

Over time, a father came to rely on the mother as someone with whom he could talk, watch television, play cards, take the children to the park, or just relax. When a father visited his children, the mother made him feel at home. If he had missed breakfast, lunch, or dinner she would often "warm something up." Regardless of the time of day he visited, he would often eat at least one meal. Isaac Little, father of two, described the friendship he has with his children's mother:

"I can't say I love her. Like a man loves a woman. But there's something there. Oh, we're not intimate. She has her own love life and I got mine. . . . I consider her a friend . . . she respects me, makes me feel at home when I'm over, and lets me be a daddy to my kids."

Eldin Tate shares a similar relationship with the mother of one of his several children:

"When I go see my children, which I do almost every day after work, it's like I live there. I go to the refrigerator and she has something for me to drink. I go sit down and she let's me take my dirty, sweaty boots off . . . We have our arguments but she know I'm a good father to the children. We know we can count on each other especially where they are concerned. That's why I say we friends."

"Friendly" relationships were also maintained by consistent phone conversations, wherein the mother would report on what the children were doing, including how they were doing in school. Such conversations would often involve arrangements for the father and children to visit, as well as informing the father when one or more of the children needed his specific attention for discipline or other everyday matters.

Primarily, mothers were "friends" when they were perceived as being "good mothers" to their children. According to these fathers, good mothers had several important characteristics: they loved their children; they took care to keep their children well fed, bathed, healthy, neatly clothed, and kept their hair combed. "Good mothers" saw to their children's needs, looked after them, and did not "bad-mouth" a child's father, at least not in the presence of the child. Finally, good mothers were those who did not let relationships with boyfriends, lovers, or current husbands interfere with their own or live-away fathers' parental interactions. Three fathers commented on what enabled them to maintain friendship with their children's mothers:

"She's got her ways but she does her best with the children. That's all that matters to me. We'll always get along as long as she takes good care of my children."

"We're good friends because I know she loves my children as much as I do. She takes care of them. Treats them all the same. You can't hate someone who genuinely loves your children because, really, she's loving a part of you."

"We made a deal. The children could stay living with her as long as she didn't have boyfriends staying all night there and as long as she didn't get married 'til after the children are grown. If she does any of this, then the children come and live with me. That's the agreement we worked out."

Additionally, mothers were considered "friends" when they did not prohibit or otherwise make it difficult for fathers to see children. Fathers who were "friendly" with the child's mother felt that their good relationship with her served to enhance their fathering. Kenny is a 30-year-old live-away father of three children ranging in age from 7 to 16. He felt that his good relationship with Shirley, the mother of his children, made it easier for him to visit them. He compared his relationship with Shirley to that which existed between his parents.

"I remember my mother and father could never get along. I think that's what kept him away a lot. He wasn't the type that liked trouble. I'm not saying he was a necessarily . . . a bad father but he could have been better if he were able to come around more . . . If he an' my mother had gotten along better. See, I'm just the opposite. Me and her get along so there's no hindrance there. So I've been able to be a better father than my father."

Family research generally indicates that fathers are more likely to be involved with children when they are on good terms with custodial mothers. It seemed as well that fathers associated good mothers with those who placed few demands on fathers' paternal responsibilities. Fathers perceived that "friend-mothers" expected them to be accessible and to spend time with the children. They also perceived that "friend-mothers" felt it important that fathers be consistent and honest with their children.

A middle-aged father of two explained: "She expects me to show up to my son's games. Go to his practices. Visit him regularly. Things of that nature."

A father of two daughters by two different mothers made a similar comment: "The mother of my other daughter, she expects the same. If I tell my daughter I'm going to pick her up at 8:00 in the morning then no matter how tired I am I better be there at 8:00. Not 9:00. Not 8:05 . . ."

In turn, fathers felt that they could count on "friend-mothers" to be honest, treat them fairly, and act to insure that their children maintained proper respect for them. Calvin provided an example:

"I know that if I miss a visit I have a very, very good reason. Their mother knows that, too. I have only had to cancel two arranged visits. She knew it hurt me to do that. But

I counted on her to tell my kids in a way that wouldn't make them feel worse and in a way that would not make me look bad as their father. See, 'cause she has the opportunity to talk me down but she don't do that."

Fathers felt that they were greatly respected by the "friend-mothers." Mothers often relied on them for advice, to make repairs to broken toys, the house, or automobile, and to help move from one place of residence to another. If by chance a father should briefly neglect his father duties, a mother would expect him to have a valid excuse. However, she generally understood or at least seemed to forgive such "brief" negligible behavior. Said one father, "I think she generally knows I'm going to stand by my kids; see, a lot of brothers don't, so she tolerates a lot from me." This particular comment suggests that black men themselves believe that men are not doing what is expected of them as fathers.

ANTAGONISTIC RELATIONSHIPS

Some fathers characterized their relationships with the mothers of their children as hostile and strained. They generally expressed strong dislike for the women who were raising their children. "Animosity" perhaps better captures these fathers' descriptions of their relationships. From men's perspectives, mothers were purposely hurtful toward them and often hateful. Seven of the reported relationships fit this category. The strong dislike that these fathers had for their children's mothers was based on varying circumstances.

Two fathers felt that they had been "tricked" by the mother, that she had purposely become pregnant in an effort to maintain a relationship with them. For this reason, these men harbored deep resentment and anger toward them. Artie Jones explained why he does not foresee a "friendly" relationship ever existing between himself and the mother of his daughters.

"I felt like she tricked me. She's sneaky that way . . . and then she planned it so I would find out about her being pregnant from somebody else. I had it in me to kill her. I mean I kept cool but there's hatred between us. Pure hatred."

Other fathers disliked the mothers because they felt that the mothers were using them for their own personal gain, without regard to the children involved. In these fathers' eyes, the relationship between father and child was maintained only as it suited the mother's needs. These mothers primarily expected fathers to provide child support, and visitation arrangements were made and set at her convenience. These fathers felt that a mother could be using child support payments "to make herself a wealthy woman."

"All she wants from me and all she has ever wanted from me is money, money, money. She think just because a black man got a job that he ought to be taking care of her."

"She gets a check every month. What does she do? Does she spend it on my boy? No. You know what she do? She go out with her friends, buy herself new clothes. Meanwhile my boy sitting there with his sisters in ragged drawers and eating Cheetos for dinner."

When these mothers were unsatisfied with the amount of a payment, a missed payment, or fathers' excuses for being late for visits they would use the children as a means to "get back at" the fathers. Most fathers disliked the mothers because of the mothers' attempts to keep the fathers from maintaining contact with their children. Again, Artie Jones provided an example.

She's angry at me so she's trying to hurt me through my son. Because she knows I want to be with him, spend time with him. She knows that's one way to hurt me. So me and her there ain't no love lost there."

When mothers became involved with other men, they sometimes altered a father's contact with their children. Fathers generally expressed no resentment about the mothers' relationships, per se, but became angry when they interfered with their own relationship with their children. Leonard explained what brought about the present antagonistic relationship:

"We was getting along all right until she started going out with that man. At first I didn't know what it was but I knew something had changed so that she was making it harder for me to see my son. I'd go to pick him up at the arranged time and nobody would be home. Or I'd ask to speak to him on the phone and she'd tell me he was asleep—-things of that nature. That went on about a month 'til her sister told me that the man she was seeing was living with her and he had told my son's mother that he didn't want no other man around. I wasn't going have that. We was friends up to that point."

Another father also expressed his dissatisfaction with his son's mother's decision to keep him at a distance:

"Oh, we're enemies. There's no doubt. She took that boy and moved him into her boyfriend's mother's house and then told me that I couldn't come by and see him."

Overall, fathers disliked mothers whom they perceived as "bad mothers." "Bad mothers" were those who seemed to care more about themselves than about their children. They were those who seemed to spend child support or other money frivolously and/or not on the children. For example, "bad mothers" were those who received welfare payments and spent money on such things as the hairdresser, manicures, liquor, or new clothes for themselves. Such mothers also did not feed their children "nutritious" meals, even when they received food stamps and other government subsidies. Other characteristics mentioned were dressing children in "shabby clothing," not transporting them to and from school in a timely manner, being dishonest when attempting to get "extra" money from the fathers, and not keeping fathers informed about children's whereabouts, behavior, or general well-being. Jeffrey Hamilton summarized the feelings of many of the fathers in antagonistic relationships:

"I dislike her because she don't care about nobody but herself. A mother is supposed to put her children first. Not her friends; not her boyfriends—her children. She don't do that. Some women were just not meant to be mothers.

That type of relationship notwithstanding, fathers generally did not see themselves eventually marrying the mother or one of the mothers of their children, although several fathers had considered marriage for at least at some point during their relationship with the mother. When asked why they had dismissed the idea of marrying the mothers, some fathers argued that the mother of their children was simply "no good." Two fathers commented on why they chose to not marry the child's mother:

"I loved my son's mother. That's no lie. I wanted to marry her. That is, until I found out she wasn't no good."

"I didn't want to believe it but the evidence kept stacking up against her. My friend told me, he said, "She's playing you. She's going out with so-and-so and so-and-so." Eventually I just had to accept that the woman, the mother of my child, was just for shit.

Many fathers doubted that they would ever marry. "Good women," several fathers claimed, "are hard to find." Such a perspective compounds past sociological discussions on the marriage squeeze among the black American population. These past findings suggest that women, because of men's high incarcerations, substance abuse, and homicide rates and their low levels of income and education have few options to marry. These fathers suggest that finding marriageable women may also be perceived as a difficult task.[3]

Other fathers dismissed marriage because they did not feel that they were ready for marriage and/or that they were not "good husband material." These fathers, ranging in age from 21 to 35, explained why marriage is not a current option for them:

"I'll tell you what a good husband is. He's a good man. He doesn't show a lot of pain. He never complains or blames anyone for his troubles. He accepts responsibility for everything—good and bad. He's supposed to be hard but he also has to be patient . . . I just don't think I'd be a perfect husband. I've got some of those qualities but not enough to sustain a relationship."

"I think that eventually I'll be ready to get married but right now I'm too wild . . ."

"If I had a wife she wouldn't be able to trust me. Right now I'm not husband material."

"I need to get my life together. Work steady. Come home at decent hours. I have to be able to do all that before I can even think about getting married."

TIME AND NEGOTIATION

Overall, fathers did not feel that their children's mothers' expectations were expressly communicated to them. Regardless of the type of relationship fathers had with the mothers of their children, most fathers explained that they were, at least initially, uncertain about what mothers expected them to do as fathers. This was the case even with fathers who appeared to play a substantial part in their children's lives.

Abel Stone, for example, explained that he visited with his daughters almost daily and cared for his 3-year-old until noon each week day. Their mother, Tanya, worked at a local university in the housekeeping department. She awoke at about 5:30 each morning, got herself dressed, fixed breakfast, dressed her girls, combed their hair, and otherwise prepared them for the day. Abel arrived at his daughters' home at about 6:30 each week-day morning. He then cared for both the children while Tanya prepared and left for work. She worked from 7:00 A.M. to 3:00 P.M. The kindergarten bus picked up their 5-year-old in front of the house at 7:30 A.M. Once his oldest daughter was safely on the bus, Abel and his youngest daughter spent the morning together. When the weather was good, the two would spend time at the playground, walk to the grocery store, or visit Abel's mother. At noon, the child's maternal grand-mother would arrive, and she and his daughter would walk down the street to her house. Abel would then walk to the home that he shares with his sister and her two children. There he would sleep in preparation for his nighttime shift as a stock clerk at a local grocery store. He explained that although he did not reside with his chil-dren, he considered them and their mother as his family. He felt, in regards to the children, that Tanya knew that she could always rely on him.

During his interview, he spoke of his and Tanya's relationship and how the present child care arrangements developed. Abel explained that though he and Tanya loved one another, Tanya did not want to marry. He explained this was due to her indepen-dence and her desire to have the house that she purchased to herself. Abel indicated that he did not "really mind" the arrangement because it enabled him to have some freedom himself "with no one fussing around." "We respect each other," he stated, "we give each other certain freedoms [and] we also expect certain things from each other."

When asked to elaborate on these expectations Abel replied: "Sometimes she expects me to be like a husband—cut the grass. Fix this or fix that . . . Mostly I think she expects me to be there for the children. To help take care of them. Take them to school or here or there. Buy them shoes if they need it. Basically, she expects me to be a daddy to them . . . spend time with them . . . so they know who I am and that I love them . . ."

When asked what he expected from her, he thoughtfully stated, "Maybe to respect me . . . be treated like part of the family . . . Let me do my role as father." Yet, Abel, like other fathers, expressed that they had not always known what their children's mother expected from them as fathers. According to him, he "just sort of had to figure out what she wanted . . . what role she wanted me to play." He recalled that her desires were unclear: "Did she want me to practically live here and help take care of my children or just stay away and wait 'til she need something." He said, "It took awhile for me to figure this out . . . Then too, at first, I didn't know what I was supposed to do as a father, either . . . trial and error."

Abel remembered feeling frustrated and searching for direction: "Early on, I would stop by to see the baby, whatever. But learned to tell when she (Tanya) didn't want company . . . and then, see . . . it just got to be that eventually she would ask for my help with certain things . . . then it got so that I would just do these things automatic. She stopped asking . . . I kept doing. So then we just started expecting that this is what I would do as my children's father."

Similar to other fathers, the present understanding and relationship between Abel and Tanya developed over months and years. Other fathers recounted their experiences:

"I knew she wanted me to be around in some capacity but it took, I'd say, about . . . several months after he [their son] was born for me to figure out somewhat what she wanted me to do . . . we didn't really talk about it."

"She would never say anything; like she didn't want me to be around . . . I started buying things for my child . . . I came around sometimes . . . we just got used to the situation without ever saying, 'Okay I should be doing this and you should be responsible for these other things for our child.'"

From fathers' perspectives, it seemed women simply expected fathers to know what was expected of them and to act accordingly, a view many custodial mothers confirmed in findings reported in the next chapter. They did not feel it was up to them to tell fathers what to do as fathers. According to one single-parenting mother:

"They know what fathers are supposed to be like . . . they can't expect the woman to hold their hand and guide them . . . They know what the man's job is . . . They just need to do it."

"If they say they don't know what they supposed to . . . as a father to their kids, they are lying. How can a man grow up in today's society and not know what a man is supposed to do? I tell you they know. You do what's right, that's all . . . that's being there to care of your kids."

Overall, it seems that mothers did not always directly tell fathers what they expected, nor did these fathers directly ask what was expected of them. The effect of this lack of communication was that many fathers had to guess the expectations of their children's mothers by, as one father stated: "[F]eeling my way around . . . like trying to find your way out of a pitch dark room . . . every now and then you bump up against a chair or table and that's good 'cause you know you headed in the right direction . . . but sure have a time finding the door."

Regardless of the state of the relationship prior to the child's birth, most children were conceived in relationships in which the father felt some affection for the woman. Among fathers' first experience with fatherhood, 25 percent occurred between couples who were living together at the time of conception; 32 percent of all fathers sired children with at least two different women, and most pregnancies and births (64 percent) occurred between men and women who were dating. Of these, only six fathers had children with women whom they had no other bond except sexual. That is to say, most fathers held some affection for women prior to conception. This is important to note because it is a finding that is contrary to the negative images portraying black men as sexual predators who are unwilling and/or unable to establish emotional bonds with women.

FATHERS AND THEIR OWN MOTHERS

Contrary to the varying perceptions of the women who were raising their children, these fathers expressed mostly feelings of high regard for their own mothers. They also seemed to feel emotionally closer to their mothers than any other women in their lives. Moreover, fathers held a considerable amount of respect for their mothers' opinions, insight, and attitudes regarding their fatherhood. The majority of these fathers had been raised in the homes of their single-parenting mothers or grandmothers. Most fathers felt they learned the most about being a good person and a good father from their mothers—even when their fathers lived in the home. When asked how he knew what he knew about being a father, Jason replied:

"Well, it would be more my mother and my father. Mostly from my mother. You have to understand my mother, she is loving about her kids. I have to rate her . . . it's those mothers of that caliber that are the top, the top. You can learn a lot from your dad, but you learn a lot about life from Mother."

Fathers were also asked what their mothers, fathers, and various other relatives expected from them as fathers. The majority of fathers only discussed their mothers' or grandmothers' views, depending upon who it was who raised them. Rarely was a father or other relative mentioned in this regard.

Some fathers had children who were being raised by the children's paternal grandmother or great-grandmother. However, these fathers expressed no more or no less affection or respect for their mothers' views on their fatherhood. Regardless of with whom their children resided, a father placed his own mother's expectations of him above any others. If the father had been raised by his grandmother, then her expectations, not his mother's, were held in the highest esteem.

Dante Rhodes specifically recalled the day that he discovered his girlfriend's pregnancy. "All I could think about . . . was 'What was my mama going to say?' just 'What was my mama going say?'"

He recalled that he waited a week before finally telling his mother about his girlfriend's pregnancy and about her plan to carry the baby to term. When he finally broke the news to his mother, he was surprised at her reaction. "She did not get mad . . . she did not get angry . . . She just said, 'Well, I guess it's about time,'" Dante said, as if still in disbelief. His mother also told him that he had a responsibility—"to be a good father."

"She said babies need a lot of things . . . but what they need the most is attention. She said a good father will spend as much time as possible with his children. When she said those things to me, I felt kind of bad but kind of good inside. See, because I felt bad that I think I kind of disappointed her, but good because I knew she was going to be there for me and my kid . . . I think that I have the best mother, the best mother there is."

Of course, not all mothers or grandmothers had positive reactions to news that their sons or grandsons were about to become fathers. At least two fathers recalled that their mothers were so disappointed that they refused to communicate with them for a time. Two other fathers remembered that their mothers berated them harshly when they discovered they were to become grandmothers. Said one of these fathers, "She yelled at me . . . she said I was no good . . . that I was just like my sorry ass daddy." Still another, who fathered his first child when he was 17, said that his mother made him move out because, "she said she wasn't supporting me and my kids."

What did mothers expect from their sons? Other fathers expressed experiences and perceptions similar to Dante's. According to many of these fathers, mothers expected their sons to primarily perform one function for their children—spend time with them. This was true even for those paternal grandmothers who were raising their sons' children.

"My mother got angry for the first time in a long time. Well, not angry, but disappointed when I went out with my buddies last Saturday instead of spending time with my daughter."

"She just wants me to get my life on track. She takes care of my child and she expects me to spend time with her and take care of myself. That's all."

"My mother, all she told me was that she expected me to be a good father to my boy. She said he was going to need me."

Mothers also expected their sons to serve as role models for their children—particularly for young boys. Said two fathers:

"My mom expects me to do what I can. She wants me to teach them how to be a man, teach them certain things, to be a role model 'cause he's in a house full of women— she wants me to teach them how to be a man."

"She expects me to teach him about being a man. Show him how to take up for himself. How to play sports. How to protect himself and stay out of trouble. Teach him what's important . . . self-respect, stay away from drugs, stay in school, how to be strong."

Mothers were these fathers' primary confidants in matters relating to their children. A mother would offer her son guidance and support if he were having difficulties with such matters as child custody arrangements, employment, or girlfriends. She was often relied upon to get a father through "rough" times. Rolly Ford provided an example:

"This thing with my son sometime get me down and I just want say, 'the hell with it.' Run away and hide somewhere. Then I go see my mom. And I don't even have to say anything. And she don't say anything. She just fixes me a plate, sits down at the table with me. She look at me. I try not to look at her. And she asks 'You having a rough day, huh?' I say, 'Yeah.' But then I feel better just knowing that she knows how I feel, but I don't have to talk about it if I don't want to. Sometimes I do talk and sometimes I don't."

Mothers would also encourage their sons to go visit their children, offer to help them baby-sit, and insist that they bring the children to their home for at least an occasional visit. In fact, several fathers, due to their antagonistic relationships with the mothers of their children, arranged visitation through their own mothers. The father's mother was often relied upon to make necessary phone calls, arrange for transportation, and even rearrange her work schedule if necessary. Arrangements were often made to drop the kids off at his mother's home. Here, children had the opportunity to visit with their father, grandmother, aunts, cousins, and various other relatives.

Fathers felt that they could always count on their own mothers, "no matter what." They felt that their own mothers would always be there for them. In turn, fathers felt for their mothers a certain respect that they gave to no other individual. Fathers endeavored to not disappoint their mothers. These fathers offered the following statements:

"My mother expects me to be a good father, so what am I going do? Even if I didn't want to pick up my son every weekend—which I do—but even if I didn't want to, I'd do it anyway 'cause I know my mama's going get on me if I don't."

"My mother doesn't ask much of me—just to spend time with my child. I do that because I don't want to let my son down, I don't want to let myself down, and I don't want to let my mother down."

Overall, most fathers expressed a sentiment similar to the one made by 26-year-old Cal Gathers:

"If my mama's not getting on me and if I know I'm doing what she expects me to do, then I know I'm doing right. If she's getting on me about something having to do with my little girl, then more than likely she's right and I better make some changes."

When asked what would happen if they were to disappoint their mothers, fathers replied that they would feel ashamed, as if they had let not only their mothers down but themselves, as well.

CHILDREN'S EXPECTATIONS

Fathers were also concerned with their children's expectations of them. They generally indicated that they believed their children primarily expected them to spend time with them. According to fathers, children wanted them to visit, telephone, attend school functions, extracurricular activities, and simply "be there" when needed. One father explained:

"My child doesn't ask a lot of me. He make it easy for me to be a good father. He just wants me to come see him, play with him, take him for a burger sometime, just basically be there as a father. He don't ask for money, he don't expect me to be Santa Claus like some fathers think they should be. Just spend time with him."

Parenting experts tend to support these observations and generally encourage fathers to spend quality and quantity time with their offspring. In their list of "Ten Things Men Can Do to Help Themselves Get More Involved," Ross Parke and Armin Brott (1999) tell fathers to take more initiative in the daily care of their children and "be available more than on weekends."[4] Fathers are encouraged to spend their free time sharing with their sons and daughters. Include your children, they are urged, whether it is in front of the television set, washing the car, or cleaning the house. A recent cultural comparison study found that at least relative to Japanese fathers, American men do spend more time with their children. But the tenor of popular parenting advice manuals and books is both class- and race- oriented. Specifically, they appeal to mostly white and/or middle-class fathers and mothers in two-parenting households. Low-income live-away African American fathers are generally not the target audience of popular paternal self-help books, or the typical subjects of cross-cultural analyses. Leisure time and "extra" time for children must be balanced with work schedules, other relationships, and aspects of everyday living. Nevertheless, if the responses of these fathers are any indication, information and advice imparted through the popular press seem to be expressed common knowledge within black communities. Fathers feel they are generally expected to spend time with their children, boys and girls.

In addition to custodial mothers and their own mothers, fathers also look to children to guide their paternal behavior. As an example, how well children had done in regards to school and staying out of trouble was a measure fathers used to assess their fathering. "Good father" status was enhanced when children did well in preschool or higher levels of education and when they "stayed on the right path." Most fathers described their children in glowing terms. Children were generally perceived as being at least average in regards to school. Children of toddler ages were described as being "exceptional," "better than average," or "smart." Overall, fathers expressed pride in their children's ability.

Some fathers had children who had gotten in "some trouble" either with the law or in school. However, such troubles were described as minor, and did not lead fathers to berate their children. However, they did sometimes blame themselves and their lack of presence in their children's daily lives.

Said one father, whose 15-year-old son was recently arrested for theft: "I blame myself . . . young men need there fathers to be role models . . . to keep them in line." He himself had spent time in prison and felt that he should have taken more time to "connect" with his son and "keep him on the straight." Several of these fathers prided themselves for properly handling the situation, being patient, or being there to help their children overcome the particular problem. Fred Masters' offered the following:

"I figure I'm doing a good job. My children are good children. My daughter, she ain't perfect but she ain't no street-runner, and my son ain't no thug or hoodlum. I have had my share of problems with them, but they have never gotten into any serious trouble."

Fathers also used their relationship with their children as a means of measuring how well they fathered. Fathers who perceived they had good relationships with their children saw themselves as good fathers. Good relationships had several characteristics. Relationships with their very young children were considered "good" when a father sensed the following: the child was happy to see him; the child seemed to have a good time with him; the child tended to do what he or she was told by the father; and the child did not want the father to leave at the end of the visit.

For older children, preadolescent and adolescent, fathers perceived a "good" relationship to have the following attributes: children insisted on their presence at certain activities; children looked forward to arranged visitation and, children turned to fathers for advice and counsel, or "just to talk." Two fathers provided examples:

"My kids call me if they have a problem. They know they can count on me. They trust me to be honest with them. I don't know of many fathers that can say that."

"Sometime she'll call me, not wanting anything, really. It just makes me feel like I'm doing something right."

Fatherhood does not exist in a vacuum. Each of these fathers was surrounded by the attitudes, behaviors, and expectations of significant others.

The expectations of some were more important than those of others. The expectations of their own mothers were sometimes more important than those of the mothers of their children. The expectations of children were also significant. The importance fathers placed on the expectations of the mother of his children seemed to be dependent upon his relationship with her, which was often tenuous. Such findings lend support to other studies examining mothers' and fathers' interaction, and its relationship to fathers' involvement.

Needless to say, the birth of a child does not always bring father and mother closer together, although, more often than not, those who were mere acquaintances at conception tended to become friends after the birth of their child. This was the case at least among those who did not question the paternity of their children. In some cases, fathers and mothers maintained intimate relations, while in others they became arch enemies. Regardless of the type of relationship held between mothers and fathers, most fathers expressed a commitment to maintaining contact with their children. And they often negotiated aspects of their relationships with mothers to achieve this goal. It appeared that what maintained fathers' level of involvement was not only their relationship with the mothers, but also their commitment to their children, their sense of paternal adequacy, and the support they received from significant others, particularly their own mothers. Except for those in antagonistic relationships, fathers perceived that their children's mothers, their own mothers, and their children primarily expected and wanted them to spend time with their offspring.

As subsequent chapters reveal, fathers' perceptions of others' expectations support their own notions of the ideal live-away father. They also tend to support the type of paternal activities they choose to engage in. But do live-away fathers and custodial actually share similar notions of what men should do for their share children? And, do men's parental behaviors meet these mothers' expectations?

5

"BLACK MEN CAN DO BETTER"
What Mothers Say Fathers Do for Their Children

*I*n earlier chapters, it was argued that low-income black families have historically negotiated parenting forms, roles, and responsibilities within austere social, economic, and political conditions. As a family form, the noncustodial father—custodial mother arrangement has historically been a significant element within black communities. The percentage of African American female-headed families maintained without a husband more than doubled between 1970 and 1990. It is also rising steadily among most demographic groups, regardless of race and income. Nevertheless, relative to dual parenting mother-father households, households with single-parenting mothers continue to be perceived as inadequate and ill-favored.

Social, economic, and political institutions continue to function in a manner unfriendly to custodial mothers. Poor mothers with few marketable or technical skills generally do not get enough through welfare and/or low-wage earnings to meet the minimum physical needs for themselves or their children. Women of color are generally relegated to the lowest paying occupations, and in the mid-1990s African American women and children experienced higher rates of poverty than did most other demographic groups combined. In the early to mid-1990s African American women heading households with children had a median income of only $10,380 (well below the poverty level for a family of four and 28 percent of that received by African American married couples with children). While education is negatively related to poverty for men, women require much more of it to avoid welfare lines. Census Bureau 1993 statistics calculated by Albeda and Tilly (1997) indicated that whether women had achieved less than high school or seventeen-plus years of education, they were more likely to be poor than were men. African American women earn about 90 cents to the dollar of European white women. The median weekly earnings of those working full time in 1993 was 75 percent and 58 percent of that earned by black and white men, respectively. The birth of children generally decreases the facility with which women can enter the paid workforce but simultaneously increases their families' material needs.[1]

As in slavery and Reconstruction, and throughout the earlier decades of the twentieth century, poor black single-parenting women continue to utilize social networks to supplement the physical needs of their children, whose daily care costs much more than what mothers get from welfare or earn through paid employment. They must rely on community support systems such as churches and food and clothing outlets that offer free or minimally priced foods and used apparel. Used baby bottles, toys, car seats, dishes, and furniture can also be located through such centers. Recent findings reported by Kathryn Edin and Laura Lein (1997) suggest that women who lack strong personal systems of support most heavily rely on such community center networks. Many mothers rely on these agencies as well as personal networks that historically consist of relatives, neighbors, friends, and the fathers of their children. But even then their parenting is strained by financial hardships. Those they receive assistance from are generally in similar social and economic restraints. Increasingly, low-income black communities are losing economic, social, and cultural assets. A declining tax base has left these communities with depressed infrastructures, few if any movie theaters or parks, and schools with underpaid teachers and out-of-date books. Predominantly black neighborhoods are often weighted down with homeless and battered women's shelters, substance abuse clinics, and liquor stores.[2]

The mothers interviewed for this study lived lives similar to those across the nation. Each of these women had received AFDC, Medicaid, WIC, and/or subsidized housing and child care at some point following the birth of their children. At the time of their interviews, 53 percent were still relying on some form of assistance. Others were generally working in low-wage jobs in the health care, food service, janitorial, retail, security, telemarketing, or other service industries. One mother managed to receive training as a forklift operator and was working part time, twenty-eight hours a week, "loading, moving, and unloading" boxes for a hardware distributor. Their average level of education was slightly higher than that of the men participating in this study. Most had a high school diploma or G.E.D. and over one-half had some formal training or schooling beyond the initial twelve years. However, several (eight) rarely remained in a single occupation or remained with a single employer for more than two years. Rather, due to varying crises and issues with work schedules, managers, and child care, they moved from one job to the next, hoping to improve their work conditions, schedules, and finances.

It is commonly believed that fathers living in households (instead of living away) will eradicate many of the ill effects to children often attributed to parenting alone. Recent programs have attempted to encourage marriage between poor mothers and the fathers of their children. But poor women gain little by marrying those who generally father their children. Like the mothers in this study, these fathers, and poor black men in general, experience low-wages, unemployment, incarceration, and other elements that do not ease family incomes above official poverty lines.

As earlier discussions point out, in our society paternal accountability and responsibility have traditionally been defined financially. State mandates and family policies continue to define the live-away paternal role mostly in economic terms. Consequently, states have developed stringent policies to diligently pursue live-away fathers for formal payment of child support. Yet, policies developed in this regard are destined to fail until they reflect the reality of life for African American families. As Geiger (1995) points out, not all custodial mothers benefit equally from current policies. African American single mothers are less likely than other demographic groups to formally identify the children's fathers, which subsequently impedes the state's ability to acquire paternal economic support.

Furthermore, the life circumstances of many African American men make securing child support from low-income live-away fathers a particularly arduous if not almost impossible task. Indeed, approximately 60 percent of all 16- to 24-year-old African American men have no work experience at all (U.S. Dept. of Labor 1990). The jobless rate for African American men is more than double that of whites. And while some black men are receiving higher levels of education and obtaining middle-class occupations, many more are sliding closer to the bottom of the economic hierarchy.

As chapter 4 outlined, high levels of unemployment, underemployment, and low wages, coupled with relatively low levels of education and high rates of incarceration, mean that these fathers are often unable to fulfill the traditional Western paternal economic provider role. In fact, Barbara Ehrenreich (1986) calculated that considering the then current median income of black Americans, it would require three black men "to clear the median U.S. family income," which was $26,433. She further estimated that it would take four men to obtain a middle-class family status. Today, little has changed. Relative to whites, black men with full-time, year-round work are more likely to receive "low earnings"—that is, annual earnings less than the official poverty level for a family of four. And the proportion of black men receiving low earnings has risen dramatically since 1979 (Hernandez 1997).

For women, the formal addition of a man in the household could mean the loss of housing and childcare subsidies, food stamps, and Medicaid.

All of this leaves us with what appears to be an unclear, inexact definition of the roles and responsibilities of African American live-away fathers. In general, what single-parenting mothers expect from them is, as yet, ambiguous and ill-defined. We know that social policies attempt to combat the negative conditions of single mother households primarily by pursuing fathers for formal payment of child support and by implementing various changes in welfare policy. In an attempt to increase the receipt of child support payments to children and their mothers, the Family Support Act in 1988 required states to strengthen efforts to identify the paternity of "fatherless" children. This legal identification would then enable the state to increase the collection of paternal child support payments. Moreover, many live-away fathers tend to pay inconsistently or not at all. In addition, while most African American births are to unwed parents, many African American unwed mothers do not officially name the fathers of their children. Thus, there is no named father to pursue for any form of child support. Moreover, high levels of unemployment, underemployment, and low wages make securing sufficient child support from African American fathers through legislated means largely ineffective.[3]

We know very little about the attitudes and perceptions never-married adult African American single mothers have of the fathers of their children, or how they expect them to behave in their paternal role. In general, the concerns of many single-parenting mothers seem to be consistent with some of the elements social policy attempts to address. Studies focusing on divorced white mothers find many are dissatisfied primarily with fathers' participation in the lives of their children, particularly in terms of the economic support men provide. Additionally, many white divorced mothers and adolescent mothers say that noncustodial fathers do not spend enough time with their children and that they would like for them to participate more in the lives of their offspring (Arendell 1986; Furstenberg 1995).

Stack's study (1974, 1986) of a midwestern African American community provides some insight into how African American fatherless families perceive and define the fatherhood role. Her findings suggested that a single-parenting African American mother generally regard her children's father as a friend of the family whom she relies upon for assistance of varying forms. Other sources offer some historical and contemporary support for these findings. Borchert's study (1980) of early twentieth-century Washington D.C., Bell Kaplan's 1997 study of black adolescent mothers, and Edin and

Lein's 1997 study examining how single-parenting mothers make ends meet, indicate that mothers rely on fathers when they can, but other males and females within their personal network are also significant. In the more recent study, Stack found that 70 percent of fathers of 1,000 children on welfare acknowledged their children and provided them with kinship affiliation. However, only 12 percent of those acknowledging paternity provided their children with economic support (see also Allen and Doherty 1996; Furstenberg and Nord 1985; Hamer 1997).[4]

For the most part, past research suggests that live-away fathers and custodial mothers may not always agree on paternal roles and functions. While mothers seem to place more emphasis on economic provisions, a few studies of African American live-away fathers indicate they place stress on both their economic and their social roles. Nonetheless, it seems that when they do play a role it tends to be recreational and social rather than instrumental.[5]

Since slavery, low-income African American women and men have lived with the reality that for many, the means to provide a consistent level of economic support for their children is often tenuous. Equally fundamental, low-income and working-class black women have historically developed creative means of sustaining their families. Given this and the history of the live-away father family form in black communities, how do single-parenting mothers define fatherhood and does it approximate fathers' perceptions? What role do these women want fathers to play in their children's daily lives? And what do they do to enhance his paternal activities? In this chapter, we find that these mothers' definitions of fatherhood are modified to accommodate their real life experiences and the behaviors of their children's fathers.[6]

"EVERYBODY KNOW WHAT MEN ARE SUPPOSED TO DO"

Chantel lived in Edwardsville, Illinois, a middle-sized town with a population of slightly over 20,000. Less than 10 percent of the population is black but the percentage has been increasing for the past three decades. The nearest major cities, St. Louis, Missouri, and East St. Louis, Illinois, are about a 20-minute and 15-minute drive away, respectively. St. Louis is the farthest Chantel has ever traveled. The city has a black population of 50 percent, most of whom are poor. She rarely exited the boundaries of Edwardsville but occasionally visited the nearby towns of Alton and Godfrey. Her family had lived here for generations and hers was the second generation raised with the assistance of welfare. Now, at age 23, she was raising her own three children with the assistance of the state and no formal child support. She had been in and out of work since she was first employed at age 17 as a waitress. Like most of her other jobs since then, she held this one for less than six months.

At the time of our interview, she had just begun work as a nurse's assistant and was having difficulty finding child care for her two toddlers and infant daughter. However, she liked the work and for the time being had arranged for her mother and brother, with whom she resided, to care for the children while she worked. "It's just temporary," she said, "until August," which at the time of the interview was two and a half months away. In the fall, her two eldest children, Franklin (age 4) and Alan (age 3) were scheduled to begin a child care and Head Start program. Still, she would need someone to watch the baby. "But I'll figure something out," she said with a look of uncertainty. She had always received substantial support from her mother. But her mother had two minor children of her own. She also worked at two and sometimes three different jobs at a time to maintain the household of three adults and five children. The family was firmly entrenched in a kin network as well as one consisting of state and community agencies. Yet most of her kin were in economically fragile positions. Some were worse off financially than even Chantel's mother.

With the birth of her daughter, Chantel expected her life would become more difficult. Temporary Assistance to Needy Families (TANF) was contingent on her maintaining employment. However, as with many mothers on welfare, how and where she could work depended on her ability to find decent child care. When asked if she received any child care help from her children's fathers, her response was a brief, "You must be kidding!"

She explained that each of the children had different fathers and only one, Nick, the father of her oldest, visited and offered support. "He doesn't have a job sometimes but he does what he can." She said his visits were fairly consistent and he would come by "at least once a week." Although their intimate relationship had long since been over, he desired to rekindle the romance, a notion she flatly rejected. "I just don't want him," she stated, "he can be there for Franklin [his son] but I have no intention of going back with him." She explained that if she did, she would just be using him, "because I don't love him and I don't see any other reason to be with a person . . . he can't really help me financially."

As for the other fathers of her children she explained that one was in jail. The other, the father of the infant, phoned prior to their daughter's birth to say that he did not want to be involved with his child. "I was hurt but there wasn't nothing I could do about it, so. . . ." Chantel reluctantly decided to have the child and raise it on her own. "I think he thought I would want money from him," she further stated. But according to Chantel, this was not her intention at all. "I just wanted him to help me out when I needed it. . . . that could mean help pay the doctor, then he should help pay the doctor, if that means she [the baby] needs new clothes then that means that too . . . or it could mean for him to just be there when I need him," she added brusquely. "I was mad at him because he could've at least offered to help."

She believed that at this point in time, she was truly on her own and expected no assistance whatsoever from two of the children's fathers. Additionally, she felt that any support she received from Nick was tenuous and would end abruptly as soon as he entered into a new intimate relationship. She spoke candidly, "He already told me that if I don't start having sex, he ain't going to be coming around here much longer." She explained that it was because of this pressure that she rarely, if ever, asked him for anything. Nor did she encourage him to visit. "When he asks to come over I just say yes . . . because I think it's good for him to spend time with his son," she said. His visits would range from one hour to all day, depending on whether he had a job. When he was employed his visits were often brief. "But he doesn't do anything but sit around the house and go to the refrigerator. Although she acknowledged his visits were important to their son, she was concurrently discomforted by his presence and did not like the way he spent time with their son. "I don't like the way he plays with him . . . he's too rough," she complained. She felt that he should understand how to interact with a small child, just as she did. "If I can know what to do, so should he."

Chantel explained that in this "small town" the pool of potential partners is extremely small. In this predominantly white, middle-class bedroom community, black youth and young adults like Chantel and the fathers of her children have a particularly difficult time. Although the district's schools are acclaimed as some of the best in the state, by fifth grade nearly one-half of all black students are failing. Those who have extensive academic difficulties are often sifted into an alternative school located in a nearby town. Whether they remain in Edwardsville or commute to the city of St. Louis, work opportunities for adults with only a high school education are bleak.

For most of her childhood, Chantel's live-away father spent time in and out of jail, an uncle had problems with substance abuse, and her older brothers lived at home juggling girlfriends and intermittent work. The fathers of Chantel's children had jobs cutting grass, or worked in nursing homes or local fast food restaurants. She expected they would never provide child support and at least two had no interest in spending any time with their offspring—a reality she felt would be more harmful to her children than the lack of finances. "Kids need to know their fathers, especially boys," Chantel said. She was hopeful that one day she would meet "the right man" and move out of her mother's home, but simultaneously recognized that the chances of this occurring were slim. Thus, she had solemnly resigned herself to the apparent fact that she would "just be raising kids on my own"—a fact of life experienced both by her mother, grandmother, aunts, and several close female friends.[7]

Interviews with the former partners of one-quarter of these fathers revealed that fathers and mothers do not always share similar views of men's paternal behavior.

Nick, the father of Chantel's eldest child, had a slightly different perception of his relationship with Chantel. He also described his visits and paternal activities in a slightly different manner. "She wants us to be a family but at the same time she wants to control when I'm around," he said. When he visits, he is reluctant to interact with her in an affectionate way because he is never certain of her feelings and how she expects him to act. "She knows how I feel about her and my child . . . I want us to be together," he said. With regard to his parenting, he explained, "I do what a man is supposed to." He continued, "I make sure my son don't need anything . . . whatever he needs I will get for him, his mother don't have to ask." On this issue he and Chantel agreed. "I take him for walks, for ice cream; play with him, you know, father-son things like that." He perceived that Chantel's primary parental role was to "let me know what he needs . . . make sure he stays healthy."

Unlike Chantel, he did not wholly see that his relationship with his son was contingent on his relationship with Chantel. But his halting discussion of this suggested that he was not quite certain of what his role or responsibilities would be if they failed to reestablish the relationship. Said he, "Well, if she don't want to be together then see . . . I won't be coming around like I do . . . but I'm not going to abandon my son . . . no, no way." He stated that although they had never discussed the matter, they would "just have to work out an agreement" with regard to his continued visitations with Franklin. However, he explained that "she needs to decide what she wants to do about us."

For Nick, the mother-father relationship was more central to his parenting than it seemed to be for Chantel. This was the case for many of the mothers in this study. That is, what was expected of fathers had little to do with their current relationship with them. Although according to Chantel, "It shouldn't matter if we're together or not . . . he should act like a father." Despite the type of relationship fathers may have perceived they had with the mothers of their children, whether it was intimate, friendly, or antagonistic; the two groups generally had conflicting perspectives on the ideal roles and responsibilities of live-away fathers. As a young mother, Chantel's description of what fathers were supposed to do was similar to many others in this study. Her thoughts on the matter were founded on "just what everybody know men are supposed to do," she said, "that's all."

Mothers were asked to discuss live-away fatherhood in their own words and using their own terminology. Specifically, they were asked to define their conception of an "ideal" father. These mothers' definitions tended to reflect the ideal of fatherhood often espoused in Western cultures. Similar to Chantel, they tended to verbally emphasize fathers' instrumental or economic roles. This seemed to be accentuated regardless of the amount of economic support mothers said they received from fathers. Fathers, on the other hand, as detailed in chapter 6, tended to emphasize the importance of social and emotional interactions with children. And, in fact, they rarely mentioned their behavior with regard to child support or economic provisions unless prompted by the interviewer. These former couples express attitudes analogous to most others:

Mother: "A father is first biological. He takes care of the child he helped bring into this world . . . By that I mean he sees to it that his children have what they need to stay healthy. For example, enough food to eat and a roof over their heads. He provides for their everyday needs."

Father: "A good father is one who understands when don't nobody understand. One to be the backbone for them to lean on . . . A guide they can call on."

Mother: "He makes sure that his kids are well fed, have decent clothes, and a good way of life . . . The father should be someone that the mother can count on to help with the children's medical, food, school, discipline and everything."

Father: "A good father puts his family first, above all else. He's a role model to his daughters and his sons. He's the strong shoulder for them to cry on. Now, he loves them unconditionally but he disciplines them when the mother ain't strong enough to do it."

Mother: "He should love his children. Take care of them by seeing to it that they want for little or nothing. He should see to their financial needs and help the mother with raising them, especially if he has sons. Then he should spend a lot of time with his sons."

Father: "The father is the one who provides provisions but more importantly he shows them the way . . . He's somewhat or should be somewhat the leader. He handles situations and keeps the family safe and together."

Mother: "The ideal father makes enough money to take care of his child and himself and is educationally prepared to handle that . . . He spends time with the child, too." *Father:* "He provides security for his children. They can count on him when there's trouble or if they're going through something. He's a source of strength. Like my kids know they can always turn to me when they're having difficulties with their mother. I'm here for them."

Mothers defined "ideal" fathers as those whose primary responsibility was to meet the economic needs of their children. This included payment of medical bills, providing for shelter, food, clothing, and other essentials. These were elements that they themselves had the most difficulty obtaining. Fathers, on the other hand, defined fatherhood in terms of providing protection and security, and serving as a role model to offspring. While one definition does not necessarily exclude the other, it may indicate a source of contention between men and women over raising their mutual offspring. However, what element was emphasized with regard to paternal behavior varied over time. From conception and beyond, mothers seemed to modify their expectations of fathers and redefine the role of "good" fathers to meet their particular experiences.

INITIAL EXPECTATIONS

"I EXPECTED HIM TO BE PART OF HER LIFE"

Prior to the birth of the child, mothers recalled that they generally expected that live-away fathers would equally provide economic, social, and emotional support to them and to their children. These expectations were founded in discussions they had with their boyfriends prior to their children's births and/or assumptions that they had with regard to fathers' paternal and relationship commitment. Prior to pregnancy, mothers remembered how trusting they were of children's fathers. These men were generally perceived as "different from others," that is, they were generally not perceived as "players," or "dogs," or men who enjoyed playing games of sexual tag with many women. Rather, mothers perceived them as basically honest, or at least more so than other men, and as gentlemen who would stand by them in times of need and trouble. Mostly, mothers felt that their relationships with fathers were "special" and different from those they may have had with other women.

Said one mother, "I just thought we was always going to be in love; that he would be there for me, you know . . . I trusted him to take care of his child . . .do all the things like teach him to play ball, buy him nice things." She recalled feeling heartbroken when her child's father behaved in a completely unexpected manner by ignoring her for much of the pregnancy and being "high" on drugs the evening their child was born. He only visited their son when the mother called and requested favors.

This mother was not alone in her experiences. As was the case with Chantel and two of her children's fathers, more often than not, the paternal behavior a mother initially expected was not fully realized after the birth of the child. According to one mother:

"Before the baby was even born, we sat down and had long talks about what we were going to do for our child. I felt good about our talks but I also had a feeling that it was just talk. Especially, because during the later part of my pregnancy he started messing with another woman. At that point, I did not want anything to do with him. All I wanted was for him to pay child support, which to this day, has not happened. However, that is all I wanted and expected from him."

The child's father had a slightly different description of how their relationship came to an end, but agreed that he was not playing the paternal role she had expected of him.

"She wants me to help take care of my son. Before Damien was born we made plans, partially fantasy but partially I wanted things to work out between us . . . for the baby . . . How things turned out the way they did is she decided to kick me to the curb. So then there wasn't much I could do. I did wrong. I admit that. And when I did wrong we just stopped communicating like we had been . . . I expected that she would eventually let me see my boy and she did. How that happened was I just kept calling to check on her and our son, broke her down. So that's what I do. I spend time with him when I can, send things over. That's somewhat different from what she really wants from me."

Another mother, Josephine Thompson, admitted that she and her child's father never explicitly discussed what was expected of him. However, she recalled that she provided him with detailed descriptions of her and their child's needs.

> "We never really talked about what he was supposed to do. In a way, I told him. See, I would tell him I need diapers; I need for you to take her to the doctor; I need for you to watch her, I need money, that sort of thing. Because I expected him to be part of her life even though he didn't live in the house. I expected him to be a mother and a father to her just like I was . . . I expected financial help."

She and her children's father, Darnell, considered themselves as friends and communicated frequently about their child's needs. Except for her emphasis on child support, his and Josephine's expectations were similar. As he put it:

> "She expected me to be a father and help her out as much as possible. I go above and beyond the call of duty when it comes to my daughter. I know I do more for her than many men out here. The only thing I knew about being a parent was from watching my mother and my uncle a little. The result was that, basically, I learned one day at a time once my daughter was born. I didn't know nothing about getting the milk warm, burping, changing diapers. But her mother expected me to help her with all that. So that's what I did at first and I continue today to do help take care of her."

Other mothers expressed disappointment in the lack of paternal behavior rendered by live-away fathers, but disappointment was generally what followed their feelings of hurt and betrayal by their children's fathers. Before mothers reached the stage of disappointment they first had to acknowledge the sadness and anger they felt when their children's fathers did not live up to their initial expectations. Generally there was no agreement on what or who was the root cause of the couples' problems. Although mothers often blamed fathers for their relationship and paternal failures, fathers rarely accepted full responsibility. This former couple related their experiences:

Mother: "I expected him to be there for me and the baby. To love us unconditionally. To help with the finances, the doctor bills, the diapers, the formula, everything. I expected him to be a good father . . . In my last trimester I told him no more sex. Well, of course, that did it. Things cooled off real quick like and he went and found him some somewhere else. That devastated me when I found out, because he always told me he loved me and that he wanted us to be a family . . . Even then though, I still thought he'd be there for the baby. But he never has been really."

Father: "We had a falling out about this and that, otherwise I think we would have eventually got married. She's the marrying type. When she told me she was pregnant I was real angry and upset. I tried to talk her into having an abortion because I knew I wasn't ready to be a father. I couldn't afford to take care of child. But she wasn't having none of that and I talked to my mother about it a little. After awhile I started to get excited about being a daddy. We made plans, where we was going to live, me finishing school, getting married. I was into it one hundred percent. But, like I said, we had a falling out and I figured she just didn't want me around her or the baby. It got to the point that every time I would try to talk to her she would be yelling at me. Telling me to go to hell and shit! I figured that was a clear message to keep away. So I just make arrangements with her mother to visit my daughter or bring her toys and clothes . . . I do this every now and then."

Overall, mothers and fathers generally did not take time to thoroughly discuss parenting and varying conceptualizations of the term. Both assumed, as do many first-time parents, that it was a task solely learned by doing. However, living in separate quarters and/or living together under financial hardship only increased the normal relationship strain created by pregnancy and childbirth. Mothers felt that there was no "understanding" or general agreement between themselves and fathers regarding paternal roles and responsibilities. If agreements were worked out, this often occurred in reaction to a misunderstanding or an angry debate about parenting. Rarely were couples proactive in setting down the rules and norms of parenting for their children. Consequently, when arguments about child care occurred they were often women making demands of fathers, while fathers attempted to remove themselves from the situation—placing the blame for their actions on mothers. These men felt they were being pushed away from their children; in contrast, mothers felt they and their children were being abandoned.

ROLES AND RESPONSIBILITIES AS PARENTS

"HIS FATHER . . . DOES VERY LITTLE"

While mothers and fathers were asked to describe the "ideal" father and their initial expectations of parenthood, they were also asked to discuss the actual roles that each played in providing for the well-being of their shared offspring. That is, what exactly do they do as mothers and fathers? They were also asked to describe the role of the other parent. The following examples reflect the responses provided by most couples:

Mother: "What I do is primarily to make sure he [son] has what he needs like clothes, pay the rent for a place to stay, food, the basics. I take care of him on the day-to-day basis, everyday. When he's sick I'm his nurse. When he has a problem I talk to him and ask his daddy or my brother too. It's my job to spank him when he needs to be taught a lesson. His father, on the other hand, does very little. I have never received child support . . . Though there has been a few occasions when he gave me ten or twenty dollars to get clothes or boots or whatever . . . What he does do is he will buy him birthday presents, take him over to his mother's on the holidays especially, take him to the movies on occasion if it's something he wants to see . . . he sees him a couple of times a month at least but that's about all.

Father: "My role is to basically be there to support my son's mother. She pretty much provides for his everyday needs. I'm there to support her getting him the extra things he needs and help to get some essentials. Then too, I also try to spend time with him and this is most important because in this way I stay in touch with what's going on in their lives and they know I'm there for them . . . So my role is to do what his mother can't or won't do . . . I take them to the show, spend time with him, get him extra things to make his life better . . . Then see, my biggest role too, is teaching him how to be a man, a black man . . . because that's something that his mother definitely cannot teach him . . . how to defend himself, how to act out here in the world, how to associate."

Mother: "With my kids I am the primary caretaker. I see to their health needs, make sure they get to the doctor, to school, pay all the bills so that we have a roof over our heads, help them with their homework as much as I can. It's rough but that's my role as a mother. I'm their mother and a black single mother and I do for my kids what my mother did for me . . . Their father, he provides some things . . . I would say the role he plays is an important one because the kids love him. He talks to them on the phone a lot. He takes them to McDonald's every now and then. He does not have the financial role as far as the kids are concerned."

Father: "My attitude about my role is this, I do what I can. I try to do the very best that I can for my kids. That means I make sure that when I have money I do for my kids. I buy them something or take them somewhere, to the museum or zoo. I talk to my kids, I'd say, about every day I'm on the phone checking on them, asking them how's school. Now, their mother, all she wants me to do is give her money, which I do when I can. But I think it's more important that I spend time with them and if they need something and she can't get it then I'll try my best to see to it that they somehow get it . . . As far as her role is concerned, she would tell you that she does everything. That's not true and she knows it. She is a good mother, though. She makes sure they have breakfast, lunch, and dinner and other material things. She makes sure they have a quality place to stay.

Mother: "I take care of my son and my daughter. I make sure that they are healthy, dressed appropriately, and all that. I make sure that they eat properly. I buy the right kind of food. I make sure that they can participate in sports and school activities no matter how much it costs because it's important that they are exposed to many different things. My son wanted to play the trumpet so I made sure that he got a trumpet. We used to have a little apartment when they were younger but it was cheaper for me to come live with my mother . . . This way the kids can go outside more. I got a swing set for them a few Christmases ago . . . My role is to take care of my kids in all ways.

"Now, my son's father really does not spend any time with him and really contributes nothing to raising him . . . He has been in and out of jail twice . . . So I recognize that it's difficult to pay child support when you're in jail. I will give him credit, though, because he asks his family to help me out . . . so I think he does what he can. My hope is that now that he's out of jail that he will stay out, stay off the streets and try to do right by his son, spend time with him. Get a job and help me with expenses. My daughter's father was killed when she was 3 so he has no role but she knows his family. They are very much a part of her life and they have always been helpful toward me."

Father of Son: "Well, my role is limited by my occupational hazards, you could say. I haven't had much of a role because, as I've told you, I've been in jail, prison. As a way to be a father, that's not the best way . . . I try to make sure he's [my son's] safe. I have my brothers and sisters keep up with him and make sure he stays on the straight and narrow. I call him, let him know I'm thinking about him. I did this even when I was locked up, I made it a point . . . Since I'm out I'd like to spend time with him more but his mother wants me to be straight first . . . Get my act together . . . Really, his mother does for all his needs, she is really like a mother and a father in the role that she plays. You name it. She does it. That's all there is to it."

Overall the actual roles and responsibilities fathers perform do not seem to correspond with mothers' definitions of "ideal" paternal behavior. Mostly, men and women described father's actual paternal behavior as that of "helper" and not full partner. Few of these fathers offered significant economic assistance on any consistent bases. Rather, the roles they played were consistent with their own definition of fatherhood, which emphasized socioemotional parental support. Yet, even in this arena fathers fell short of their own and mothers' goals. Both men and women felt fathers were not doing as much as they possibly could for their children. Fathers were mostly helpers, picking up somewhat where they felt mothers slacked or were unable to perform. But men tended to report that they were better fathers than their own fathers were to them. And mothers, though expressing general disappointment about not having more in terms of father involvement, tended to express some satisfaction with fathers behavior, particularly if they were providing the minimal amounts of both economic and visitation.

Said one mother, "he could be worse, so I have to be thankful for that." According to her, the father of her child did not drink heavily, had a part-time job, supplied her with emergency items upon request, sent money "when he can," and visited and/or called at least once a week. In other words, while they did not modify their notions of "ideal" fatherhood, mothers seemed to alter their expectations of fathers so that they better reflected the context of life in their communities and in their own households. Said one mother, "In a perfect world I would like to have my baby's father take care of me and my son financially, buy us a house, you know . . . but in this world you have to understand that ain't going to happen, that's a fairy tale . . . so you get to thinking that this man is as good a father as my baby's going to get."

ENCOURAGING FATHERS' PATERNAL RESPONSIBILITY

"I TRY TO GET HIM TO SPEND TIME WITH HER"

Mothers indeed expressed a general frustration with fathers, but that frustration was intermingled with their frustrations about living in poverty and barely "getting by." Nevertheless, most felt they should do their best to encourage fathers' economic and social participation in the lives of their children. Several mothers discussed their methods of encouraging men's paternal behaviors, as follows:

"Mostly, I just try to get him to spend time with her. Show her that he loves her . . . I ask him to help out [financially] but only when I know it's something Jewel [daughter] really needs. That way I know he'll give it to me. Any other time he sees me as hounding him for money."

"If I ask him for money and he says 'I don't have it,' then I try not to make a huge deal of it. Otherwise, we start arguing and shouting and the result will be what? He won't even come around to see Marcus (son) anymore . . . I try to keep things even and stable so when I tell him he should pick up Marcus, there won't be no hassle about it."

"See, men will come around when they want something. And you know what they usually want. But then as soon as you ask them for something, they're gone. Ask them for money and you'll see they forget your name, their child's name, your phone number. So you have to let them think they're in control. Let them give you things when they feel like it. Ask them for things at just the right time. Otherwise, you ain't going to get anything from them."

"I let him be part of the family. For the kids' sake. Even though sometimes he helps with the payments and sometimes he doesn't."

Mothers generally felt that without their verbal encouragement and/or their use of various subtle strategies, fathers would pay little or no attention to their offspring. Fathers' own descriptions of their paternal feelings and behaviors often did not lend much support to mothers' claims. However, some fathers did interpret mothers "encouragement" as an effort to control their behavior and curb their freedom. Two fathers explained:

"Most times, when I call, she's pissed off at me because I called late, or I changed my mind about something, or didn't return her phone call. That's usually it—that I didn't return her phone call right away. I say, 'We ain't married! We ain't in a relationship! I don't answer to you!' The only reason I tolerate her is for my son. Other than for him we probably wouldn't associate. She has yet to comprehend that she can't tell me what to do. She makes it hard for me to be a father sometimes."

"She tries to get me to do right by her and my children. She makes me take on my responsibilities with them. She does her best at that . . . I pick them up from school, make sure they always safe, cook, put them to bed . . . I don't think I'd be a good father if Candor didn't force me from the start . . . She's a good mother . . . The problem is this, though; when we argue, it's usually because she thinks I'm disrespecting her by my lady friends. But I never bring women around my children, never. I don't smoke or drink around them either . . . But, you see, at the same time I can't let her try to control my life . . . not just because we have children together."

Fathers expressed a general fear of being "tied down" to family. While mothers conducted the day-to-day activities of parenthood, fathers tended to value the freedom that accompanied a live-away parenting status—not that they did not aspire to have a "traditional" family. But most expected that it would be with someone other than the current mothers of their children. Many also indicated that marriage would require a significant improvement in their financial situation. For men, their liberty often took precedence over women's expressed desire for them to be more accountable and attentive to their children. Mothers often found themselves "putting up" with poor paternal behavior in an effort to maintain some bond between fathers and children. They felt they valued the father-child bond more than the fathers themselves. Mothers often expressed frustration and resentment for fathers' seemingly ambiguous attitudes.

IMPROVING PATERNAL PARTICIPATION

"BLACK MEN TODAY ALWAYS HAVE EXCUSES"

Both mothers and fathers agreed that men could do much more to meet their paternal obligations and improve participation in the daily lives of their children. Mothers tended to feel that fathers could, if they so wanted, "focus more on their responsibilities," "spend less time satisfying their own needs" and "make more of an effort" to meet the needs of their children. Fathers generally agreed and admitted they could do more for their children, but cited many external barriers that hindered their ability to do so, a topic discussed in detail later. Mothers, too, recognized barriers to men's paternal behavior but generally felt that these could be overcome "if fathers put forth a sincere effort." Three couples talked about what fathers could do better:

Mother "The first thing he could do better is to get out of jail and stay out of jail. This certainly would make a difference in my eyes as far as his children are concerned. I understand the world is not kind to black men. However, at some point these men need to decide what's best for their children. Jail is not the answer. In Keith's case, he had choices. He chose the wrong way and now me and our child are suffering because of it."

Father: "I do my best for my child given my life circumstances and situations I've gotten myself into. I've had hard times all my life and I just went the way of my father, ended up in jail a couple of times. I think that if my father had been around more for me then I would have been a better man to Freda and a better father to Jellissa. People are the product of their environment and I'm no different. Right now I'm trying to do better by them. All I ask is for them to have a little patience with me."

Mother: "I would like for him to spend more time looking for a better job. More time playing with his son and seeing to his needs. I've told him that . . . He'd rather be out hanging out with his boys, going to the clubs, having different women. If he wanted to he could give me a little money every week or month and just be around his son on a consistent basis. But he doesn't want to. No, he ain't got time for that. I told him he's going to regret it because one day his son's not going to want to have anything to do with him."

Father: "I think I do pretty good as fathers go but there's always room for improvement. That's how I look at it. It's hard to be a father when you don't live in the same household as your child. Then what I have would be his, automatically . . . I think if I lived in the same household then I wouldn't have to go out of my way to spend time with him because I'd be around, part of the furniture. As it is, though, that's not the case. Now, to see my boy I have to arrange it around his mother's schedule or my schedule. So if you look at it from that angle, then you might say I do pretty good as a father, given the circumstances of living apart. I can do better only if the circumstances change themselves."

Mother: "Understand that I think he does a good job as a father, especially compared to other men out there. But black men today always have excuses. Even if they don't live with their children that doesn't mean they have to be a part-time daddy. They keep blaming everyone else for them not doing what they're supposed to do. Black men are always complaining about the white man keeping them down, they can't find a good job, they can't get no good education, they can't buy a car. All that may be true, but what's stopping them from getting a second job, or taking night classes. Black men can do better if they want to and my daughter's father is no different. Women are tired of their sorry excuses for not being a daddy all of the time. Excuses don't pay the bills or help a child feel better when her daddy forgets to call."

Father: "Yeah, I think I can improve, definitely. Me and her have talked about it some . . . what I can do better and what she can do better. She's understanding of my situation and my habits, that's why she'll always be my lady. My daughter, she thinks the world of me. She is the joy of my life. She's the reason I decided to change some of my habits, stop hanging with the wrong crowd so much. So things are changing that will help me be a better father to her."

From mothers' perspectives fathers seem to invariably have excuses for not providing what they contested was optimal care for their children. Even though fathers admitted they could do better, they also said that there were internal and external factors such as work schedules, bad habits, and jail time, that prohibited them from doing so. These mothers say they understand the hardships that these fathers, as well as many black men, experience. Yet, they also express a weariness with the justifications men regularly provide to defend their decision not to be better parents. For many mothers, being a good father is largely a matter of choice, which few external barriers can control. "See," said one mother, "mothers ain't allowed to have excuses." She was essentially arguing that fathers should not be allowed excuses either.

OBTAINING CHILD SUPPORT

"BLACK PEOPLE, WE HANDLE THINGS ON OUR OWN"

Given their consistent emphasis on the importance of fathers' economic provider role, mothers were asked whether or not they formally pursued fathers for formal payment of child support. In general, most mothers expressed a reluctance with regard to seeking legal assistance. Yet, six mothers had attempted to obtain consistent child support payments through the courts or state collection agencies. These women explained why they chose such formal means:

"I knew he could afford to take care of his child. That's what he's supposed to do. I knew he wasn't going to pay just because I told him to, or because his mama told him to; all those avenues had been tried . . . He's too selfish. So I took him to court."

"He was taking care of his other children and I knew he could afford to take care of this one. I talked to him a lot. I warned him about what I would do. I told him I'd sue his ass! He didn't believe I'd go to an attorney . . . but that was the only way . . . I didn't really want it to be that way because I knew once I made the decision, he would essentially be out of our lives."

"I felt like I should give him a chance to be a good father. He kept telling me that once he got another job he would help out. I was very, very patient with him. I did not want to take him to court for the money. I think, mostly, I was afraid of losing him . . . But, after awhile, I felt like this was the only way I could be sure I was going to get help. I really needed the support."

While these few mothers chose a legal option to obtain child support, all perceived it as a final resort. And, generally they only utilized the option after months of informal negotiating and communication with fathers proved unsuccessful. And each perceived that the fathers of their children were capable of providing much more money than what the gave informally. However, most mothers chose not to pursue child support through the legal system. Several mothers explained:

"Black people, we handle things on our own. We don't need lawyers or judges. The first thing they're going to do is throw the man in jail. Then what? I still don't have money coming in. And worse, now baby really ain't got a daddy."

"Well, I didn't see a need for all the trouble. He does what he can. Nobody can make him give more than what he has."

"At first, I thought he was going to be there for us . . . that he'd do his best. I didn't think it was necessary to get a lawyer. I didn't even think about it . . . Now, I just don't think it's worth it because there are too many bad outcomes possible. One, they could arrest him. Two, my daughter won't have the opportunity to get to know him better. Three, he will truly, truly resent it and then I won't get any help."

These and most other mothers felt that even if they sought legal action, little would result. Many felt it would be a "waste of time." Given their work and family commitments, "time" was an element these women felt they could not spare. They understood that formally seeking child support would require numerous meetings with welfare officers, attorneys, and several court dates, all of which would necessitate their missing work and losing wages. In addition, they expressed a fear of alienating the father by forcing him into a public forum. Further, a few mothers feared the father would be taken into legal custody for nonpayment and subsequently cut the father-child bond. They also feared that an award of child support would be accompanied by a revocation of welfare benefits, an apprehension founded in the realities of welfare policies and actions.

For most mothers then, these "costs" outweighed any potential benefit they might receive from an award of child support, particularly since they also tended to believe that little if any child support would result from court actions. For many mothers, the best and most reliable options to secure any form of paternal support involved informal communication and persuasive approaches. "At least this way," said one mother, "I know he will at least come and visit his son."

WHAT ABOUT MARRIAGE?

In the United States we tend to define the ideal family as one consisting of a biological mother, father, and their children. Many of us hold to this ideal despite the fact that since the 1960s the probability of marrying has declined. African Americans in particular are less likely to marry than white Americans. At present, the majority (58 percent) of African American households with children are headed by single-parenting women (Chadwick and Heaton 1998). Regardless of income and education levels, even those African Americans who marry are more likely to separate and divorce compared to other demographic groups. Yet, black women and men continue to have children and, as Andrew Cherlin aptly states, "making the transition to parenthood without marrying is now the predominant experience among blacks." "Marriage," he adds, "has become disconnected from childbearing" (1998:148).

Consequently, child rearing has followed suit and become increasingly disconnected from formal marital unions. This is particularly true for low-income black families. As a group, they are less likely to marry than those with working- and middle-class incomes. Research suggests that high rates of black male homicide, incarceration, and joblessness make for a very small and decreasing pool of marriageable men. But evidence presented by these mothers and fathers suggests that other elements may complicate the issue of marriage.[8]

Women, for example, often have strong ties to their mothers, sisters, brothers, other kin, and/or social service agencies that enable them to sustain their families regardless of the level of their children's fathers' engagement. This is not to suggest that these mothers live in comfortable or even adequate circumstances. Quite the contrary, many lived at or below the margins of poverty. Assistance from relatives tended to be social, emotional, and in-kind rather than cash. Furthermore, those family and friends from whom they sought and gained assistance also tended to exist in dire economic straits.

Said one mother, "My mother, she will help me if I ask her but I know that [if] she give money to me then that mean she [is] going to be borrowing it from somebody else." Another mother explained that it was not her mother but her maternal aunt who provided her with the most assistance, "I've always been close to my aunt, she raised me . . . when I need something for the kids she'll do her best to help me." This same mother also explained that her aunt had two adolescent children of her own to provide for "so she can't do as much for me as she probably would."

Still, in contrast to recent welfare policy, mothers did not feel marriage to the fathers of their children could contribute significantly to their families' well-being. Said a mother of twins, "My mother raised me, her mother raised her . . . They all did it without a man." Another mother explained, "They [men] nice to have around sometime but they can bring a lot of problems into a house . . . you have to tolerate a lot to live with a man." Still another mother offered deeper insight, "Men always want to have control in the house but they don't want to do anything to help out . . . like pay the bills, clean up after themselves, help with the kids."

All in all, most mothers did not seem to feel it necessary that fathers live in their children's homes to be good fathers. Fathers tended to agree. "But if it were a perfect world," sighed one father, "my kids would live with a mom and dad in the house." Another father explained that this was simply not the circumstances in black communities. "Mothers raise children . . . Fathers help out and do what they can."

These mothers' specific definitions of "ideal" fatherhood tended to reflect dominant norms within traditional Western standards of fatherhood. Their definitions of ideal fatherhood contrasted sharply with those expressed by fathers. On the surface it appeared that, similar to white divorced mothers, these African American never-married custodial mothers tended to define a "good father" primarily in economic terms. In this vein, a good father was one who provided adequate financial support for his children's care and well-being. However, unlike white divorced mothers of past studies, these mothers expressed a reluctance to use legal channels to pursue fathers for formal payment of child support. In fact, the majority chose not to do so at all, for fear of causing legal difficulties for live-away fathers or jeopardizing the paternal-child relationship (Arendell 1986). However, mothers in this study separated their "ideal" from their reality and the possibilities existing therein. Understanding the economic circumstances of black men, these women placed more significance on fathers' social presence than child support—though each was considered important. They expected fathers to financially provide when they could, but to be consistently physically present in their children's lives.

These mothers distinguished between their ideal image of fatherhood and its reality in their own lives and communities. They generally felt live-away fathers rarely met their standards. Mothers generally acknowledged the existence of hardships and disadvantages for African American men in the labor market. Yet, they simultaneously expressed a frustration with men whom they felt did not work hard enough to overcome the various obstacles confronting them, particularly given fathers' financial responsibilities to their children. Mothers were also frustrated because they felt that they themselves faced many obstacles and hardships but yet were not deterred from meeting the needs of their children.

Fathers, on the other hand, tended to define fatherhood primarily in terms of their expressive roles. These fathers discussed the importance of being a role model, a guide, and source of social and emotional support for their children. In terms of providing economic support or child support, these fathers perceived their function as one intended to support their children's mother in her role as primary caretaker. In this regard, many provided toys, and purchased clothing and miscellaneous items for children on an "as needed" rather than a consistent basis. These fathers correctly perceived that while they emphasized social and emotional paternal roles, money was an element that many mothers needed. Many fathers admitted shortcomings in their paternal behavior and felt they could improve. However, contrary to most mothers, who equated paternal improvement with consistent economic support, live-away fathers equated it with spending more time with children and various other social elements. Men who acknowledged paternal shortcomings perceived them as consequences of past or current circumstances and "situations" which they often felt were beyond their control. Despite explaining their paternal inadequacies on external terms, these men generally felt that given their circumstances, they were performing "better than most men" with regard to fatherhood.

Overall, it appears that African American, never-married, custodial mothers really want financial support from noncustodial fathers. However, mothers in this study separated their "ideal" from their reality and the possibilities existing therein. Understanding the economic circumstances of many low-skill black men, these women placed more significance on fathers' social presence than child support—though each was considered important. They expected fathers to provide financially when they could, but to consistently be physically present in their children's lives. The problem, as they see it, is that they often receive neither on a consistent basis.

The problem for policy makers and social work practitioners who primarily emphasize paternal economic responsibilities is that mothers are willing to forego economic support in lieu of the social and emotional support fathers provide. These findings suggest that while mothers express an interest similar to the state with regard to child support, they simultaneously "understand" that fathers are not likely to provide child support regularly. Furthermore, mothers are generally quite reluctant to pursue any legal recourse to obtain such support for fear of jeopardizing the paternal-child bond, the fathers' freedom from the criminal justice system, or their own relationship with the father. Indeed, evidence indicates that low-income fathers are more likely than those with higher incomes to be arrested for nonpayment of child support (Hill 1997). And having low incomes or being in poverty are conditions African American men experience disproportionately. Thus, mothers tend to settle for what they can get from live-away fathers and generally do not make adamant economic demands of them. Rather, they attempt to encourage fathers to play a social role with their children, and call upon them for economic support only when they are fairly certain it will be received.

While well-intended "efforts have been aimed at showing how U.S. social welfare philosophy and policy have affected people of color, rarely, if ever, are the cultural values or worldview of people of color used as a conceptual foundation to describe how social welfare philosophy and policy should look" (Schiele 1997:23). Neither mothers' nor fathers' attitudes, definitions, or behaviors with regard to paternal roles and responsibilities are completely compatible with the goals of the state. In the eyes of many African American women and men, what is best for their children often has only partially to do with economics. Rather, the presence of fathers, and the social and emotional bond that develops within a father-child relationship are integral to the well-being of "fatherless" children, and it is a support fathers can provide independent of their economic circumstances. However, that mothers and fathers do not seem to agree on the type or extent of paternal economic, social, or emotional engagement suggests that the role of live-away fathers remains unclear. Despite an established history of noncustodial father-custodial mother family forms, low-income black Americans are still negotiating appropriate parental roles and functions within these systems.

PART 3
Being Fathers

Live-away, low-income black American fathers do not have an easy life. They are America's public enemy; they descend from a history of tenuous economic and social circumstances; they experience high levels of incarceration; they face unemployment and relatively low levels of education and income. As men though, they are expected to be financially responsible for their children. They are generally blamed for the increasingly high rates of poverty among African American children. Yet, they increasingly find it difficult to meet their financial obligation to their children. And their general roles and functions as live-away parents are not clearly defined within their relationships with their children's mothers. Other than child support, public institutions provide little support to guide and define the criteria for "good" live-away parenting. How then do low-income, black live-away fathers decide on what is or is not appropriate parental behavior? The answer to this question, replied one father, is: "It isn't easy."

In part 3 of our story we listen as fathers describe what it is that they do as fathers for their children (chapter 6). But men's parental engagement occurs at varying levels. Some men are there everyday. Others have no involvement in their children's upbringing. Some felt overwhelmed with life issues and chose to withdraw from parenting altogether. In chapter 7 these fathers discuss their often heartrending decisions to disengage as parents and become daddies their children may never get to know. In chapter 8 we learn that regardless of their ideals and goals as fathers, men's desire to be good fathers is one fraught with hurdles. Still, many fathers persevered and overcame seeming limitations to what they considered the best possible daddies to their children.

6

WHAT FATHERS SAY THEY DO AS DADDIES

*I*n the earlier part of this story we found that custodial mothers and live-away fathers did not always share similar notions about parenting. Mothers in fact, sometimes expressed dissatisfaction with fathers' parental behavior and attitudes. And fathers sometimes misjudged mothers' expectations of their parenting behavior. Still, we are left with several important questions. What do fathers say they do for their children? How do they define their paternal roles and functions? Despite the views of mothers and the general public, do fathers think they are fulfilling their parental roles? In this chapter, black live-away fathers describe the most important aspects of their parenting role. Most significantly, they define their own standards of "good" fatherhood for black men who live-away from their children. Here is Dimitri Stiles of St. Louis.

During the first two months of his daughter's life Dimitri Stiles had a regimented daily routine. "I had to be at work at 6:00 A.M.," said Dimitri, "so I would get up early, drive to work from Alton and I would get off from work at about 6:00 P.M. and drive back to Alton. Then I would drive to St. Louis where my daughter was in the hospital." From birth, his daughter Tonya had severe medical problems. "They didn't know if her kidneys were going to function; it was as if she had one big kidney," he explained. He would sit at the hospital all night long and "just hold her." Tonya's mother, Kansas, was not as attentive. She had wanted an abortion but Dimitri had convinced her to carry the child to term. "I didn't believe in abortions," he said. "This was my child and maybe my last chance to have a child." Kansas agreed to give birth to the child only under the condition that Dimitri would be the baby's primary caretaker.

Just prior to Tonya's birth, Dimitri and Kansas began sharing a home. Their cohabitation lasted less than seven months. During that period he worked twelve-hour days. "Soon as I got in the house long enough to take a bath," he said, "she put this baby in my arms because she cried all day long while I was at work." At night

Tonya's father was primarily responsible for her feedings. "There would be nights at two o'clock in the morning [Kansas] would wake me up when the baby cried," he stated. "[Kansas] would say well you know you were the one who wanted the child so you get up and take care of her." Dimitri explained that the late night feedings persisted even though Kansas knew he had to be at work by six o'clock that morning. Despite the anger and frustration this caused him, Dimitri claimed, "I told her no matter what it is I will do anything for my child."

In addition to the hectic and weary schedule, Dimitri said he began to experience verbal and physical abuse from Kansas. "Sometimes I'd be laying in the bed and she would just plank me . . . you know and I would just lay there and let her hit me to the point that I would really get tired of her hitting and would get up and I would hit back." As the violence escalated, Dimitri began to take respite on the weekends—visiting bars and staying out late with friends.

Eventually, he moved out and began to reside with his mother and stepfather. However, his schedule changed little. He would work eight- to ten-hour days and spend at least six hours caring for his daughter and sometimes her half-sister. "I don't live there with her but I'm with her a lot, you know what I mean," he elaborated. "When her mother goes out or to work then I'm there . . . I'm her Rock of Gibraltar, her main disciplinarian, her moral teacher, I mean I'm her father in every sense of the word."

Still, Dimitri conceded the circumstances of his fatherhood are not ideal, and admitted to looking forward to weekends and the few week nights that he could glean "time off" from paternal responsibilities. "Even so," he said, "I would rather be a full-time father like having a mother and father in the home." This, he explained was always what he wanted for his daughter."

In individual interviews and focus group discussions, other fathers expressed similar hopes. Said one father: "I think that's just part of the American dream—the image of the family with the mother, father, and two-point-three kids." "But," claimed another, "not to say it's a pipe dream, but if it don't come true you still supposed to do as fathers are supposed to do."

PAST RESEARCH

Clearly, past research seems to substantiate the negative image of black fathers. The little research that exists on noncustodial fathers suggests that in general most fathers tend to have little contact with their children and play only a minimal role in their children's lives. Fathers who live with their children tend to be more involved with boys than with girls, but such findings are mixed in regard to noncustodial fathers. Nonetheless, it seems that when noncustodial fathers do play a role it tends to be recreational and social rather than necessary sustenance. Moreover, it appears that many noncustodial fathers tend not to meet responsibilities or child support obligations and pay inconsistently or not at all.[1]

Yet, there are some studies that suggest that black noncustodial fathers do play a substantial role in the lives of their children. A study of 100 black adolescent fathers found that 18 months after a child's birth, the majority reported visiting the child at least three to six times a week (Rivera et al 1986). Their visits included diapering, feeding, playing, and outings. Only 2 percent reported having no contact with their children. Allen and Doherty's more recent (1996) study supported these past findings. Among their sample, adolescent black noncustodial fathers tended to place strong emphasis on "being there" for their involvement with their children. These noneconomic forms of father involvement and father-child relationships often are overlooked by policy makers and researchers. Ongoing studies by Sara McLanahan, Irwin Garfinkel and other researchers with "The Fragile Families and Well-Being Study," and others indicate that low-income, noncustodial fathers are significantly involved with their children, at least up to a year after the child's birth. Roles of the noncustodial father seem to vary widely. Liebow's urban ghetto study of black "street corner" men found that noncustodial fatherhood consisted of a range of varying father-child relationships. While some fathers acknowledged paternity, others did not. Some fathers had no contact with their children while others had affectionate relationships. Overall, as Liebow contends, "Some fathers are not always 'absent' and some are less 'absent' than others" (1967:73).[2]

BARRIERS TO THEIR FATHERHOOD

The extent to which some noncustodial fathers are absent from the daily lives of their children and the extent to which they participate in the nurturing and social and emotional well-being of their children may be a reflection of obstacles and hindrances that occur within their social and economic environments (a subject discussed in detail in chapter 8). Umberson and Williams (1991), in their interviews with 45 divorced noncustodial fathers, found respondents reported a variety of "ecological barriers." These were primarily a lack of time, physical distance from children (e.g., living across town, in a different city, or in another state), and financial constraints that placed limits on their ability to visit their children regularly.[3]

Overall, black men in American society are expected to have certain attitudes regarding the care and well-being of their children. As fathers, they are expected to behave in a manner prescribed by dominant Western norms. In fact, black noncustodial fathers often are perceived as "bad" fathers because they appear to reject or neglect the very functions of fatherhood set forth by the Western "ideal"—such as the role of breadwinner. They are perceived to have no concern for their children's social or economic well-being and they receive primary blame for the increasingly high rates of poverty among black children and the increasing rates of welfare dependency among single black mothers and their children. Yet, black fathers have historically been denied the means and opportunity to successfully and consistently function in the manner prescribed by the Western "ideal" of fatherhood. Given these past and present conditions for black men in America, these low-income black live-away fathers were asked to describe what they do as fathers and what they considered to be the most important aspect of their parenting. Specifically, they were asked to discuss and define their roles and functions as fathers who do not live with their children.

WHAT BLACK LIVE-AWAY FATHERS SAY THEY DO AS FATHERS

As expected, the functions and roles of fatherhood for these fathers varied from the "Western ideal" of fatherhood. In fact, these fathers' view of fatherhood contrasts sharply with the traditional paradigm (see table, opposite page). Fathers seemed to accept the "Western ideal" of fatherhood in general, but did not accept certain aspects of the "ideal" as important as they are popularly perceived by the public majority. Some elements were not considered important at all.

These fathers primarily based their ideal of fatherhood on their past relationship with their own fathers. As children, most of these men grew up having noncustodial fathers. They based their role and function as father on what they felt their own fathers did or did not provide for them when they were children. Their role and function as a father was essentially founded on what they perceived they themselves needed from their fathers when they were children.

IDEAL FATHERHOOD: ROLES AND FUNCTIONS

"IDEAL" FOR BLACK LIVE-AWAY FATHERS	DOMINANT "IDEAL" OF FATHERHOOD

1. Caregiver
   Spend time with child
   Provide emotional support
	1. Provide Legal Endowment

2. Discipline	2. Provide Economic Support

3. Formation Function
   Serve as role model
   Serve as teacher/guide
	3. Provide Protection

4. Economic Support	4. Caregiver
5. Provide Legal Endowment	5. Formation

Overall, the functions and roles of black noncustodial fathers fell into five distinct categories. In order of importance, fathers considered their primary roles and functions to be as follows: (1) to spend time with children; (2) to provide emotional support; (3) to provide discipline; (4) to be a role model; (5) to teach boys how to be men and girls how to be young ladies; (6) to provide economic support.

SPENDING TIME WITH CHILDREN

By far the most important function of fathering for these noncustodial fathers was to spend time with their children. The importance they placed on this aspect of fathering was generally associated with the lack of time their own fathers had spent with them when they were growing up. Many were attempting to be better fathers than they perceived their fathers to have been. Scott Bennett, a live-away father of one, explained:

"I guess I do what I do as a father because growing up as I did, remembering all the mistakes that were made by my father and promising myself that I would never, never, let that happen . . . there was a lot of bad things, my father wasn't there for us physically when I was growing up."

When children, many of these fathers yearned to spend time with their fathers and for their fathers to pay more attention to them—visiting, taking them to the park, watching them participate in various school activities, particularly sports. Dennis Bradshaw spoke for several when he said:

"See, my father didn't do for me what fathers are supposed to do—take me to the park, teach me how to shoot hoops—little things." Dennis explained that it was his mother who tended to take him to football, basketball, baseball games, and other sporting events. He said that his father's absence "hurt," but at the same time it didn't because that's just the way it was. He related this experience to his present-day paternal attitudes and behaviors and stated with conviction: "I don't want to be that kind of father to my children." According to him, the most important fatherly role is to "spend as much time as possible doing the things that other fathers that live with their kids take for granted."

For these fathers, "spending time" was used as an almost catch-all phrase. Primarily it meant that a father would simply take the time to go and be with his children, or rather make himself present. When they spoke of "time" these fathers spoke of it in general and not necessarily in regard to a particular activity. It could mean talking with their children on the telephone, playing basketball, taking them to the park, taking them to the mall, sitting around the house watching television, and/or playing video games. Generally, fathers spent the same amount of time with sons as with daughters, though the activities often varied as the children grew older.

Carl Henry explained how he spends time with his sons and daughters from two different relationships:

"I try to treat my children the same—boys the same as girls, and one set just like the other." He said that when they were young they generally enjoyed the same types of activities. Both the two boys and the two girls "liked to get dirty at the playground," and that is where they spent a lot of time. He recollected his weekly paternal routine: "One weekend I'd pick up this set and the other week I'd pick up the other." He acknowledged that the schedule was "hard and tiring," but said it was simultaneously well worth the effort.

"Spending time" did not require a specified amount. In fact, the amount of time spent with children varied considerably among noncustodial fathers, from spending no time at all to seeing their children everyday. The amount of time generally depended on how near they lived to their children, their work hours, and how many sets of children they had. However, many fathers saw their children at least bimonthly. Well over half (76 percent) visited with at least one set of their children on a weekly, biweekly, or everyday basis.

Those who visited with their children about once a month ($N = 21$) or less still considered "spending time" to be the most important function a father could perform for his children. However, fathers who did not spend time with their children generally saw themselves as "not a good father" regardless of the circumstances that kept them away, all of which is discussed in detail in a later chapter.

PROVIDING EMOTIONAL SUPPORT

Second to "spending time" with their children, these fathers considered their provision of emotional support the most important function of fathering. This, too, was another aspect of the father role that contemporary noncustodial fathers learned through observing and experiencing what their own fathers did and did not do for them when they were young.

Calvin Kelly, a live-away father who grew up with his father in the home, commented on how he came to view emotional support as an important function of fatherhood: "My father, a lot of it comes from him . . . he worked all the time but he was still there for us, emotionally, we could always count on him."

A son of a noncustodial father, Paul Rowan explained that he never received the type of support from his father that he had longed for: "My father, he never stood up for me, never supported me . . . I mean maybe he did but he never said it and I never felt it." He continued, "I could have brought down the Ten Commandments from the highest mountain, and I don't think he would've even given me a pat on the back." These circumstances left him with an "empty feeling" that clearly drives his own paternal behavior. "My kids," he said, "will never know that feeling, never."

The emotional support these fathers provided took various forms. Fathers commended children for getting along well with their siblings. Also, they often took their children's side when they felt the mothers' restrictions or views were too harsh. Joe Carver, a live-away father of two teenage children, provided an example:

> "My daughter wanted to go to a school dance . . . Her mama told her she couldn't go . . . I thought my daughter's request was reasonable. I mean she present a more than fair argument about why she should be allowed to attend this dance. Her mama was just being stubborn because she just afraid to see her grow up. So I stepped in and presented my views so that my daughter could go to the dance without angering her mother and making the situation worse."

Fathers also encouraged their children to do well in school, expressed admiration of school accomplishments, praised good grades, and attended school functions when possible. According to one, Tyler Sanders:

> "I want her to know that I care. I'm a caring father. I care about everything she does or will choose to do. Most important I let her know that I love her no matter what. When she gets good grades I take her out for ice cream. When she gets bad grades I still take her out for ice cream but we talk about what happened at school that term."

Such was the sentiment expressed by many live-away fathers. The provision of emotional support generally meant that the child could count on his or her father no matter what—in good times as well as in bad.

> Wayne Chapman worked and lived in a small town, seventy miles from the large urban center in which his two daughters resided with their mother. He and his girls spoke on the phone at least once a week but rarely had face-to-face visits. He recalled what happened when he found out through a third party that his eldest daughter, then age sixteen, had become pregnant, given birth, and put her baby up for adoption—all without his knowledge.
>
> "I told her why didn't you tell me. You know. She said well she didn't want me to know because of how I would react. But I couldn't do nothing' about it. There wasn't no need for me to run down there acting like I'm the big bad father and so and so

and so and so. So I walked up to the child I hugged her. I told her I'm not mad at you but you could have told me. You could have told me. That's what I'm here for."

When these fathers did not visit their children as often as they would like, they attempted to insure that their children's emotional needs were being met by someone who could play this role for them. When Glen Porter was placed on criminal probation and assigned to a treatment center for substance abuse, he feared that his daughter would not receive proper care from her mother. Although he did not live with his daughter prior to these circumstances, he was able to call and visit as often as he wanted, which he did on a consistent basis. At the treatment center, he was unable to visit and phone calls were limited. In his absence, he asked his sister and brother to "keep an eye" on his daughter and make sure that she was "making out okay." They gave him reports on her behavior but also spent time with her at the movies, the zoo, and other places of recreation.

Other fathers also relied on relatives to help meet children's needs. Thomas Allen provided an example:

"If it's an emergency I will try to be there for my children in a matter of a couple of hours. That's how long it takes me to drive to [the city] from here. Otherwise they can always contact me by phone at anytime. If I feel like they need a shoulder to cry on or some help with something and I can't get there for awhile, like maybe because my wife or youngest son is sick or what have you, then I just go to the next person, which is my mother. I call my mother and ask her to go over there and find out what the kids need, or to take them where they need to go."

PROVIDING DISCIPLINE

These fathers considered disciplining their children a primary function of their fatherhood. They generally agreed that children needed someone to teach them right from wrong in a consistent and fairly strict manner. According to one father, "Punishment has got to be consistent and pretty hard." The type of punishment tended to vary in accordance with a child's transgression. Some fathers only used spanking, while others restricted their children's activities. Still others used a combination of the two.

Regardless of the punishment, fathers generally believed children needed strict discipline. According to Theodore Chambers, "if the child do not have somebody to do this when they young they not gonna have the difference between right and wrong properly instilled as they get older."

Most fathers felt that the disciplinarian role was not being performed adequately by their children's primary caretakers.[4] This was true whether the child resided with the mother, maternal grandmother, paternal grandmother, or another guardian. The fathers themselves felt that they often had to assume the task. Vernon Carter commented on the disciplinarian skills of his children's mother:

"Mothers are too close to their children to give them the discipline they need. I'm sure if I was in their place and was with them all the time I'd give in a lot, too. But it can't be that way. Children need to learn right from wrong early and if mother won't or can't do it then it's up to the daddies."

Despite this expressed willingness to assume such a role, disciplinarian was not one of these fathers preferred roles and it was not one that they assumed very often. They generally preferred to leave such actions to the children's primary caretakers. One father stated that he found disciplining his daughter difficult because, he said, "I feel like I'm not around her enough [so] that if I did discipline [her] she might rebel or some sort and I couldn't stand that not being there with her all the time . . . I don't want her to rebel against me." Subsequently, he rarely restricted her activities and only gave spankings at her mother's request.

When fathers chose to discipline, it tended to be because the child engaged in some negative behavior of a serious nature. Kevin Atkins recalled what prompted the last punishment he gave to one of his daughters.

"If I remember correctly," he stated, "my six-year-old went in a store with her mother and I guess you could say had stolen something." The crime was not discovered until the child returned home. At this point, Kevin chose to give her a "little talk about right and wrong" and tell her of his disappointment. Lastly, he "discussed some of the consequences that she might incur if it happens again." He also explained, however, that this was not the type of punishment he received when a child. "I remember getting whoopings for just putting my elbows on the table." He admitted that if his child were a boy the discipline would be much harsher, "but with girls you've got to respect that femininity . . . they are different from boys and they learn from being told."

Other fathers' comments confirmed the gender disparity with regard to punishments, particularly spankings. Fathers tended to believe that spanking was more appropriate for younger children, particularly for boys. One father explained that regardless of the infraction, boys needed consistent physical punishment at a young age. "You have to get their attention quickly and teach them to follow the rules," he explained. Said another father, "Boys need to learn that no matter how tough you are, there is always somebody tougher . . . spanking gives them that lesson early in life."

One of the primary values that fathers hoped to instill through discipline was "respect." These fathers felt that children did not have "proper respect" for their mothers or other adults—all of which, as they perceived it, resulted from their children's mothers' poor disciplinarian skills. They attempted to get mothers to do their part in gaining and maintaining respect from their children. Brian White described the behavior of his son:

"This boy tells his mama 'No!' He throws temper tantrums in the middle of the store with her. She tells him one thing and he'll do another. On purpose! Just to show her that he gonna do what he want. I told her she better start whooping him before he gets too big. Otherwise, she ain't never gonna get no respect from him or those other kids."

These fathers insisted on respect from their children. They expected that children would not "talk back" to them, that children would do what they were told to do, that children would always be truthful, and that they understood that their father would not tolerate what he considered to be inappropriate behavior. A live-away father of one adolescent boy and two adolescent girls explained his expectations:

"My children can do anything. They may break windows, stay out too late, get in fights, whatever. I don't ask them to be perfect and they know this. I will always help them with any trouble they get in. But one thing I will not tolerate is for them to lie to me or show me any disrespect. They know better than that."

BEING A ROLE MODEL

These fathers felt it important that they function as role models for children. Most attempted to monitor their behavior around children. In general, they defined a "good role model" as one who stayed out of trouble, avoided the use of drugs, cared about others, and always tried to do what was right. Other than these attributes, functioning as a role model included a variety of behaviors.

Fathers consciously attempted to monitor their behaviors when in their children's presence. Some tried to maintain self-control when angry or otherwise upset. For several men this was particularly difficult, especially when having to associate with their children's mother, her boyfriend or husband, or other relatives with whom they did not get along. Nevertheless, fathers said they made efforts not to argue in the child's presence. Jim Carrolton stated that this was a challenge because he and his children's mother do not agree "on much of anything." He explained:

> "It's not easy, Lord knows. Sometimes I want to kill her. But I figure I have to be civil for my children's sake. They don't need to know that Mommy and Daddy can't stand each other. They'll figure that out for themselves, in time. If I go there yelling and screaming at her every time she make me mad those kids would be afraid of me . . . It ain't worth it."

Fathers also made efforts to avoid making negative comments about their children's mothers to the children or in their children's presence.

> One father often contemplated about whether or not to inform his daughter about how he truly felt about her mother, who he felt was always sleeping around. "In fact," he said, "I had a hard time believing that she [his daughter] was mine." He said he became angry each time he thought about it and his frustration with the circumstances was evident in our interview:
>
> "I want to tell her that her mother ain't no good and that's why things are the way they are . . . but she don't need to know that, hear it, or see it. I want to protect her from that knowledge. I feel like that's one of the reasons that I have to stay in her life—so she'll have at least one good role model."

Fathers tended to view their dating relationships with women as behavior of which their children did not need to be made aware. In general, they did not want their children to meet their "women friends" unless the relationship was extremely serious, stable, and marriage was imminent. There were two reasons for this. They did not want their children to become too attached to women who were not likely to remain in their father's lives. They felt that their children had enough negative aspects in their lives and did not need the added instability of such relationships. Second, fathers themselves did not want their children to think that these types of relationships were preferred over long-lasting, stable relationships between one man and one woman. Therefore, they endeavored to keep the children's contact with successive girlfriends to a minimum. Again, Jim Carrolton explained:

"I don't want them to see me with this woman this day and that woman that day. It shouldn't be that way. I want them to see me with just one woman; the woman. That's all. I want them to see a perfect world so that they try to have a perfect world themselves one day."

In regard to modeling a work ethic, these fathers tended to dislike being unemployed, working part-time, having to work two or three different jobs, and/or having to work arduous hours. However, they generally concluded that such diligence and honest hard work would be viewed positively by their children. They also hoped that their children would want to be like them in this regard. A father explained:

"I have to work. If I don't work I don't have any money. No, I'm not an engineer or whatever, but I'm honest and I just want him to look up at me an just be proud of me for what I am and for what I'm doing an what I've done for him. I want him to see what I'm doing as good."

Most of those who earned a living through illicit means attempted to keep their children unaware of this fact, and they did not want their children to become involved in this way of life. A father, who worked part-time at a garage and sold drugs to "help with expenses," explained how he has attempted to be a role model for his children:

"You know, I was enrolled in college for awhile. It's hard to believe, I know. So I tell my children about that. I even took them to the school. I tell them it's important to stay in school. They see their daddy is doing all right. They think I just work at the garage and I wish that were true. I want them to see me as a good role model. But I can't make a living at a garage part-time . . . because of my record I don't see my work status changing in the near future. So I just tell them, and show my kids the best parts, leave out the bad, and help them do better than me."

TEACHING BOYS TO BE MEN AND GIRLS TO BE YOUNG LADIES

These fathers felt it essential that they teach their children how to behave in a proper masculine or feminine manner. This was more so the case for boys than for girls. Fathers felt that mothers could not properly teach boys how to be men. One father offered:

"I'm not saying a mother can't raise a son. My mother did it with me . . . What I am saying is that there are certain things that a woman just can't teach a boy. There are some things that he can only learn from his father or another man."

In their eyes, a boy's knowledge of masculinity or how to be a man must come primarily from another man. Fathers made a point of teaching their sons the proper way to go to the bathroom, to sit, how to play various sports, how to defend themselves, and how to interact with women. Below are representative comments made by some fathers on mothers' ability to teach masculine behavior to their sons:

"You see this is a rough world out here. Boys can't get by doing what they mamas do. Daddies got to be around to show them how to go to the bathroom—he can't be sitting down to go pee in the men's room, you understand."

"She can teach him quite a bit, but she's not going to go out there and teach him how to play basketball, football, and all that."

"If a bully is picking on him in the street, she can't protect him from that. He's got to know how to defend himself. That's where I come in. Now, women can fight, mind you. But she can't fight for her son when he's in the street."

In regard to how to interact with women, fathers insisted that they, rather than women, were their son's best authority on the subject. Brian White stated:

"I teach him how to treat women. I give him advice when he asks for it. I tell him what I would do in a certain situation. Because I treat women good. I don't disrespect them. I want him to do the same. But at the same time I tell him that they got to respect him."

Another father expressed a similar sentiment:

"When a man's dealing with a woman—it doesn't matter what their relationship is—she is going to try and control him. She's going to try to be the boss. Now, it's up to the man to stand up for himself, for his manhood, and make sure that he maintains his status in the relationship. Now, my son's mother can't teach him that because she's a woman. Only I or another strong man can tell him how it is and how it is supposed to be."

Fathers tended to be less strict in regard to their daughters' strict adherence to proper feminine behavior. For example, they were probably just as likely to take their young daughter to a baseball game as their young son. However, they did prefer that their daughters hair be allowed to grow long rather than being cut short. They also insisted to the mothers that their daughters learn how to behave like "young ladies," as in sitting with their knees together. Many fathers also preferred that their teenage daughters not wear make-up, too much jewelry, shorts or short skirts, low-cut blouses, or clothing that, as one father put it, "clings to their bodies." When their daughters did dress in such a manner, fathers blamed the mothers. One father stated:

"She gets it from her mother. That's how her mother dresses. So it don't matter what I say. She don't see it as wrong because that's the way her mama clothes herself. I think they even share clothes. It's a shame the way mothers are raising their daughters."

Fathers also did not want their daughters "hanging out on the streets" with their friends. In regards to their daughters' involvement with young men, fathers generally disapproved but acknowledged that there was little that they could do to keep their daughters from dating or even having sex. Raymond Terry, live-away father of adolescent Shalonda, expressed his paternal fears:

"I don't like it. I'm scared for her. I worry that some boy is just gonna be using her. I know how they think. Boys at that age are only interested in one thing. But I can't keep her locked up. Kids have sex. There's no stopping it. I have to respect her as a young woman and trust that she'll respect herself."

When they felt that their daughters needed to be counseled or felt that their daughters needed to talk to someone on matters of dating and sex, fathers generally relied on the child's mother or a female relative to talk with the child. Virgil Franklin summed up the thoughts of several fathers of adolescent girls:

"Well, I don't think it's my place to talk with her about sex. If she wanted to talk with me she could. But my feelings are that she's a young lady and her talking with me would embarrass her and I'd be embarrassed too."

PROVIDING ECONOMIC SUPPORT

Providing their children with basic necessities, such as shelter, food, clothing, and money was one of the least important primary function for these fathers. Fathers who earned steady and relatively moderate wages tended to view these provisions as an essential function, but also tended not to place it above other elements in regard to their role and function as fathers. Most of the fathers in this category were employed in the military or within other state agencies. Here, paying child support was something over which they had little control, as child support payments were garnisheed from their wages automatically and sent to the child's primary caretaker. These few fathers tended to view child support as a matter of fact. As one father stated: "It's just something you have to do." When asked if they would provide child support if it were not required, one father gave the following response:

> "I would, but you see not because I think that they wouldn't be all right without it. I know their mother can support them just fine. It would mainly be because I know that that's what society expects. I'd be seen as less of a man if I didn't . . . No matter, how much love and attention I was to give to my child. It's crazy cause really that's all my child wants from me."

Several fathers viewed paying child support as a means to make up for the more important elements of fatherhood that they, for whatever reason, were not providing. Said one:

> "I'd probably give more right now if I had it. I think spending time with them is the most important thing but, since I don't live close enough to visit, I have to make up for their loss somehow. Paying child support—that's the easiest way for me."

Of those fathers who provided consistent child support, few approved of how children's mothers used the funds. Again, Virgil Franklin provided an example:

> "She pays off her credit cards every month—that's all I see. Buys silly, useless things. My children don't need that. Love is much more valuable than all that silly stuff she buys."

Another father felt similarly:

> "I go over there and that boy be dressed in hand-me-downs—holes in his clothes. I said, No sir, all that money I'm sending and this is the best you can do."

Overall, fathers expected mothers or other primary caretakers to provide for the majority of their children's needs whether or not the mothers received consistent child support from the children's father. Fathers who provided no child support or inconsistent financial assistance to one or more sets of children (83 percent) were confident that their children's subsistence needs were being met. Mothers of these children were generally receiving some form of welfare assistance—Aid to Families with Dependent Children; Foodstamps; Women, Infants, and Children, and/or housing assistance. Such public programs provided a minimal monthly income (varying by state), food, and sometimes low-income housing, child care, health care and other benefits. At the very least, mothers of children received assistance from a variety of their children's relatives. For example clothing, furniture, toys, linens, and books were often passed from one family to the next. Generally, fathers in no-income or low-income circumstances tended to view the mothers' receipt of welfare as a matter of course, as an acceptable means by which to support their children, and something over which they had little control. One father explained that his child and her mother received government assistance because there were no other options. "I don't make much money," he said, "and I'm trying to get it together, get my G.E.D." This father, like most others, earned wages that were barely sufficient to meet his own daily needs much less those of his children. When asked how they felt about others financially supporting their children, several men gave the following responses:

"Right now, my mother's taking care of her because she can do a better job of it than I can. It doesn't make me less of a father, because I give her a lot of love and attention."

"We both know that this is the way that it has to be. We'd like to be a family, but we can't afford it financially. This summer I'll move up to full-time, so I can help out a little than what I do, but right now that's just the way it is."

"Somebody has to provide for the child. It's not the child's fault that I can't maintain work. It's not the mother's fault. So I have to feel good that at least I know that their basic needs can be met. If not by me, unfortunately, then by somebody else."

Regardless of their income level, most fathers felt it their responsibility to have some involvement in guaranteeing their children's needs be met. Fathers would often drive or escort their children's mother to the welfare office or post office to register or pick up benefits. Fathers would also attempt to get those things that mothers could not purchase or otherwise obtain through welfare assistance:

"Whenever she needs something all she has to do is tell me. She knows I'll get it. Diapers, clothes, whatever. I'll get it."

Fathers also ran errands for their children's mothers, picked up their children from school, and/or did the shopping.

"Their mother can't do everything. Except that I don't live there all the time. I'm like the baby-sitter, the cook, the cleaner, and the delivery man. I do all those things that a father and a mother's supposed to do."

"I don't have much to give as far as money goes and I can't deny it—I probably never will. But otherwise I do whatever I can for my child, whatever I can."

For the most part, the provision of child support was not a primary concern for many of these fathers. This seemed to be true regardless of the amount of money fathers earned in the past twelve months. Those that paid child support did so consistently and in set amounts. For some of these fathers, child support payments were taken from garnisheed monthly or bimonthly earnings and were sent to the mothers of the children through state agencies. But these tended to be fathers who held relatively steady employment. Yet, even among these fathers, child support was one of the least important aspects of their fathering.

American society expects black fathers to assimilate and adopt mainstream conceptualizations of proper attitudes and behavior. Yet, many researchers have argued that the social structure continuously denies them the means by which to live such a lifestyle. Furthermore, black men are expected to assimilate into the dominant society and accept mainstream values and conceptualizations of fatherhood as if these ideals accurately reflect their own reality. These fathers seemed to adapt the Western "ideal" of fatherhood to their own experiences and realities.

While the role of provider is a primary element of the Western ideal, it appears to be of least importance to these black noncustodial fathers. For the most part, these fathers accepted and expected that others would meet the daily subsistence needs of their children, though they might assist themselves. Nonetheless, these fathers perceived that they played an essential role in the lives of their children. These fathers valued what they felt they were denied by their fathers. Primarily, they insisted that spending time with their children was their most essential fatherhood function. This was regardless of how much time they spent with children or how much money they were able to provide for their children's care and well-being.

Most importantly, these fathers did not seem to consider their role or function in their children's lives as one that could be fulfilled by the children's mothers. According to them, a man's presence, his love, and his affection were essential ingredients for the proper upbringing of a child and the primary characteristics of a good father.[5]

In 1996, Wade C. Horn, a member of the Council of Families in America, declared that fatherlessness was "*the* national crisis" in the United States.[6] His comment was part of a growing trend within the public discussion on American family values and decline. In the past decade, social commentators, politicians, social researchers, and activists have been developing programs, convening conferences, studying and defining discourse on the disturbing consequences of father absence from the home or "fatherlessness." But the notion of "fatherlessness" is quite vague. American family structures historically have never been uniform and, as the men and women in this study indicate, there are varying degrees of good parenthood, much of which has little to do with men's full-time presence in their children's households. Nevertheless, patriarchal notions of the family man remain implicitly pervasive. Within African American communities, the call by the Million Man March and Black Nationalists for men to reassert their position in families is accompanied by a call for women to support them as family heads. This is quite problematic when low-skill, low-pay employment available to poor and working-class people demand that women parent as the co- or sole provider for their families. It is made more complex when neither fathers nor mothers, alone or together, are able to meet the economic needs of their children. It is also complicated by the ability, need, and/or desire of many men and women to nurture their children outside traditional nuclear and patriarchal family structures. Needless to say, the struggle to define the role of father and fatherlessness in an ever-changing political economy will continue to be a struggle. However, if the responses of lower-income fathers of this study are any indication, black live-away fathers are already one step ahead.

7

LIVE-AWAY, BUT ABSENT?

*J*ust before Father's Day, 1999, *USA Today* devoted a section to reports on the state of fatherhood in America. One report indicated that while the "proportion of children with absent fathers is growing most rapidly among whites, it is a *crisis* for American blacks. . . . 70% of black children are born to unmarried mothers, and at least 80% of black children can expect to spend a significant part of their childhood years living apart from their fathers."

In and of themselves, these statistics can seem staggering, particularly given the negative connotation accompanying the word "absent." However, as the findings and chapter 6 suggest, living away from one's child does not always equate to absence. Many black live-away fathers remain involved in their children's lives. Among those within this category, the most important thing fathers can do for their children is to provide them with their time and attention. Among other activities, many of the men reported they took their children to parks and theaters, talked with them on the telephone, brought them gifts, and disciplined them when necessary. Moreover, findings recently reported by Sara McLanahan (1999), director of Princeton University's Center for Research on Child Well-Being and co-investigator for the Fragile Families Project, indicated that 80 percent of the five hundred non-custodial fathers in her ongoing study helped the mother of their child during pregnancy, and planned to help raise the child in the year following its birth.

Despite these accounts, many mothers and children well know that not all men display consistent paternal behavior—at least not in the sweeping manner described in chapter 6. There are men who rarely if ever attend their children's school activities, privately converse with them, take them out to lunch, buy them gifts, or visit them on their birthdays. Current research findings note that less than 27 percent of children over the age of four saw their fathers at least once a week in the past year, and about 31 percent had no contact at all. Some may say that it is the fathers of these children that stereotypes seem to capture most accurately. These are the images cast in the public mind when *USA Today* and other media encourage terms like "uncaring," "deadbeat," "fatherless," and "absent" to seep their way into popular fatherhood discourse. And it is for fathers like these, it seems, that the public expresses the most disdain. But such terms alone tell us little about the circumstances and experiences of men who rarely if ever see their children. Yet many assume that they are, as one mother in this study stated, "all the same."[1]

This chapter focuses on the experiences of men who seem, quite literally, "absent" from their children's lives. Specifically, it explores the circumstances of fathers' lives and the paternal choices they make in this context. It looks at those fathers whose contact with their children occurred about once a month or less over the course of the year just prior to their interviews ($N = 21$).[2] Of these fathers, approximately 80 percent visited with their children less than ten full days during this period. And for most, this pattern of contact was established within one to two years after the child's birth. Why do some black live-away fathers disengage from their children? And why does their absence persist over time? The reality of their fatherhood lies in the descriptions and words they themselves provide.

BECOMING A PARENT AND BECOMING ABSENT

When Tony Barry was released from jail (three months prior to his interview) he was hopeful. "I'm going to remain on the straight and narrow, get a good job, start being a father," he remembered thinking. He shook his head in dismay as he recalled that he was barely 19 years of age when his first child, Nicole, was born. That was seven years ago. He met his daughter's mother, Chandra (then 16), through his younger brother, Eric. Within weeks he was meeting her after school, treating her to the movies, and engaging in sexual intercourse. "You know how a man is taught to never show love for a woman? Well I was never really like that." He said he was generally shy around most women and his sheepishness was apparent throughout the interview.

Tony and Chandra fell in love quickly and within six months she was pregnant. He had mixed feelings about the prospect of parenthood. "I knew the time wasn't right for me to be a father." He was also afraid of what his mother would say. "She told me don't be going out messing with them girls . . . she like ingrained that in our mind," he said, speaking of himself and Eric. Tony recalled some of her exact words: " 'You better damn well wear a condom,' " and " 'I can't afford to take care of nobody else's kids!' " This was a message he often received each time he left the house. "She wanted me to go to college and not get caught by some woman," he said, shrugging his shoulders. His shyness inhibited his dating, and he did not do much of it while in high school. Rather, he spent his free time with friends who "mostly would be together conversing and joking."

Sometimes he dabbled in petty criminal activities. While most of his friends "did it to try attract the ladies," Tony said that his main objective was to have money to buy music and help his mother with groceries and bills. Unlike several of his friends he completed high school, doing so with a solid "B" average. He had wanted to enroll in the state college for the following semester, but said he did not know how to apply or whom to ask for help. He spent his post-high school summer months smoking and peddling marijuana, "getting into trouble," and falling in love with Chandra. Although 16-year-old Eric managed to get a job washing dishes at the Magic Wok Restaurant, Tony knew very few youths who worked during the summer months. From what he could tell, there were very few employment opportunities in or near his predominantly black residential area straddling the outskirts of the middle-sized midwestern inner city. He said he and his friends would sometimes catch the bus about a block east from his home and visit the closest malls. For the most part though, their free time was spent in their own neighborhood at one or another's houses, or walking the streets.

Although asked directly, Tony spoke very little about his girlfriend's pregnancy during the interview because, he said, "I don't really like the way I handled things during that situation." However, he reluctantly shared some of his memories. He explained that the news of Chandra's pregnancy was given to his mother by a friend of the family. "I did *not* want her to find out," he said. "I guess I was hoping it [the pregnancy] would just go away." When his mother asked if he had fathered the child, Tony denied culpability. "I basically lied," he said, "told her that I didn't know who the father was."

Afraid of his mother's disappointment and his own ambiguous feelings, he did nothing to rectify the deception. He acknowledged that part of him daydreamed about being a "father" (in the traditional sense of the word) and marrying Chandra. Another part feared the potential wrath of his mother and attempted to create ways to avoid her. Still, a third part did not know how to think about the situation or proceed "one way or another."

The responses of others were mixed. His mother did not believe his lie. She expressed her anger and disappointment by not directly speaking to him "for about a month." He never confessed the paternity of his daughter to his mother and she never explicitly brought up the subject. Rather, she would ask if he had "seen Chandra lately," or mention that she had run into her at the supermarket. Meanwhile, his closest friends congratulated him on his paternity, two of them were fathers themselves. "They said things like 'It's about time.'" Chandra's family, which consisted of her mother and two sisters, were angry with her, but he sensed no ill-feelings directed toward him.

Things changed little when the baby was born. He admitted that he wanted to see the baby, "to see if she looked like me," but felt that to do so would be committing to a paternal role in her development. "I didn't know what to do," he stated matter-of-factly. "So I just didn't do anything one way or another." He would visit Chandra on occasion, and inconsistently purchased Nicole gifts on her birthdays and at Christmas. "I bought diapers sometimes, too," he said. In sum, his paternal behaviors added up to various thoughts, hesitations, and inaction.

An interview with Chandra allowed her to provide more information about Tony's absence during this period. Initially, she expected him to spend more time with their daughter Nicole, and publicly and joyfully acknowledge her as his daughter. His lack of eagerness to say and act accordingly only frustrated and angered her. "I knew his mother was giving him a hard time," she said, "and I was really mad at him for not telling her that he was Nicole's daddy." Other than the request for his public announcement of paternity, Chandra had difficulty concretely defining exactly what she wanted from her child's father, both in the past and particularly in the present: "I've always just wanted him to be there, for me and her," she said quite generally.

She also recalled understanding his reluctance to do this in his youth, "I know his friends, they acted the same way, being all macho . . . " Nevertheless, she interpreted his lack of action as a rejection of her and their baby. "It seems our daughter would've been enough to make him forget about being one of the boys." She was disappointed, and consequently after Nicole's first birthday, did little to encourage his involvement. "When he came over, which was hardly ever, I wouldn't say much to him. . . . just ask him how things were . . . That's it." She said he had little conversation to offer and "really we just drifted apart."

In some ways, Chandra's response reflected those of other adolescent single mothers. Most want and seek live-away fathers' involvement with their children. In addition, they often feel deceived and/or very pained when fathers ignore them once they become pregnant. Chandra, too, felt hurt and betrayed by the lack of attention she received from Tony once she announced her pregnancy and that she decided to keep the child. Unlike most of the five hundred fathers in McLanahan's ongoing study, Tony did not clearly articulate an intent to assist her throughout her pregnancy or with raising their child.

Adding to the complexity of the situation is the negotiation of the maternal and paternal roles themselves. Mothers and fathers often do not clearly articulate the parental roles and functions they expect the other to perform. The work of Madeline Kornfein-Rose (1992) suggests that mothers who elect to have children out of wedlock may not have a clear definition of the role they want fathers to play, particularly those who were in relationships with fathers for less than six months prior to the pregnancy. Although Kornfein-Rose's work (1992) provides little explanation for this, these parents provide some clues.[3]

Both Tony and Chandra explained that having children was not a subject they discussed prior to the pregnancy. Their conversations were generally about movies, music, friends, and day-to-day activities. Moreover, throughout the pregnancy and following Nicole's birth they never explicitly discussed what the expectations would be for either of them as parents. Such conversations could have provided Tony with direction in terms of parenting. Chandra was certain he did not want to discuss the matter, and wanted to avoid the potential conflict the topic might bring to their relationship. He, on the other hand, expected that she would introduce the subject, or "handle it on her own."

According to Chandra, in the year or so following Nicole's birth, when Tony phoned "he would talk about everything *but* the baby." Tony, too, recollected his few conversations with Chandra and confirmed their content. "Well, I would ask her about her mother, her cousin," he said bashfully. "I really wanted her to talk about the baby . . . she never did . . . she just didn't." He admitted that he could have asked her directly about his role but explained that he was afraid she would ask him questions or give directives about his intentions as a parent that he would not know how to respond to. "I thought maybe I could just go and visit with Chandra and the baby would be there; this way I would get to know the baby . . . without it being a big deal and all."

A second interview with Tony intended to follow up on questions generally sparked by the interview with Chandra, and to clarify aspects of the initial discussion. Throughout both conversations, Tony rarely mentioned his daughter by name. When asked how he generally referred to Nicole when he spoke of her to others, his thoughtful response seemed to reflect a distance. "I guess. . . . mostly I just don't call her anything . . . I just say she is doing fine or 'How is she doing?'" Before his incarceration ten months ago, Tony would see Nicole out walking with her mother and on each occasion they would greet him. On their initiative "They wave . . . maybe speak," he said. When asked if he thought he would ever play more of a role in his daughter's life, his reply suggested he felt the decision was completely out of his control. "Well, see that's nothing I can predict off-hand. . . . It'll depend on if she wants me in her life." For the time being, he thought it best to wait for a cue from his daughter and/or her mother—rather than initiating paternal behavior on his own. One of his final statements reflected the sense of uncertainty and lack of direction that seemed to guide his actions for much of his early adulthood. "As soon as I settle in and figure how to get my life together," he said, "then I'll be a father that she [Nicole] can look up to."

Meanwhile, Chandra was still waiting for Tony to take the first step with regard to contacting and parenting their daughter. From her perspective, his initiative is the only means by which the hurt and betrayal she felt years earlier can be undone. She is doubtful that he will actively pursue his fatherhood. In fact, she said unequivocally, "I'm not holding my breath."

PLACING ABSENCE IN CONTEXT

Researchers and social work practitioners often recognize the paucity of social and emotional support systems available to single-parenting women. However, the lack of similar resources available to live-away fathers is also dire, and may contribute to their parental disengagement. Charles Ballard's center for fathers in Washington D.C., and the Fathers' Center at the Lutheran Child and Family Services, East St. Louis (Illinois), are only two of the many centers founded and operated under this assumption. Their positive outcomes, and these fathers' descriptions, provide evidence that becoming an uninvolved father for some may, at least in part, be due to a lack of personal guidance and direction. When they felt overwhelmed with thoughts and feelings about fatherhood, many fathers expressed a sense of isolation and indicated they had few individuals to whom they could confide. Moreover, as literature on black masculinity suggests, men are generally discouraged from sharing their troubles, sadness, or insecurities with other human beings. Thus, these men internalized feelings of indecision and uncertainty—feelings "sucked in deep inside of you so your pain is unnoticed," as Mark King, a father of one, explained.

In a poignant self-analysis, Tony suggested that if he had someone with whom he could have "connected on a psychological basis . . . [and] . . . talked to about what was going on inside my head," he probably would have been more paternally assertive during Chandra's pregnancy and after the birth of Nicole. "I was ignorant really," he continued. "I didn't listen to my mother or no adult." He explained that though his paternal uncle lived three blocks from his home, they rarely had much in common and conversed only on occasion. "I just felt like even though it [the pregnancy] was a situation I created and . . . ultimately I would have to be the one to fix it . . . but at the time I didn't know how to do that . . . [and] . . . I was embarrassed that I didn't know what to do. . . . That's why I say I was just young and ignorant."

Tony attempted to explain his absence by emphasizing his lack of personal initiative. Upon closer examination, it appears that his paternal disengagement occurred within the context of an economically impoverished home life, inadequate academic experiences, few significant employment opportunities, and an immature intimate relationship. All of these factors seem to have complicated his feelings of paternal uncertainty.

Research indicates that those with clear definitions of academic goals and a means and opportunity to achieve them are more likely to do so, and less likely to engage in behaviors and make decisions that deflect their success.

Although Tony received excellent grades in high school and aspired to attend college, he was ill-prepared for an academic life beyond his initial twelve years of education. He had not enrolled in college preparatory courses, nor did he recall receiving formal academic guidance, all of which would have assisted his application to colleges and universities. His mother felt strongly that he should attend college but, he explained, "she didn't know how to guide me [toward necessary paperwork, funding opportunities, and searches for appropriate academic institutions] . . . it wasn't her fault." She herself had dropped out of high school at age 16 when she became pregnant with him. Not only was she unaware of how to access higher education for her son, but her long and tiring work hours gave her little time to adequately investigate the matter or forcefully and consistently encourage Tony to do so. Inadequate parental support and a lack of professional support from the educational system left Tony with little guidance about how to define or pursue his future.

Tony had also grown up in stark poverty. He recollected the pressure he felt to earn money for the family. He remembered that at age 14, he was once hired to deliver newspapers. He was fired within three weeks when someone stole the newspapers that were intended for him to deliver. Other than "delivering newspapers, running errands, car washing, and bagging groceries" he knew of very few employment opportunities. And "even these are hard to get," he said.

Since delivering newspapers, he has worked at few formal jobs. "She didn't tell me to make money, make money," he said of his mother almost defensively. He was nevertheless well aware of its scarcity in the household, and the lack of funds available for staple food items, toiletries, clothing, and utilities. He felt "tied up in knots whenever the electricity was turned off ... [or they] ... had to borrow change to buy toothpaste."

His plight was no different from that of many other young black American men. In high school he thought that a high school diploma would expand his occupational opportunities and enable him to improve life circumstances for himself and his mother and brother. He quickly found however, that few employers opened their doors to him. Overall, it seemed to him that with regard to drastically improving his circumstances and/or becoming more involved in his daughter's life, his options were quite tenuous, limited, and often beyond his control. Although he rarely thought about it, he generally felt his daughter was well taken care of by her mother and maternal grandmother, both emotionally, socially and economically. "They both work and she [Chandra] gets aid. . . . so what little money I get, I share with my mama."

He was hopeful that he would one day have a full-time job and that his earnings would increase to eventually stabilize his mother's plight. His situation did not look promising. With little work experience and only a high school diploma, it will be difficult to find secure employment.

Recent studies indicate that for young black men with these economic and academic characteristics, unemployment has increased dramatically in the past three decades. And even among those who manage to obtain employment, few will earn enough to bring themselves and their children out of poverty.[4]

As for performing his role as father, Tony said that at the time of Nicole's birth, "I didn't know how to do it at the time; there were too many things that was up in the air and confusing about my life." As for today, he explained "I still don't really [know]."

PASSIVE DISENGAGEMENT

Some fathers reported expressing open excitement about the prospect of fatherhood. Unlike Tony Barry, most professed their full intentions to participate in their children's upbringing, at least at the outset. However, several recalled that at the time of their children's births they, too, did not know how to negotiate their paternal roles, and found themselves being overwhelmed and bewildered by fatherhood. For 30-year-old absent live-away father Gary Moss, these feelings fused with other elements to push and pull him away from paternal involvement.

"I remember being excited about the prospect of it [having a child]," he said. Simultaneously he "didn't know what I was supposed to do next." When his girlfriend gave birth to their son in 1993, the ambiguity of the role remained. He said, "I just did what I thought was expected." That is, he went to the hospital, bought diapers, and played with the infant during his regular visits. But the child and his mother resided with her mother and two sisters. Gary said he always felt out of place, "like a third wheel," in a house full of women.

He suggested that his feelings were a consequence of his and the child's living arrangements. The two did not have the opportunity to reside together. He was quite conscious of how easily the child and the mother developed their own standard routines. He was also quick to notice that even the mother's cousin was more familiar with the baby's care than he was. At times, he felt as though his presence was an inconvenience to the four women who were regularly in the household. Overall, it seemed to him that his parenting was not a necessity. "I felt like, well, hell, why am I here?" he recalled.

Like Tony Barry, Gary's disengagement was fairly passive. With little explanation to his son's mother, he simply began to visit less and less. Within "six or seven months" after his son's birth, he "pretty much stopped going by." He visits with him "a few times a year."

A first-time father at age 24, Oliver Graham also recollected feelings of anxiety and uncertainty about his paternal functions. He explained that he had looked forward to co-parenting his child even though he was "a little nervous." Despite these feelings, he felt prepared "to do what I was supposed to do."

His girlfriend, Sheri, and their child shared a home with her mother and siblings, who did little to make him feel confident in his role as father. Anxiety developed into extreme ambiguity once his child's maternal relatives bluntly discouraged his visits. Almost immediately, he sensed they disapproved of his intentions to be an involved parent and preferred that he not visit his son as often as he did.

Sheri explained the hostility toward him stemmed from the fact that he did not have a job, and that soon after the child's birth he had been arrested for illegal possession of a firearm. Regardless of her family's position, he acknowledged that Sheri reiterated time and time again that his lack of employment and his legal infraction were irrelevant to his fatherhood. She was quite supportive, and he recalled her telling him "to just be there for her and the baby . . . just do what I can, when I can." He appreciated her words, but they were not enough.

"I'd come over, ask 'Is Sheri here.' . . . .and instead of being polite they would sometimes close the door in my face." While they would announce his arrival to Sheri, he was forced to wait for her in the apartment hallway. And once inside the living quarters, he found that the mood was invariably "uncivil," and "nobody barely said a word to me."

Oliver reluctantly found himself making fewer visits, and spent more and more time at home or with his friends. "She [Sheri] started to get angry at me all the time," which he understood but, "felt there was little he could do about it." Eventually, the two ended their relationship; his contact with his daughter is only at her mother's instigation.

UNPREPARED FOR FATHERING

Some fathers claimed that it was not uncertainty alone about how to behave as fathers that led them to remove themselves from their children's lives, but rather unpreparedness for the parental role. Being "unprepared" generally meant being *surprised* by the lifestyle changes a baby demanded from mothers and themselves.

Danny Godfrey summarized the thoughts of several others when he recollected the dramatic transformation that occurred once his girlfriend became pregnant. The two had dated for well over a year. They lived in the same neighborhood, worked shifts at a Denny's restaurant, and took the same bus route to and from work. They had little money to spare and thus recreational activities generally consisted of the movie theater, browsing the bookstores and malls, visiting friends and relatives, and sitting outside and talking "about getting married and other things."

"When she got pregnant we stopped going out like we used to . . . and after a while we stopped having sex," he offered. He understood her loss of interest in sexual activity, but remained unclear about her reasons for not wanting to "go out." "You know when you work all day the highlight of your day is seeing your baby [girlfriend] . . . going out." He felt that her pregnancy ended one of the small joys that they practiced as daily rituals until about two months into the pregnancy. He was reluctant about becoming a father—particularly given her behavioral change, but remembered thinking things would return to normal once the child was born.

"But," he said, "once she [his daughter] was born the only time we spent together was with the baby . . . all we did was talk about the baby." After their daughter's birth, the couple also had no privacy. They could not afford to get their own apartment, and each continued to reside in their parents' homes.

His girlfriend and the child shared a two-bedroom apartment with her mother, an older brother, and a younger sister. Danny lived with his mother, stepfather, younger cousin, and his sister in a two-bedroom home. The new parents also had little support from friends and relatives—a factor also mentioned by several other fathers. It was rare that anyone would agree to baby-sit, and his girlfriend did not feel comfortable leaving the child with "just anybody."

Like other fathers, Danny found it difficult to learn to parent in the presence of others. "It was like everyone was watching to see if I picked her up the right way, changed the diaper the right way." He found the situation oppressive, and found himself spending less time with his girlfriend who, he said, seemed to handle the situation much better than himself. His girlfriend continued to encourage him to visit, but he abashedly began to "dodge her phone calls." To further avoid her and any confrontation his paternal disengagement was certain to unleash, he sought and got a new job at a Holiday Inn far from her place of employment. The two eventually talked, but the conversations never gave him peace of mind.

"I never told her I didn't want to parent," he said. Rather, he attempted to explain to her that he could not negotiate how to be a father in what he felt was a stifling environment. Over the course of two years, her phone calls grew less and eventually stopped altogether. "Sometime I want to pick up the phone . . . I want to call her . . . see my daughter," but he said, "I'm afraid things will just be the same . . . I can't be a good father under those conditions; that's not how I see fatherhood." He expressed a great deal of love for both his daughter and her mother, and felt that things would have turned out differently had they had more resources at their disposal.

ACTIVE DISENGAGEMENT

The highest proportion of absent fathers ($N = 11$) seemed to experience passive disengagement from their paternal roles. Still, a minority of fathers professed they made a conscious, clear decision to remain aloof and distant from their children. Three men explained this was their attempt to protect their children from their harsh and sometimes dangerous lifestyles.

Leonard Evans began a frank discussion of this decision when he stated, "I knew that's what I had to do for my sons." Leonard had dropped out of high school at age 15, had begun "hustling" and participating in small robberies "at least a year or two before that." He stated that prior to being incarcerated for six years for armed robbery, he visited his sons "about once a week or more." During this period, his infant son and his two-year-old son were "the joy of my life." While he was incarcerated, his sons' mothers brought the children to the correctional facility on occasion, but such an environment was not conducive to parenting. Despite the recent development of fathering programs in some U.S. prisons, Leonard's experiences were not unlike those of most fathers in prison. His time with the boys was limited, and interaction at times felt forced. Contacting them by phone was not always easy because "their moms would move or sometimes the phone would be disconnected, I just never knew."

Released from prison at age 26, he reluctantly realized that the only way he could survive and provide for the things he wanted for his sons was "to go back to my old habits." He explained that even if he sought legal employment, his prison record would markedly limit his options. He made contact with his sons' mothers, "just to check on them [the boys]," he said. Whenever he could the ability, he would send both children money, and various toys and games on a regular basis. However, this has been the boundary of his contact with the children. "I want them to know who I am . . . that I love them" he said sadly, "but I don't want them to grow up [to be] like Dad."

Robert Clayton, too, has been deliberately disengaged from the social aspects of parenting for his child's safety and well-being. He placed his decision in context of his own difficult childhood experiences. For him, the most important aspect of fathering was something he was afraid to provide—time. In lieu of this, he decided that he would insure that his son receive an excellent education and "never want for anything." He explained that his emphasis on education was probably due to his regrets about his own academic failure.

Robert recalled having aspirations of becoming an artist or writer. "I was real smart; I liked to draw; I got good grades in grade school and I won an award for a short story in fifth grade." However, he was not encouraged to pursue his talents. In fact, he was held back in sixth grade. His mother was surprised when she learned he had failed. "It's not that my mother wasn't aware, it's just that she didn't know the extent of how bad I was doing." He explained that he could not really explain why he did so poorly but remembered having a teacher who told him he was stupid and needed to comb his hair. "I think that was the start of it, really."

He recalled that it was about this time that his height and weight seemed well above average, and he began to feel awkward in public. Rather than being placed in "regular sixth grade" the second time around, he was placed in special education classes. "See, I knew I didn't belong there," he said, "and so did my mother." But he explained that school officials ignored his mother's pleas to place him in more advanced classes. "I would go to school with all these kids who had emotional problems or were retarded. . . . it was ridiculous . . . I was helping them with their homework while nobody was teaching me anything."

At age 14, he decided to drop out of school. His mother would get truant notices in the mail, which he discarded before she returned home from working two jobs. He spent his days and nights "hanging out" and "sightseeing." Before long, he and other young men were committing petty crimes. To account for the money he was suddenly bringing into the household, he told his mother that he had a part-time job at his uncle's barbershop. "I don't know if she just believed me or was just too tired to investigate," he said with a smile.

Standing over six feet and weighing over two hundred and fifty pounds, 18-year-old Robert was hired as a bouncer for a local night club. However, within a year he was charged twice with assault, and served time in jail. He later drifted into various "hustles." By age 22, he estimated that he was earning "about fifty grand" a year. At age 23, his son Marcus was born. At age 25, he was once again jailed for assault and sentenced to three years in prison.

He did not offer much information about his relationship with Marcus's mother except to say that "she meant a lot to me at the time." He blamed himself for the relationship's failure and said, "I was a ladies' man . . . [and] didn't respect her like she deserved." She visited Robert during his detention, and attempted to convince him to live with her once he was released. He stayed with her and Marcus briefly upon his release, but explained he soon moved on because his livelihood was not conducive to family life; the danger brought by many visitors entering the home he shared with his son posed a "very real threat" to the child's safety. For this reason, he moved out and took up residence with another long-time female friend.

Prior to the move, he contemplated seeking a legal occupation. "I sincerely thought about it, then I realized I don't know how to look for a job." He offered an additional explanation, "I don't want to give up the car, the gold, and all that." These were items he felt could not be earned through the regular employment accessible to ex-offenders. "I done made my choice a long time ago and it's not a bad way of life," he said, "for me." However, he felt his son deserved an easier life, starting with a good education. With the money he had provided, Marcus's mother was able to send him to a private Catholic school for a few years and he received good grades. Robert realized, though, that no amount of money would make up for his paternal absence. "All he needs is me, but I don't know no other way, really . . . If I spend too much time with him then all that's no good will rub off on him." He explained that it was better for his son if he simply stayed away.

Two fathers who had problems with substance abuse also consciously remained absent from their children's lives.

Griffin Stanley was one. "It's the drugs," he explained; "when they're in my system I'm no good for nobody. . . . least of all my kids." He thanked God several times for their mother, who was able to refrain from using heroine herself long enough to regain custody of their three children. "She's a good woman . . . she just started using because I did," he said.

Custody of the children was lost when the youngsters were found abandoned in a park, well after midnight; the oldest daughter was 8 years old at the time. High on drugs, their mother, Trina, had forgotten where she left them, and Griffin was in jail at the time for driving without a license. Trina was arrested and the children were placed in foster care. Griffin did not find out about the incident until his jail release five days later. Even then all he could think about was how he was going to get drugs while Trina was incarcerated. "That was my lowest point," he murmured. "I was deeply. . . . afflicted." Nevertheless, he felt that some good came from this bottommost circumstance.

"It made Trina get her head straight," he said proudly. Under court orders she successfully completed a treatment program—a process which took over three years. At the time of Griffin's interview she was living in a three-bedroom apartment (which she shared with a cousin), and working in a laundromat. He was willingly in a drug rehabilitation facility, and had not seen his children more than "about three or four times" in the past five years.

He could not say for certain that he would ever be able to be more of a father to them. He candidly said, "I'm completely disgusted with myself," and reiterated time and again that he did not want them to be around him until he was free of his addiction. At the end of the interview he was feeling hopeful and looked forward to seeing them again. But he said these feelings come and go.[5]

RESISTANT DISENGAGEMENT

For some fathers, paternal disengagement was, from their perspective, due to the mother's decision to exclude them. Once exclusion occurred, many men had a difficult time finding their way back into their children's lives. Some felt they were doing the best they could possibly do under the circumstances; however they still did not feel good about the role they played as father.

Dwayne Hayes was one such father. At the time of an initial interview one early Sunday evening, he had just returned from purchasing his son's birthday gift—a Tonka dump truck—which he planned to package and mail the following day. He seemed a proud father of 4-year-old Jeremiah. "I like being a father," he offered. "I could talk about my son to anyone, anytime." During a subsequent interview, Dwayne talked about Jeremiah's favorite activities, how he was doing in preschool, and how much taller he was than other boys his age.

A hint of sadness crept into Dwayne's voice when the discussion turned to his fatherly activities and the frequency of his visits. "His mother has pretty much kept us from being together," he sighed. He explained that "Jeremy" was the product of a year-long relationship with his girlfriend, Patricia, that went sour once the pregnancy occurred. "At first we were both excited or," he added, "at least I was." He continued, "I started spending more time at her apartment, and it was almost like we were becoming a family." They talked about getting married, but the possibility of nuptials seemed ludicrous to Dwayne as the pregnancy advanced. "It was like she would use the pregnancy to get her way," he spoke with some anger. "She started getting lazy and even stopped working" at the floral shop within walking distance from the apartment Patricia shared with her mother.

Dwayne began to help Patricia with her portion of the rent and groceries. Times became difficult because he was also maintaining his own separate residence. "At first I was okay with the situation . . . I didn't know much about pregnancy. . . . I thought 'Hey, if she doesn't feel good about it then she shouldn't be working.'" He said that during the first five months she made a lot of unreasonable requests of him and these demands increased over time. "She would ask me to buy her new clothes; she wanted me to pick up food for her *all* the time; I would take her mother to the doctor; just all kind of things," he said, the exasperation evident in his voice. Concurrently, she seemed to lose all energy, slept quite a bit, and became disgusted with sex. To his chagrin, she also refused to go for walks—one of their preconception enjoyments.

By the sixth month of her pregnancy, he was working two jobs. His primary occupation, one that he had worked at since high school, was in a K-Mart's auto service center. With tight budgeting, he was able to afford an efficiency apartment, and had saved up to purchase a used Toyota truck. At age 31, he had also begun taking classes at a junior college. "Before she got pregnant I had enrolled for some general education courses." His intent was to become a "full-fledged mechanic."

Patricia's economic needs forced him to put his studies on hold; instead of taking classes, he began a part-time job as a retail store stock clerk. Increasingly, he found himself hating her and she began to dislike him as well. "We used to be able to talk; we laughed a lot," he said forlornly. "Once she became pregnant, she just became evil. It's like she wanted to fight and argue all of the time." Looking back on the situation, he admitted that he knew very little about women's hormonal changes and the fatigue that often accompanied pregnancy. However, he explained, "I don't think that any amount of hormones could account for that evil behavior."

He also discovered around the sixth month of pregnancy that the money he gave Patricia was actually being used to buy her and a male friend alcohol and marijuana, habits that existed prior to the pregnancy. Although he remained excited about having a child, he realized that he should have gotten to know her better before they had a child. By the time Jeremiah was born, he was the only subject they could discuss with civility. While it was clear that they were no longer a couple, he never thought that she would keep him from his son. Yet, less than two weeks after Jeremiah's birth, there were signs that Patricia intended to do just that.

She refused to take his phone calls, and would not respond when he knocked on the door. "She wanted child support and that was it; she did not want me near my son." Her male friend and mother shielded her from Dwayne's anger and frustrating attempts to visit with his son. They both intercepted phone calls from him, and refused to allow him to speak with Patricia. They also prevented him from entering the house, and refused to answer the door when he visited. Her aunt was the only one who whole-heartedly supported his efforts to visit Jeremiah. "She said that she knew Patricia was wrong." She also explained to Dwayne that Patricia never wanted a baby, and had considered an abortion, but her mother, a devout Catholic, refused to help her with the cost.

A brief interview with Patricia confirmed this claim. Rather than explicitly talking this over with Dwayne, Patricia began to blame him for her predicament. Although she felt love for him, she began to hate him as well. "I just didn't want to be a mother," Patricia explained in an interview. "I felt pressure to have the baby." She felt pressure not only from her mother but also from Dwayne. "He didn't say, 'Bitch, you're going to have my baby' . . . it wasn't anything like that." But his excitement when she announced the pregnancy and his enthusiasm about parenting suggested to her that if she aborted the child, their relationship would be over. In addition, she would have had to borrow money to pay for an abortion. "So I decided to just have it," she stated bluntly.

She said that during the pregnancy Dwayne began to look at her with disgust, and she was certain that he was seeing other women. He disputed this accusation with the following response: "Whenever I worked late, or if she called my apartment and I wasn't there, she would jump to the conclusion that I was out with some other woman." Patricia also explained that with the pregnancy it seemed that Dwayne became too controlling, "He would give me money . . . then wanted to tell me how to spend it." She admitted to using alcohol and small amounts of marijuana but said, "I knew I wasn't doing enough to harm the baby . . . he made it a big issue because he wanted control."

A month following Jeremiah's birth Patricia sought and gained a restraining order against Dwayne. "He was always hassling me . . . He thought he could come by yelling and carrying on whenever he felt the urge . . . I didn't want him in my life." Rather than violently protesting the restraining order, Dwayne decided to seek an attorney. "I've seen my uncle go through something similar," he said. "The justice system is going to do whatever the mother wants . . . men don't automatically get the right to raise their kids." Dwayne said he has paid child support since his son's birth. He has kept meticulous records of checks he has written to Patricia, the dates and amounts of which he read over the phone. He managed to convince her mother to allow him to visit with Jeremiah once a month. An arrangement was made for him to visit with him at Patricia's aunt's apartment. Although Dwayne is dissatisfied with the arrangement he said, "it's better than nothing." He continues to work two jobs; continuing his education is on indefinite hold. However, he is hopeful that his attorney, whom he pays in installments, will be able to help him obtain full custody of the four-year-old.[6]

Dwayne's goal to become engaged in his son's life and obtain full custody is part of a growing trend. Fathers seeking and obtaining custody of their children are on the rise. From 1995 to 1998 the proportion of single-parenting fathers increased 25 percent. Yet, not all of these absent live-away fathers sought legal charge of their children. Nonetheless, they still wanted to be a significant part of their children's everyday lives.[7]

Said one father: "I just want to hear his voice, pick him up and take him to see Grandma . . . I miss him." Yet this father, like several others, indicated that irreparable relationships with their children's mothers was primarily to blame for the distance that was created and persists between themselves and their offspring.

According to another father, "When she [his child's mother] got this new boyfriend, she basically just pushed me out of the picture . . . threatened to get a restraining order." He had no concrete proof of the order. But he thought it best to "stay out of trouble," particularly since he was not unknown to the local police department. "She used my record against me, to keep me from being able to visit my daughter."

Still another father suggested that his girlfriend was angry with him and was using their daughter vengefully, "She knows how much Kyerra [his daughter] means to me and that's really, really the only way to get at me . . . hurt me." He said that she occasionally calls him and makes requests for money or various items—all of which he readily provides. "I do it because I know my daughter needs these things . . . her mother is just crazy." On rare occasions these requests provide him with an opportunity to briefly visit with Kyerra. "At least she knows I'm her father. . . . one day she'll want to know more and I'm waiting for that day."

Similarly, 36-year-old Dwight Wells, an assistant driver for a beverage company—with less than a high school education— paid over $400 a month in child support. He recalled that the last time he saw his two children, ages 11 and 13, was two years ago on Father's Day. Although the court set his visitation for Easter, three weeks in the summer, and a week during the Christmas holiday, he said that their mother consistently violated the terms. "She tries to keep them away from me," he said. "It just seems that she would rather have them think that I'm a deadbeat dad."

WORK, OTHER CHILDREN, AND PROXIMITY

Fathers, whether "absent" or not, faced barriers that contributed to their lack of presence in their children's lives. Namely, men indicated that long, arduous work schedules, physical distance from their children's home, cohabiting girlfriends, and other children were elements that made it difficult to stay in touch with their offspring. While many of these elements created difficulties for several fathers, few described them as the explicit or primary reason for their disengagement.

One father was compelled to disengage himself when he was laid off from his Southwest Texas construction job of three years. His cousin, who lived in the Midwest, was able to get him a job doing similar work at his place of employment. "I had to move," he said. "It was either that or unemployment." His new job paid nine dollars an hour. However, he could barely afford to visit with his children as much as he once had. In the past five years, he could afford to take time from work and purchase travel fare for only one visit a year. How his now adolescent children feel about visiting him is one of the primary problems, he said. "Once you loose contact with them; they grow up; they grow away from you; you're no long a part of their lives. . . . and you can't undo it."

Another father's explanation for his absence encompassed several elements.

At age 43, Jeffrey Campbell was working as a roofer's helper. "I get up at daybreak, work until sunset," he said. Feeling exhausted following each day of work, he generally showers, cooks a quick meal, sets his alarm, and falls asleep in front of the television. With a tenth-grade education, he has had many jobs in his lifetime, most of which have been in the construction field. However, his work schedule and daily routine have changed little in the past six years.

In his previous job, "digging ditches," he hurt his back and was unable to work for eight months. He received a small insurance settlement from the company that employed him at the time and was able to live on the cash amount for a few years. When it was time to return to work, the doctor suggested he find a less strenuous means of employment. However, construction seemed to be all that was available. Each day he went to work and returned home with severe pain in his lower back. It was during the period of his injury ten years ago that he began to lose regular contact with his noncustodial children. "I was always tired and angry because of my back and also my finance situation," he said. "I just didn't have the energy to deal with anybody."

To add to his problems, he was residing with his girlfriend, who had two twin toddlers of her own. "I was trying to be a family with this woman and her kids, but I was neglecting my own." He explained that his girlfriend did not mind occasional visits from his children, but she did not want him going to their home or sending them money. Rather than argue with her, he chose to avoid the conflict, concentrate on healing his back, and try to make things up to his then 9- and 10-year-olds when he had more energy.

However, time went by quickly, and his decision to reject his children did not sit well with their mother. "Prior to that she didn't ask for child support . . . we just had an arrangement where I would give her what I could." But after he ceased his visits, and the children's visits to his home also abruptly ended, she took the matter to court. Although he was unemployed at the time, his children's mother was awarded child support. Since she felt she would no longer have his personal support with their children, she took the boys and moved to a city three hours away, where she would have familial support. With his ailments, his lack of income, problems with his girlfriend, and the children's move, a full year went by before Jeffrey began to see his children again on a regular basis. Because of distance and work schedule, Jeffrey said he now sees his children on New Years, Father's Day, and his birthday, "and a couple days in the summer if they feel like it."

Jeffrey Campbell's experiences provide a segue to another element that seems to contribute to a father's disengagement—"other children." Although none of these fathers married the mothers of their live-away children, some did cohabit with and/or marry other women. Some of these women brought children into the relationship. With others, relationships produced new offspring. Still others remained childless. However, those with children proved to add a particular complication to fathers' routines. Regardless of how children came into the relationship, fathers often found it difficult to negotiate parenting between their new families and their noncustodial children. Fathers indicated several reasons for this: (1) women in new relationships did not approve of fathers visiting the homes of the children and their mothers; (2) it was difficult to manage time between two sets of children, and (3) fathers felt more attached to and accepted by the children with whom they were now living. For most fathers, a combination of each of these elements contributed to their lack of involvement as a live-away parent.

New relationships often complicated fathers' lives and often served to encourage fathers' disengagement from their live-away children. "My old lady she's the jealous type," said one father who offered to explain his reluctant departure from the life of his noncustodial son. "She said she did not want me going around where my son's mother lived," he continued. He explained that his current partner (from whom he had recently separated) became quite hostile when he tried to make contact with his son. "From her way of seeing it, I was going over there [to his son's] to visit his mother . . . she thought we still had a thing going on."

Other fathers had similar experiences with their current partners. They explained that these women were not only jealous but also seemed to resent any gifts or money fathers attempted to provide to their live-away offspring. Said one father, "She would try to convince me that his mother didn't need the money, or that she was using me to buy her stuff." According to another father:

"She [current partner] cussed out my daughter's mother when I took her [daughter's mother] some cash. She wanted me to use all my money for this house [current] and her and her son . . . like my daughter didn't exist." In some respects he agreed with his current partner. There was very little money to go around and certainly not enough to provide for two sets of children. He added that despite his current partner's wishes and his minimal resources, he continued to sneak small gifts to his daughter. As a compromise, though, he elected to not spend time or money traveling to visit the little girl because it would bring too much disruption to his current household.

Fathers often felt they were caught in the middle. If they did not visit with their children, custodial mothers would express disappointment and anger. However, if they did visit with their noncustodial children, their current partners would express feelings of betrayal and hurt. Not knowing what to do and with little formal knowledge to guide them, fathers generally found themselves slowly and eventually retreating to what they perceived was the most comfortable option. "It was easier to just let it go [not see his live-away son] than to put up with the bullshit that I got from her [current partner]," explained one father. "At least," said another father, "I'm here for one of my kids."

Attitudes of current partners in and of themselves were generally not the sole reason for fathers' disengagement. Rather this element tended to interplay with fathers' own feelings about live-away parenthood and their willingness or ability to provide support and care to their noncustodial children. According to Richard Thompson, the child he produced with his current girlfriend felt more like "his child" than the one created six years earlier with his former girlfriend.

"I just don't feel the connection with her [noncustodial daughter] like I do with my youngest child," he explained. He is convinced that difference lies in the fact that he never resided with his first daughter, "so there was not a bond there that developed between us." He acknowledged that the birth of his second daughter made him "feel like a father is supposed to feel . . . I can see her when I want, spank her when she's bad, hug her when she's good, whenever I want," something he said has always been lacking with his first daughter.

His current partner did not discourage or encourage him to maintain contact with his live-away child. "I think she is just happy with the way things is right now . . . she understands the situation for what it is . . . she knows I don't have much to offer my daughter . . . and we don't really talk about it that much," he said.

With the birth of his new daughter and the time she demanded, he simply lost track of his noncustodial daughter. He had heard from a friend that his ex-girlfriend and their shared child had moved from their old apartment. However, he never took the time to locate them and decided that his absence was best for his older child's well-being. "She don't really know me, no how," he said, "so I don't know what I could really do for her as a father at this point."

"TIME IS SLIPPING AWAY": PERSISTENT DISENGAGEMENT

Said one father, "Well I see him [his son] none, nada, not at all . . . I want to because I know that's what he needs from me more than anything else, but I'm just not a good father, a lousy father." He explained that on the day his now 9-year-old son was born, he "was out with friends. . . . I didn't find out about him for about a week after." He was 22 years old at the time, unemployed, and regularly shifting his residence from an older cousin's apartment to his mother's rented home.

Like several other men, Victor Barnes was not sure how he was supposed to respond to the news. "Hell I didn't know what a father was supposed to do anyways." He remembered visiting the baby and his mother on and off for a few months following the birth. "I brought little gifts; a rattle that said 'I love Daddy,' " he smiled. Still, other than "just holding him," "changing his diaper," "tickling him," and buying him a few playthings, he was uncertain of what was required.

Unable to articulate this to anyone in particular, Victor found himself avoiding an increasingly uncomfortable situation. "If she [the child's mother] paged me, I'd go over, see what's up," he said. Other than that, he went on with his daily routine. Thoughts of what he should be doing as a father preoccupied his mind for months after the birth, but eventually it became easier to stay away and push the thoughts aside. Yet even now, he said, it remains difficult. "I still think about my son . . . how I'm screwing up his life by not being there." He added, "time is slipping away."

When asked what would make him a good father, Victor replied: "I just need to go see him and stop putting myself down about the past. I know he don't care why I didn't come see him last week, last month, or last year. He just cares why I ain't coming to see him right now! I know because that's the way I felt about my father. All I wanted from him was time . . . I guess now I'm afraid he's going to look at me like I look at my father. . . . most the time that ain't good."

Time was a factor that appeared to work against the bonds between absent live-away dads and their offspring. The longer fathers were not in contact with their children, the more difficult it was to define their roles as fathers. Victor, the father above, recalled that he spent a lot of time imagining "what to say and do" with his child, rather than carrying out the act. As months and eventually years went by with little or no communication, the more complicated his imagined scenarios became.

"The more I waited [to call his child and the mother] the more explaining I knew I was going to have to do." He also noticed that on those rare occasions that he visited his child, the more distant and unfamiliar the interaction became. Increasingly, he found it difficult to ascertain what he was supposed to talk about or do to make his child feel comfortable and enjoy their outings.

Other absent fathers expressed similar concerns. "It's not like everybody thinks. . . . that men don't care about their kids [and] don't think about them," said Kyle Foster. "But it's more like . . . once you make the mistake of not being involved [in your child's life], it's hard to get the mindset to get re-involved." By this he meant "psychologically it's harder for you and your kids . . . [because] . . . nobody's used to being around each other."

Attempts to connect and reestablish bonds with children were further complicated by the routines children established with mothers, various relatives, and men who had assumed the paternal functions in place of the natural father. Once confronted with these situations after attempts of engagement, fathers often found it easier to return to the status of an absent live-away dad. Randy Roman explained that "it seemed there was no place for me, she [his daughter] was doing her thing, her mother's boyfriend was playing the daddy, so I have no purpose." He said after several emotionally draining and unsuccessful attempts to develop a relationship with his 8-year-old, he decided "to let it go."

Fathers who were uncertain about their paternal roles in the past only heightened the ambiguity by their prolonged distance. One father, Clyde Donnelly, explained that ten years went by before he attempted to reestablish contact with his 12-year-old daughter.

"I heard that she was pregnant . . . I thought she might need me." He had seen her off and on, on rare occasions since her birth. For many of the reasons expressed by other fathers (including a stint in prison), he remained absent for a greater part of her life. "I just stopped visiting," he said. "I stopped calling her mother, and [she] stopped wanting me to come over." Feeling emotionally drained by verbal battles with his daughter's mother, he discontinued his attempts to visit. He tried to send financial support when specifically requested. This halt in visitations occurred "about eight years ago," he reported.

Since that time he has had another child with a different woman. He has remained in constant contact with his second child, a boy, and the event of his birth forced Clyde to think more about his firstborn. He said he began to reflect on the effect his life choices had on his daughter. "There are a lot of young people who need their fathers," he said.

However, thinking about making contact and actually performing the feat were quite separate affairs. Once Clyde found out where she and her mother resided, he went by their home. He had intended to call, but they had no phone. His daughter barely said a word to him, and he felt he was carrying the relationship on his own. He offered to take her to the movies, walk with her to the store, "but it seemed every time I said 'Let's do this or the other' she had something better to." Clyde didn't think that she disliked him. Rather, he felt she "just didn't know me and didn't know if she could trust me." Also he explained, she had an established routine. Surrounding her academic schedule were girlfriends, boyfriends, and chores she had to do for her mother and siblings that generally precluded any activities he planned.

Over the years, Clyde too had established a routine. However, it was completely devoid of parenting his daughter. Like other fathers, the decision to reunite with his child meant he would have to relinquish certain liberties. He admitted that while his feelings were hurt when his daughter sometimes declined his invitations, he simultaneously felt relieved. "I mean I could stay home and watch TV or read," he explained, which is what he often did when he was not working.

A peek into a maternity ward waiting room would confirm that the initial anxieties about parenting expressed by these men are no different than those experienced by most new fathers. But the confluence of varying personal, social, and structural circumstances make paternal disengagement or "absence" one of several possible outcomes for this particular category of live-away fathers. Their decisions about how, when, and if to parent depended in part on the cooperation and encouragement they received from their children's mothers and the family members who resided in their children's households. Refractory family members often discouraged fathers from visiting their children by heightening the awkwardness and ambiguity they already felt about the fatherhood role in such cases. Fathers often felt out of place and more like visitors than family members when inside their children's homes. Poor communication between the fathers and mothers of their children about parenting expectations also contributed to fathers' anxieties. For some fathers, poor relationships with their children's mothers contributed to their paternal detachment.

Fathers' internal anxieties about parenting were compounded not only by personal relationships but also by struggles to maintain other commitments and their own economic stability. Familial poverty and poor academic and economic opportunities limited many life options for these men. In addition, it placed many of them in contact with the criminal justice system, which only served to further distance them from their children.

While some fathers silently removed themselves from their children's lives, others openly disengaged from their parenting roles. Still others felt forced to assume an absent father status. Regardless of how their paternal disengagement came about, the longer it lasted the more difficult it became to assert and/or reassert their fatherhood. The form of disengagement also did not always coincide with what these fathers actually did as fathers. The behavior of such fathers illustrates that "absence" can be a nebulous term. While these fathers had virtually no physical contact with their children in the past year, some provided them with gifts, phone calls, and/or payments of child support. Others provided nothing at all.

Nevertheless, fathers across this varying spectrum of absence expressed ambivalent—and, in some cases, outright anguished—feelings about being or becoming absent. "What hurts most," said one father, who had not seen his 13-year-old daughter since her second birthday, is that "we'll never know what its like to be father and daughter, daughter and father."

8

"AIN'T NOTHING LIKE TRYING TO BE A FATHER AND TRYING TO BE A MAN"
Barriers to Being Daddy

*F*ew would argue that parenting is often an arduous task. Even in two-parent households, adults are challenged to meet the needs of their children and simultaneously manage their work schedules, shopping, housecleaning, relationships with relatives, and find time to monitor their own physical and psychological well-being. Relative to the past, today there are increased obstacles to parenting, particularly for lower-income parents. A decline in real wages, fewer opportunities for well-paying blue-collar employment, a rise in temporary and part-time jobs means that men and women have to work more hours outside of the home to sustain the physical needs of their families. Subsequently, they are spending fewer hours of their days and weeks with their children.[1]

For fathers who live away from their children, the responsibilities and joys of parenting are equally if not more difficult to realize. When fathers live in homes separate from their children it means that they may miss the opportunity to visit with their children at what may otherwise be taken-for-granted periods. Time before and after school, time in the evening before bed and the many other small blocks of time likely to accompany a custodial parent status are not provided a nonresidential parent. For many reasons, despite their intent, these fathers often found it difficult to follow through with parenting activities.

In chapter 4, I discussed how father's relationships with the mothers of their children often served to hinder or strengthen paternal activities. But the custodial mother—noncustodial father relationship alone provides us with an incomplete picture of the context of fathers' lives. Myriad variables cloud the issue of parenting and compound personal and familial choices. In this chapter we examine the circumstances of fathers' work schedules, intimate relationships, and other elements that often inhibited their ability to maximize their paternal roles.

According to Warren Wilcox, live-away father of two, "Nobody said being a parent was easy . . . but when you young, you don't think about how hard it is to do," he said wistfully. Thirty-one at the time of his interview for this study, Warren reflected on his younger days. He was 19 when his first child was born. Deborah, the mother, was 20 at the time and this was her second child. "In my mind I imagined it [fatherhood] would be like on TV. When they show fathers on TV they don't show the stress he be under trying to accommodate everything."

Warren was unemployed when he and Deborah began dating. "I was in between jobs," he explained. "I think that was when I had gotten fired, I was kind of depressed," he remembered. This is what his life was "mostly like." He had a difficult time maintaining full-time employment and generally took odd jobs here and there as opportunities presented themselves. He had worked in construction, in restaurants and bars, collections, sweeping floors at a local sports arena, and at various other low-wage jobs. He managed to find out about jobs through friends and relatives. However, the work was generally minimum wage and/or "off the books." Subsequently, employers would demand that Warren be on call, work odd hours, and/or work thirteen and fourteen hours daily.

Such demands were characteristic of several men's employment experiences. Employers often attempted to underpay them or avoid paying them for their labor altogether. This was particularly true, said one father, if employers knew workers had a record of incarceration and little opportunity for legitimate work.

Warren explained that there were many times when he had to "hunt down" and "threaten" the employer to receive his agreed upon earnings in a timely manner. He had been to jail twice for assault since the birth of his child. "See you want to talk about barriers," he continued, "ain't nothing like trying to be a father and trying to be a man. See the two don't always go together. If you do one good, then that means you probably doing poor in the other, you see." He explained further, "To be a man you supposed to work, provide. But if you do that then that means you don't be around for your child . . . The way work is situated, the way I'm situated here is that if I'm going to make enough money to support my son, like a man is supposed to do . . . Then that means I don't have time to do what a father is supposed to do . . . I'm busy hustling and trying to make cash . . . That's all my time and all my energy, see?" When I'm not working I try to spend as much time with him [son] as I can."

Warren shared a home with his Uncle Merl and Aunt Vivian, which had made
spending time with his son an ordinary daily activity. The house was within walking
distance of the store top apartment in which his son had lived for most of his life.
"He'll stop by after school, sometime on the way to school. Sometime just come by,
speak, for dinner . . . Other times he'd be wanting to stay all night . . . he's a good boy."

Many men in America increasingly experience the tug-of-war between
work and fatherhood. As the economic cost of raising children increases
and real wages continue to decline, fathers have to spend more time in the
workforce and less time with their children. Simultaneously, popular discourse is encouraging men to take more responsibility for the social and
emotional aspects of parenting. Other fathers in this study reported feeling
the frustration of trying to earn a living and be a father, elements they perceived as often contradictory to one another. Said another father, "When I
work twelve hours a day digging ditches or whatever they have me doing
that day, then I'm too tired to pick him up [four-year-old son]."

In other words, work schedules and demands often served as barriers to
the socially supportive aspects of fatherhood that these men felt were of
utmost importance. But their paternal roles were often complicated by their
relationships with their children's mothers (as discussed in chapter 4), children by more than one woman, a lack of reliable transportation, and many
other factors.

At the time of Warren's interview it was a hot summer month, and economically, times
were "going all right" for him. He arranged to take turns with his uncle, selling snow
cones a few blocks from the St. Louis Zoo. "It's good money this time of year . . . you
just got to have enough change, you got to have ingredients, and you got to make sure
you have enough water to drink," he said laughing. However, as things would have it,
his son's mother recently relocated to the county's far north to take advantage of a welfare to work opportunity. She and her children now shared a two-bedroom home with
a cousin and spent most of their time miles away from Warren's neighborhood. "I'd
say it's about, hmm. . . . an hour drive from here [his home] to where they at now . . .
longer, if you take the bus." That's not a long time however, he explains, "when you
have to wait for a bus and work, it takes a lot out of your day . . . Time I need to make
money."

With the change in living arrangements, he expects that unless he can find work
further north, he will only see his son "a couple of times a month," relatively less than

the almost daily visits they used to share. Warren closed the discussion of work and its relation to his role as father by talking about his intentions to maintain paternal involvement: "I'm trying to see what I can do to be closer to him . . . I'm flexible with work . . . I can do just about anything somebody wants to pay me for."

In these fathers' environments there were tribulations and circumstances that hampered their parenting options and often limited their ability to maximize their involvement with children. Said one father, "It takes more than just wishing to be a good father . . . It takes superman skills." He was referring to the many turns and twists in everyday life that create hurdles to being "the type of father every kid should have," said another father. Turns and twists take various forms. In chapter 4 I examined how fathers' relationships with the mothers of their children assisted or hindered what they did as fathers. Other barriers to paternal activity could be placed in the following general categories: (1) a lack of time due primarily to work, (2) proximity or physical distance from children and available transportation, (3) economic instability, (4) having two or more sets of children, and (5) households and relationships with intimate others.

LACK OF TIME

Time is an element that many parents feel they lack. Black lower-income families have little time for leisure activities and spend a great deal of their waking hours working outside of the home. As mentioned, for live-away fathers, parenting experiences are further complicated by their removed residential status. Fathers expressed experiencing a lack of time for several reasons: employment, responsibilities for maintaining their own households and intimate relationships, having two or more sets of children by two or more different mothers, and a combination of all of the above. Thus, while each of these elements is discussed in separate sections below, they all interact and create a context of parental options for live-away fathers.

WORK SCHEDULES

Most of these fathers who were employed worked in occupations demanding much time and providing little pay and/or benefits. Many fathers held more than one or two jobs to compensate for their low pay and to make ends meet. Several fathers with full-time occupations also worked part time. Several fathers who could not find full-time employment worked at two or more part-time occupations. Regardless of whether they were part time or full time, these fathers' work schedules were often inconsistent and provided little flexibility.

With great sadness one father recalled a time five years past, when his first daughter, then age 3, became ill with pneumonia and complications from a heart condition. While he was at work, an ambulance was called and the little girl was rushed to the hospital. Her aunt telephoned his place of employment to inform him of the situation. However, his supervisor refused to excuse him from work and did not permit him to use the telephone to check on his daughter's condition. He explained, "[the supervisor] just basically said that if I leave I lose my job." On probation for possession of stolen property, he decided it best to maintain his employment. Six hours later, he completed his shift and caught a bus that placed him about two blocks from the hospital. He recalled the dread he felt as he walked the remaining distance to the emergency room. Upon his arrival he learned that his daughter had died of heart failure 45 minutes earlier. Although he said he has found joy in being a father to his two other children, he continues to feel regret and guilt about that single day five years ago. "I was too late," he said; "Too late to hold her and tell her how much I love her . . . I wasn't there when she needed me most."

While the account above is one of the most tragic collected for this study, many fathers felt the strain and frustration that accompany inflexible employment schedules and work environments. Fathers' parenting was also structured around inconstant or rotating shift schedules. Shifts would often be changed every day or week or month.

Art, a father of two young children, explained that he worked as a janitor for a preschool during the day and then took a thirty-minute bus ride across town to work cleaning bathrooms and floors at a sales office. However, his work schedule at the sales office changed from week to week, depending on whether or not the owners were in town. "I'm not sure what they do is legal," he added and explained that they often left town on very short notice, often neglecting to inform him. "I don't know if I have to work or not until I get to the office . . . if the doors are locked I go home . . . If they are unlocked then I get to my job," he said. He speculated that the owners did not trust black men enough to provide them with keys to the business office.

Another father worked as a security guard with eight-hour shifts that rotated every two weeks. Still another worked at two fast-food restaurants cooking, cleaning, and stocking. "Sometimes, my schedules conflict because the schedules are always changing [from one week to the next]. Sometimes they schedule me for twenty-three hours and sometimes it's twenty-eight. If I worked full-time for at least one company it would be easier, because then I would probably be able to have at least one schedule that stays the same," he explained. Consequently, his visits with his children were inconsistent and dependent on the number and hours of days he was scheduled to work.

Many fathers worked evenings and/or weekends. Such schedules usually did not coincide with children's school or vacation schedules. Changing work schedules, rotating shifts, and evening work hours limited "when" and "how often" fathers were able to spend time with their children. Evening hours and weekends were the times when children were out of school. However, they were also the times when fathers worked at part-time jobs, "picked up" overtime hours or other types of work, or relaxed and slept in between jobs and shifts. Even some fathers who saw their children on an almost daily basis perceived "a lack of time" as a hindrance to the ideal fathering they would like to provide. As an example, one father cared for his children five days a week. The children would come to his house immediately after each day of school. He fixed them a snack, helped them with their homework, and watched cartoons with them. Around 6:00 their mother completed her shift as a nurses assistant. She then picked the children up and took them home, which was approximately five minutes away from the father's apartment.

"See, it would be good if I could spend more than an hour or two a day with them. But most weeks, at the end of the week, I feel like I been stretched from one corner of the earth to another. There is not enough time in the day to work, pay the bills, go to the grocery store, do this here and that and be the perfect father. But I try to come close . . . I could use a 100-hour day instead of a 24-hour one."

Some fathers reluctantly admitted that reporting "a lack of time" was something they had some control over but found difficulty making choices about how to spend the little leisure time they had in a day. For example,

Juan, father of 11-year-old Tiffany explained that "after I complete what I got to do [work] I rather sometimes just chill on my days off . . . I don't want to be bothered by nobody . . . I don't want to see nobody." He said that he often felt guilty for choosing to spend his free time alone instead of with his daughter. He attempted to make sense of the dissonance these thoughts created for him. "I'm not making excuses . . . It's hard to explain . . . It's like I want to see her but at the same time it's like I don't have a lot of time to get my personal sh— done . . . so when I choose to take care of my business the trade off is I don't have time to do what it takes to make that [seeing his daughter] happen . . . If I spend as much time as I should with her then other things get behind."

Fathers often expressed mixed feelings of sadness, frustration, and guilt when they made decisions to forgo visits with their children. This was particularly true when mothers did not perceive their alternative choices as legitimate. According to one father, "My son's mother, now she don't work, but she always wanting me to swing by there and take him . . . She don't care what I'm doing, she don't care about my life, she don't care how she inconvenience me . . . just 'come over here and get him.'" However, he did not seem to consider how parenting and its inconveniences were more of a responsibility for the mother of his child than for him. He would often take pause and deliberate on whether or not to return her pages and phone messages because from his perspective, she was constantly reminding him of his parental responsibilities and his failure to live up to his promises.

Regardless of how little time fathers perceived they had to spend with their children, few fathers felt that "a lack of time" in-and-of-itself, created a significant barrier to fathering. In fact, fathers were quick to chastise men who they felt "made excuses" for not being more involved with their children. One father summed up the feelings of most in this regard. He asserted that while time is generally a problem it does not keep him from being a "daddy" to his children:

"If I didn't want to be a daddy to my kids I could. I could easily blame it on work. Ignore my kid's needs, saying: 'Uh, no I can't take you here because I got to work,' or 'I'm sorry you going to have to ask your mama to help you 'cause I'm too tired to drive over there.'"

Like other fathers, this father reported he made the most of what little time he had to spend with his children. He explained that his occupation and the amount of money he earned inhibited the amount of time and energy he would like to devote to his children.

"If I were a doctor or lawyer I could set my own work hours, see my kids all the time—but it ain't going to happen and ain't no use in me wishing. I just have to be thankful for the time I do get to spend with my kids and then make sure I'm the best father I can be whether I'm with them or not."

Still, fathers were not completely satisfied with the time they had to devote to fathering. Ideally, most explained, they would see their children on a daily basis. Or at a minimum, once a week. When describing how they made decisions about visiting, fathers who were legally employed generally talked about their choices in the context of the work schedules. But they also made their choices in the context of the type of work they did.

Dixon, father of 6-year-old Brittany, explained that "the reason me and her mother don't live together no more is because of work." He said that his job as a roofer's helper kept him dirty and tired. "I'd come home with tar under my nails and on my clothes. She said I smelled bad. I would get up at sometimes 4:30 in the morning and be gone until 9:30 that night. We had to work from daylight until it got dark. The only days we [he and one other helper] had off was when it rained. Rainy days and snow days, that's the only time I had free to spend with her and Brittany."

He admits though, that even on these days off his back and knees would often ache. Thus, he would reluctantly choose to use the time off from work to simply lay on the sofa to rest and watch television rather than interact with members of the household. By the time she was six months old, he had moved into his own apartment. This meant he spent fewer hours with Brittany. Additionally, he and her mother could not seem to agree when or if he should maintain contact with his daughter at all. This was eight years ago and since then he has changed employment. However, while his employers have changed he has remained in the construction field all of his jobs have required strenuous physical activity.

JOB STRESS

The physical demands of men's labor were often accompanied by emotional toll. Many of these fathers worked in occupations that required their subordination to others. Few were supervisors or managers who held a significant degree of autonomy or decision-making authority on the job. Rather, they were working in low-level service-type jobs or trades that required they record their work hours and breaks on time cards, obey commands, and follow directions. Moreover, none were union workers and so their positions had few protections from employer whims and indiscretions. At the least, these men did not feel they had any means of legally rectifying any harm they felt employers unduly imparted.

As a possible consequence, men often expressed feelings of frustration and tension when describing their work environments. They worked in jobs that required long hours, physical labor, and the ability to please not only employers but clients and customers as well. Whether they were feeling poorly, were tired, or had worries external to the job, they were expected to "put up a front" and pretend to enjoy their occupations. This emotional toll, however, is not reflected in their earnings. It is a job requirement that if not performed properly could quickly result in termination.

Philip provided an example. He recalled going to work at Denny's Restaurant less than thirty minutes after a heated argument with his daughter's mother. "I was in a bad mood," he said, "but you can't let customers know your feelings like that." From where he stood, customers "don't care . . . They just expect you to smile and grin . . . If you don't laugh at their jokes then they don't tip you or they think you got an attitude and report you to the manager . . . He don't care neither."

Philip explained that most days are like this. "You go to work, you don't really want to be there, you don't make any money, customers are rude, but you don't have a choice . . . you just force yourself to smile through the day."

Other fathers report similar experiences and explain that after a day of "putting on" for employers and customers they often feel emotionally depleted and lack the energy and willingness to interact with others, even their own children, for sustained periods of time. These men reported they were regularly victims of individual discrimination from fellow bus travelers, bus drivers, store managers, and the many others they happen by or interact with on the way home from work.

"After work, I just mainly want to be left alone," said 29-year-old Donald, live-away father of twin 8-year-old boys. "Even if I go by their house, I just might sit there like in another world, while they be playing around me."

"It's sad really," said 33-year-old Steve, who works as a car wash attendant and gas station cashier. "I spend so much time trying to stay out of people's way and stay out of trouble that it drains most of my psychological and physical energy," he continued. "It's sad for my girls because all they see of me is the tired me . . . The me that says 'I've got a headache' or 'I just need to get some sleep *then* I'll come visit,' " he said, recalling several times when the intended visits never occurred.

Fathers expressed feelings of guilt about not having enough time and energy to give to their children. "A lot of it is really psychological," said Frederick. "I'm not physically tired but sometimes I just don't have the mental energy to do the father thing . . . I mean, I don't like that about me but I don't know what to do about it," he said, seeming to blame himself solely for the weariness that often occupied his days.

PROXIMITY AND TRANSPORTATION

For several fathers proximity or physical distance was the primary obstacle to their full involvement with their children. Some fathers, particularly those in the low ranks of the military, had to move a great distance from their children to accept or maintain employment. Some fathers lived three or four hours away, others lived in a different region of the United States, still others moved from one location to another as their military occupation demanded. These fathers claimed that if they lived closer to their children they would be able to be "more of a father." Listen to this father:

"I feel like I'm missing a lot. I didn't get to see her first step. I missed her first birthday. And now, like she's going be in the Easter play at church and there's no way I want to miss that. If we weren't separated by thousands of miles then her daddy would be there taking pictures, getting all nervous for her, like all the rest of the daddies."

Other fathers who viewed proximity as a problem lived in the same city as their children but lived on the other side of town or in small towns nearby. These fathers explained that a lack of transportation coupled with the inability to consistently coordinate their schedule with the mother's hindered their ability to spend time with their children. The fathering of live-away fathers who lived across town and worked were doubly hampered in this regard, particularly if their work was in still some other part of the city. A 28-year-old father described his circumstances:

"I could see my girls more if (1) If they lived closer to me, (2) If I didn't work so many hours, and (3) If I didn't have to drive for an hour everyday, up there and back, to get to work. See, I work in a different area from where my house is and from where they live. And they live in a different part of the city from me."

One father explained how his situation was made more complicated by the condition of his vehicle.

"What I got is . . . you've seen the truck on *Sanford and Son*, right . . . ? That's what I drive, everyday . . . An old jalopy. Sometimes she works and sometimes she's temperamental, and sometimes she just doesn't work. So when I say it takes me an hour everyday of driving you can double and triple that on some days because of my transportation problems," he said, with a hint of self-ridicule and matter-of-factness in his voice. As a result, he visited with his son about three times a month.

Public transportation was the primary mode of "getting around" for many of these fathers. While this form of travel was monetarily inexpensive, it was quite costly in terms of time and convenience. However, purchasing a vehicle, particularly a dependable one, was not an easy matter for low-income live-away fathers.

As Roy clearly explained, "You can buy a car for fifty to one-hundred-fifty dollars if you want . . . but you get what you pay for." He recalled an old Buick Riviera that he had purchased for $220. "I had saved a little something and I added that to what I just got paid," he stated proudly. He then recalled his plans to visit his girlfriend and first newborn daughter, "I was going to surprise her [the child's mother] by pulling up and honking the horn. "I was feeling good about having some money in my pocket."

He purchased the car from his father, a man whom he said was well known for his ability to hustle. However, at the time of the purchase six years ago, he was "barely twenty" years old and had not believed most of the things rumored about his father. "That is until he sold me the damn car," Roy said. "It started right up, I paid him the cash and started driving . . . Then bump, bump, bump, clack, clack, clack it started falling apart . . . I didn't even make it to my mother's driveway and it was just five blocks from my pop's," he chuckled and shook his head seemingly in continued disbelief. He then recounted his father's refusal to take the vehicle back and return his money. "This is what he told me, he said 'You got to learn to be smarter with your money' . . . he said 'It's a father's job to teach you that.'"

Therefore, when Roy needs to travel from one part of the city to another he either walks, takes the bus, borrows his mother's car, or asks for a ride from friends and relatives. When his daughter began kindergarten he managed to pick her up daily by catching a two o'clock bus at the stop two blocks from his downtown job. He then transferred to a second bus that dropped him off about three miles from her school. He jogged and walked the distance to her school. Except when he missed the bus, or the weather was uncooperative, he generally arrived at her school by three-thirty. "I was hardly ever late picking her up," he said proudly. Although the schedule seemed a bit hectic and tiring, he recalled that at the time, "I never really thought about it much . . . I just did what I had to do so that she wasn't waiting at school."

Overall, fathers found that reliable cars and other major purchase items were difficult to come by, particularly because they tended not to have the cash or credit to purchase from a reputable dealer or individual seller. The costs of living coupled with low wages, time in the criminal justice system, and few significant employment opportunities left many with little, bad, or no credit at all.

One father, Bruce, recalled having to make the decision to either pay his mother's electricity bill or that of his daughter and her mother. He chose the latter because, as he explained it, if his mother's electricity were turned off she could have it restored almost immediately by opening up another account with the utility company in her three-year-old niece's name. More important, he did not want his daughter to have to live without electricity. He also feared her mother would restore their account by using his daughter's name, which could eventually ruin her future credit with the utility company in the event the bill wouldn't be paid. Regardless, the decision to offer financial assistance meant that he fell behind on payments for several of his personal monthly debts, including his automobile liability insurance on a 1986 Dodge, which costs $71 monthly. His income was approximately $230 a week. His utility bill dilemma was typical and he did not expect that there was ever a day when he held a status of good credit. In fact, he had never owned a credit card or legitimate employment that paid much above minimum wages. Subsequently, he and most fathers were unable to purchase "decent" vehicles, and tended to rely on the bus, city rail system, or the good will of others to transport them from here to there.

Small items too were not always affordable. One father told of his desire to one day purchase an electric razor. "I just wish right now I could buy it but it would take away my money for other things," he said. Microwave ovens, washers and dryers, and other items that could assist in making their days more efficient were reserved for those with steady incomes and credit. "Usually, I spend one day a week going to the laundromat or if my mother's machine is working then I'll go there and wash my clothes and iron and get my clothing neat for work," said Roland Bailey, father of one. He considered these "run-around-days" because he was generally visiting various places trying to secure the goods and services he needed for the following week, paying debts, purchasing lottery tickets, confirming rides to work, and the like.

ECONOMIC INSTABILITY

Not all fathers were as organized as Roland was. In fact, the lack of steady employment coupled with their poor credit rating contributed to the instability some fathers experienced. One father, Jerold, provided an example.

Jerold lived day-to-day not knowing for certain where he would be sleeping from one month or week to the next. Out of work for four years and with no savings, he moved from one residence to another, living with friends, relatives, and sometimes girlfriends. Wherever he resided, he offered his services in exchange for the permission that was granted for him to stay. At his cousin Bernadette's, he provided childcare for her two sons while she worked nights. He also helped her maintain the interior and exterior of her rented house. During this period, his 8-year-old daughter would visit with him regularly and often spend the night. She attended the same school as her male cousins and they were instructed to walk home together after classes. He moved out when Bernadette's boyfriend moved in and settled with another cousin, Nadine, where a similar arrangement of exchange was made. However, the two adults bickered constantly and after nine months Nadine decided he would have to leave.

From there he moved twice more. Although he always remained near his daughter's home, his visits with her generally depended on his living arrangements and the services he negotiated for his room. At one point, he was unable to visit with his daughter because he had offered twenty-four hour care to his grandmother's elderly next door neighbor. The gentleman was soon moved to a nursing home and about three months after the start of the arrangement, Jerold was forced to move elsewhere.

He eventually settled into his elderly uncle's home, a small two-bedroom brick house in need of substantial repair. He offered to do work on the house in exchange for a room. Every month his uncle would purchase whatever supplies he could afford so that Jerold could carry out the process of fixing and remodeling the home. Jerold also began picking up odd jobs around the neighborhood and earning a meager but growing income. Through word-of-mouth, people in the community learned they could depend on him to "fix almost anything" in or around their homes, including their cars.

At the time of his interview for this study, his daughter was almost 12 years old and lived about six blocks away. Since living with his uncle, Jerold saw her at least twice a week, if not more. On weekends, she would sometimes help him with his odd jobs, though he realized that her interest in boys and gossiping with girlfriends was making time spent with him less interesting. Nevertheless, he insisted that he would remain with his uncle "for as long as it works out," because the arrangement offered him some stability and he was now beginning to find a balance between his work, his own personal needs and problems, and his fatherhood.

In the company of relatives, roommates, or a girlfriend were settings that seemed most comfortable for fathers when interacting with their children. Several of those living alone felt that there homes or apartments were not the "right atmosphere" for their children's presence. Others expressed an uneasiness at having their children visit them and see them in their living quarters and/or they felt there was little for these children to do other than watch television. Said one father, "I don't have a good TV." He demonstrated this by manually turning the knob on the older model set from one fuzzy black and white screen to another. "There ain't nothing for my kids to do here," he added.

Fathers also tended to survive on the bare necessities. Lonny, live-away father of one, lived in a rooming house.

His 10 x 11 square-foot room came furnished with a twin-sized bed and a single pillow. His coffee maker and digital clock were plugged into what appeared to be the only working electrical outlet. His closet had no door or clothing rod. It was filled to the top with neatly stacked blue and yellow Chiquita Banana boxes that served as a bureau for clothing and other belongings. A community bathroom was two doors down the hall. He explained that his son sometimes spent time here but they generally spent their time together outside of these walls. They visited others, went to the movies, rode the bus, or sat outside and grilled hot dogs.

Another father, who shared a home with a couple and one other gentleman explained: "Right now I'm not really living the way I want to . . . There's too many people goes in and out of my place sometimes . . . It's not as clean as it could be for her [daughter]."

Another father explained that of his three sets of children, two were in foster care and the other was in the custody of his brother and his wife. "I messed up," he said. "I wasn't there for them so you know, they [the state] had to step in and take care of things," he offered with dismay. He had fathered four children with three different women. Two of the women had problems with drugs. The other was mentally challenged. He himself suffered with bouts of depression that required medication. He had attempted suicide twice in his life, had been placed under psychiatric care in a state institution, and had slept on the streets more than once.

At the time of his interview for this study, he was staying with his niece helping to maintain the old house she had inherited from her mother (his sister). He helped pay the bills with his monthly disability checks and other meager government assistance. He wished he could do more for his children and he desired to be a better father. "I think about all of my kids," he continued, "but the only one I really see is my son, he's with my brother and sister [in-law] . . . so that's why I get to see him." As far as the other children were concerned, he explained that he was not certain how to formally initiate contact with them.

TWO OR MORE SETS OF CHILDREN

Fathers' familial systems take many forms. For these fathers, some structured their paternal role around one set of children, while others had two or more. Some fathers lived with at least one biological child or girlfriend's child and had one or more sets of children with whom they did not reside. Fathers with two or more sets of children, that is one set of children by one mother and another set with still another woman, found it difficult to divide their time between one household of children and another. The task was particularly difficult when the households were not located within close proximity of each other.

> "I see my son almost everyday. I work about a block, two blocks from their place. Now, my daughter I'm lucky to see her once a week. Her mama done found a place out on the South Side. I feel like I should see them both the same amount but I'd have to divide myself in two to accomplish that."

Some fathers attempted to maximize the time they spent with their children by bringing two or more households of children together at once. Fathers felt most comfortable with their children in their mother's or other relative's homes. Therefore, gatherings of children generally took place at one or more of these locations and usually occurred on weekends and/or holidays.

> "I made a promise to myself to see my kids at least once a week. No matter where they are at or what work I'm doing that is what I have always done. My mama helps me out. She lets me bring them all over to her house on weekends. We grill hotdogs, rent movies, sometime I'm able to take them to the arcade, stuff like that . . . It works out for everyone this way. Their mamas get the weekend to themselves an' my kids and I get to spend quality time together . . . And they get to know their brothers and sisters."

Some live-away fathers reluctantly visited with one set of children while spending virtually no time at all with another, though this was not the preferred arrangement expressed by fathers with two or more sets of children.

When such circumstances did occur they were generally the result of a father's physical distance from the one household and his relatively closer proximity to the other. However proximity was not the only obstacle to their fathering. In addition to proximity, fathers seemed to associate the time they spent with one household or another with one or more of the following: a negative relationship with the mother of the children, the mother's marriage, or her live-in boyfriend. One father summarizes the feelings of several fathers who tended to spend more time with one set of children than with another:

> "I could go and see them at least a couple a times a month if I really took the time. But I really feel like she [the mother] doesn't want me there, especially since she done got married. She just wants them to be one big happy family. I feel like I have to respect that—give them some space. I want the best for my girls. But at the same time I have to keep in touch with them so they know me as a father and then they'll come to me when their older and have a problem."

Not all fathers expressed such tolerance and easiness with circumstances and individuals that seemed to purposely exclude them from their children's lives.

> "I haven't seen my son in . . . three, three and one-half years. His mother basically, she didn't want me coming around. But at the same time she refused to bring him to me . . . I told her a boy needs his father but she wasn't hearing it . . . Just selfish."

RELATIONSHIPS WITH INTIMATE OTHERS

Research suggests that within a live-away father's environment the attitudes and behaviors of his current partner affect his fathering behavior. When a man enters new relationships or remarries he may feel less committed to his children from previous relationships. Cohabitation and remarriage—due to the complexity and constraints of balancing time between families—may decrease father's involvement with their children. Seltzer and Brandreth

(1994) recently found that relative to fathers who remained single following divorce those who remarried or cohabiting found managing time for their children more difficult. Relative to those who did not live with children, those remarried or cohabiting live-away fathers who lived with other biological children or stepchildren were more involved with their cohabiting children and had more positive attitudes about their fatherhood.[2]

Although these men had not experienced legal marriage or remarriage many had experiences with cohabiting and/or intimate relationships with women other than the mother of their children. These intimate relationships contributed to the complexity of their lives as fathers. "When I first started seeing her [his girlfriend], I told her about my children," said one father. "She act like she so pleased that I take care of them, understand? . . . Then as soon as we get serious and things start to take off; I'm thinking about us being serious, she go and tell me I spend too much time at my children's house . . . when I bring them over here [his house] she say 'Why they always got to be over here?' "

Fathers in such situations said they felt caught in the middle.

"I want to do right by my children but I want to keep peace in my house," said Juan, a father of two live-away children. He defined peace as being able to come home from work and relax or not hearing any arguing or nagging from his cohabiting girlfriend, or the children's mother, or sometimes the children themselves. Peaceful moments were a rarity, especially on weekends or evenings when his children were around. "See they always trying her [girlfriend] and she don't know how to handle them," continued Juan. The children, ages 8 and 9, would seem to purposely do the opposite of what they were told, or would ignore what his girlfriend was saying all together. That the children's demands and behaviors were a constant irritant to his girlfriend was only part of the problem and perhaps was simply the way the actual problem manifested itself.

According to Juan, "She's jealous of my relationship with my children . . . We have a powerful relationship." Overall, he believes his girlfriend thinks he spends too much time and money on his children. She would prefer that he invest more of each in the family and home they created exclusive of his offspring from another relationship.

The struggle to negotiate his parenting and intimate relationship was tense—so much so that Juan would often avoid the situation by spending time at his mother's home about two miles away. Or, he would take his children to Burger King instead of having them over for dinner and to stay the night. He recognized that these two alternatives were qualitatively different, "I like to have them at the house then we get the bonding in . . . We spend hours talking and watching sports . . . we work out problems . . . things like that," he said. He perceived simply "taking them out to eat" as something uncaring fathers would do. In other words, fathers who are serious about being involved with their children did more than simply provide them with recreation. "That's like a payoff . . . Saying here I know I been wrong for not spending time with you so I'm going to take you out to dinner or to Six Flags, or to a show instead of spending some serious time with you," he explained.

Other fathers too found structuring fatherhood roles and functions was difficult when they were in relationships. From the perspective of many fathers, their children's mothers were more likely to perceive fathers' girlfriends as a problem than they were. But girlfriends also enhanced fathers relationships with children, especially when they encouraged them to be "more of a father" or visit with their children.

"She taught me to be a better father than I was . . . I didn't understand the meaning of the word until she told me," said George. He explained that his girlfriend encouraged him to pick his children up from school, bring them over for visits, and call them regularly. "She said it was wrong to not show them what it means to be a father," he said, verbally reminding him of the lack of feelings he felt for his own live-away father. "I never really knew my father," he offered. " I mean I knew his name, I knew where he lived, I knew his other children, but I was not allowed to get to *know* him," he explained further. "I just don't think my father knew how to love me at the time I was coming up," he said, recalling how on the few occasions they were in the same room his father barely acknowledged his existence. "He would ask me how I'm doing, 'What you been up to,' that sort of thing," George recounted, "but he never hugged me and he never made me feel like he wanted to be my father." George remembered that as a youngster, he "hated" his father but as he grew into adulthood his feelings changed to indifference. In his words, "If he [father] told me he had cancer right now, today, I wouldn't care."

Given his experiences with his own father, George feared that his children would develop similar feelings toward him if he did not maintain involvement. However, after ending his romantic relationship with their mother he found it difficult to be around his children. "I didn't know what to say or what to do with them besides taking them to the park," he said. He found his visits uncomfortable and as time went on his contact with the children became more sporadic and undependable. When he met his girlfriend, he was on the verge of discontinuing the father/child relationship altogether. "Not purposely or consciously . . . just the way things was going," he said. However, his girlfriend forced him to think about the ramifications of his withdrawal from his children, "I just needed that support that she gave me," he said. "Before, I was always afraid of my kids rejecting me or not liking me . . . Now I know that the only way they going to love me, is for me to be there for them no matter what," he stated and then chose to close discussion on the matter.

Overall, this study suggests that African American fathers are often confronted with numerous elements that serve to discourage their social and emotional behavior as fathers. The findings reported in an earlier chapter support past research indicating that mothers often act as gatekeepers, inhibiting or enhancing the role fathers play in the lives of their children. The environment that fathers felt most encouraged and enhanced their fatherhood were ones in which they were friendly with the mothers of their children and ones in which they did not experience multiple employment or multiple sets of children, and where they lived relatively close to their children's homes. Here, most fathers felt that mothers encouraged them to provide consistent social and emotional support to their children, to spend time with children and to be a part of their children's daily lives.

In contrast, antagonistic relationships coupled with multiple employment and multiple sets of children were least inviting and most discouraging for fathers. Here fathers felt that mothers were only interested in the economic support they expected fathers to provide and communication between the two was often cursory and/or limited. This often left fathers with a sense that their social and emotional paternal involvement was unwelcome and uninvited. Other than the experience of antagonistic relationships, fathers felt that most barriers did not completely prevent them from being involved with their children. Nevertheless, upon further examination of their ecological environments in this chapter, we find that fathers structure their parental activities around work schedules, a lack of well-paying and/or stable employment, the lack of a stable residence, intimate relationships, and other elements—all of which in some measure discouraged their involvement and/or dampened their relationship with children.

Regardless of income, education, and occupational levels, most live-away fathers must find a way to effectively parent the children with whom they do not reside. But the experiences of the fathers in this study suggest that inconsistent and inflexible work schedules in particular make it diffi-

cult for fathers to visit with children for long periods of time and/or in constant manner. In addition, economic instability seems to compound the
negotiation of fatherhood roles and behaviors. Daily activities revolve
around not only concerns about their children's well-being but also encompass men's transportation needs, quests for employment, and necessity to
secure food and shelter. The circumstances of poverty and unemployment
are not that uncommon. Homelessness and the lack of a permanent residence among African American men, women, and families for example, are
a growing phenomena. Its rise in the past fifteen to twenty years is due to a
shortage of affordable rental housing, a decline in real wages, and an
increase in poverty.

In a study of eleven communities and four states, the National Coalition
for the Homeless found that from 1987 to 1997 shelter capacity more than
doubled in nine communities and three states. In two communities and two
states, shelter capacity tripled. Men are more likely to live without a permanent residence than women are and African Americans make up almost 50
percent of the estimated homeless population. African Americans too, like
other disproportionately poor populations, are overrepresented among
those who suffer from job-related injuries and mental disorders. Relative to
black women, males are more likely to be admitted to hospitals for mental
illness.

Fathers, then, are faced not only with meeting the needs of their children
but managing their own physical health and psychological well-being under
impoverished conditions (Taylor 1992; Cockerham 1990; Brown and Gary
1987). A summary of these and other literature on blacks and mental health
suggests that the prevalence of mental disorders among African Americans
are more clearly associated with poverty than with race itself, though there
exists some research to suggest that institutional and individual racism is
associated with elevated levels of stress among people of color.[3]

Overall, it seems that fathers are negotiating what they do as fathers in
consideration of limited economic and social options and opportunities.
Spending time with children is structured around survival. And for fathers,
their own survival is often more immediate than their parenting. This study
provides support to the findings of Steir and Tienda (1993), who suggest
that African American fathers make great efforts to maintain ties with their
children. It also provides evidence for their argument that a lack of economic child support is no indication that African American fathers are
marginal members of their children's family system. Although the public
tends to characterize African American live-away fathers as uncaring and

uninterested in the care and well-being of their children and places primary blame on them for their children's negative life circumstances, these findings provide little to no evidence to support such assumptions. These fathers say that their exists few if any barriers that could completely eliminate the care they feel for their children, nor are there elements that could in and of themselves, wholly impede them from being involved fathers. Barriers were not perceived as permanent obstacles. One father's words provides an example of how most fathers felt about the various barriers to their fathering:

"These things are like small bumps in the road. They might stall me a little but they ain't going to keep me from being a daddy."

Still another noncustodial father likened his experiences to a football game:

"It's like . . . I'm the quarterback. The ball's in my hands. I know what my goal is but it's not easy getting there. Sometimes my passes are intercepted, I'm tackled. But nothing can keep me down. I just get up, dust myself off, and come up with another play. Because my eye is always on the goal."

When asked to explain his football analogy, this same father responded with the following:

"You see I have control over how I want to be as a father. I know I want to be a daddy to my kids. That means I want to be there, to love them, to support them. When something knocks me down, like my car breaks down, I'm out of work, or my son's mother gives me a hard time like she does sometimes, I have the choice to just stay down or get back up. It would probably be easier to stay down—no hassles—my father was that way. But that's not my choice. My goal is to be the best father possible to my kids. So I don't let anything prevent me from doing that."

CONCLUSION: "GOT TO MAKE FATHERHOOD WORK FOR US"
The Meaning of Fatherhood for Black Men
Who Do Not Live with Their Children

*O*ur story about fatherhood for low-income black American fathers is drawing to a close. It began by asking the reader to look at fatherhood through the eyes of this category of men. Specifically, the audience was asked to place paternal attitudes and activities of these fathers in the context of their surrounding environments and then, given the circumstances of these environments, understand parenting from their perspectives. These tasks are complicated by the barrage of public reports about high school drop-out rates, teenage pregnancy, gang violence, and stark poverty among African American children. Headlines blame fathers for their children's poor life circumstances. They are considered deadbeats, absent, and common villains.

The findings from this study of black live-away fathers move us forward in the public debate about black men and their families. They broaden our analyses and lead us to better understand that low-income black live-away fathers, like all other fathers, continuously negotiate their parenting within particular social, political, cultural, and economic circumstances. These circumstances consist of historical and contemporary social and economic injustices, cultural misrepresentations, unrealistic public expectations, and vague parental agreements with the mothers of their children. In this final chapter, the reader is again asked to consider the context of black live-away fatherhood and its meaning in the fathers' world. What follows is a brief explanation of why low-income black fatherhood for them appears to contrast with the dominant paradigm. Finally, this chapter discusses the implications of these findings for social policy.

FATHERHOOD ON THE MARGINS

"The world is a beautiful place," said one father of two, "if you can ignore the trash on the streets, if you can afford to pay the rent every month and eat . . .

and then after all that, if you can still see your kids smile at the end of the day, the world is a beautiful place." Many black, low-income, live-away fathers experience life on the boundaries. Socially, economically, and culturally they hold a marginal position. The men interviewed worked for low wages and acquired low levels of education. They worked in jobs that required erratic schedules, demanded stringent emotional and physical labor, offered little opportunity for advancement, and afforded them little respect.

Most fathers expressed a desire to one day acquire a single job that would enable them to spend greater leisure time with their families and earn enough money to provide sufficiently for them. Said one father, "I just need to make enough so life is not a struggle . . . so I don't have so many worries." Their occupational aspirations did not seem unreasonable. A few shared their desire to become airplane pilots, corporate CEO's, and self-employed owners of profitable upscale businesses. However, references to these types of positions were generally made in jest and described as "dream" jobs.

Given their backgrounds, these fathers genuinely and realistically aspired for working-class employment. They verbally listed companies such as Coca-Cola, the U.S. Postal Service, United Parcel Service, city sanitation work, and other service or blue-collar occupations. They perceived that these employers would provide them with financial stability, family wages and retirement, paid vacation, health insurance, and other benefits. These were accouterments their low-wage labor, underground employment, and/or unemployment did not render. Fathers told of a few men that they knew who held or once held these types of occupations. "My uncle, he used to work for the telephone company before they laid him off . . . it was a good job, too," one father reported. "He bought himself a nice house . . . he bought his wife a nice car . . . beautiful." A thirty-six-year-old live-away father recalled his childhood neighbors building a new house "with a finished basement and a pool table" when the father was promoted to a supervisory position in a local glass manufacturing plant. Most surmised that these better-paying positions were today difficult to come by, and were virtually nonexistent in the areas surrounding their communities.

They were correct in their assessment. Such manufacturing plants and employers continue to move away from cities and communities that house a disproportionate number of poor African American residents. Many of these fathers lived in East St. Louis, Illinois; Houston, Texas; Chicago, Illinois; St. Louis, Missouri; Detroit, Michigan; and other cities that at one time held economic promise for low-skill workers. Not having access to employment with higher wages and better benefits pained fathers. Said one father,

"It's like it makes you feel bad when the snowcone van comes around and you don't have money to give to your child for snowcones . . . and yet and still, he sees all his little friends get to buy a snowcone." Another father recalled the anguish and guilt he felt when he did not visit his daughter on her birthday because he had been fired from his job and could not afford to purchase a birthday gift. "I figured her mother would go off on me for showing up without the present that I had promised," he said sadly. He found out weeks later that the mother of his child was angry not because he did not provide a gift but because he had chosen to simply not attend the celebration at all. In addition to the poor pay and low benefits of employment, these fathers, like black people in general, were faced with racial prejudices and individual acts of discrimination in their everyday encounters at work, on the bus, in stores, and on the streets.

WHAT FATHERS DO

For many black men, their situation has demanded that they develop an "ideal" of fatherhood at variance with dominant cultural and institutional norms. Ironically, their status has provided them with some freedom to set their own code of conduct for proper paternal behavior. This freedom has also enabled low-income, black live-away fathers to develop their own identity outside of mainstream expectations and norms. They are, as Le Roi Jones (1963) explains "natural nonconformists" because "being Black in a society where such a state is an extreme liability is the most extreme form of nonconformity available."[1]

Regardless of black men's uncertain status, social policies, cultural media, and social institutions direct black people to assimilate and adopt European American mainstream conceptualizations of proper attitudes and behavior. Yet, many researchers have argued that social conditions continuously deny them the means by which to live such a lifestyle. Consequently, black men are expected to assimilate into the dominant society and accept mainstream values and conceptualizations of fatherhood as if these ideals correctly reflect their own reality.[2]

Social researchers and social policy creators tend to view fatherhood in a manner significantly different from that held by the men in my study. Family policies generally reflect a patriarchal perspective that is much in keeping with the historical "ideal" of a father as family head. In this study, black live-away fathers have chosen an alternative to this tradition.

CAREGIVING AND FORMATION FUNCTION

According to the fathers in this study, "ideal" live-away fathers are those who spend as much time as possible with their children. This, they perceived, was their primary paternal function. A review of parenting literature indicates that the amount of time fathers spend with their children is less important than the quality of their interaction. Even without this formal knowledge, most of these fathers attempted to involve themselves as much as possible in the daily aspects of their children's care. Fathers reported managing various responsibilities for their children's care. They picked their children up after school, counseled them, and listened to their concerns. They prepared their meals and helped with homework. When they felt mothers were weak in terms of disciplining their children, they stepped in to fill the void.

Similar to married fathers who reside full-time with their children, these men interacted with children in recreational activities as well. While they took them to various public events, they were more likely to entertain their children with low-cost activities. Such activities would include visiting with relatives, playing cards, eating lunch occasionally at McDonald's, going to the park, or simply taking a leisurely stroll. These findings strengthen research indicating that many live-away fathers may involve themselves extensively in children's caretaking. Moreover, these findings indicate that fathers may continue their involvement throughout their children's development—from infancy through adolescence.

This contrasts with studies indicating that among those experiencing divorce, noncustodial fathers decrease involvement with children over time, particularly those who were "very" involved with children prior to divorce. What this may also suggest is that if the two groups were empirically compared, never-married black live-away fathers may be more "consistently" involved with their children than those experiencing divorce. Research also suggests that married fathers who reside with their children spend about one-third of the time mothers do in direct interaction with their offspring. Additionally, they are less likely than mothers to take on responsibilities for child care, such as changing diapers, giving meals, and making medical appointments. Rather, play time takes up much more of their time with children. Many fathers in this study reported spending time with children. Their involvement was at varying levels. Some never visited their children while others cared for them on an almost daily basis. Moreover, for those who visited or cared for their children one or more times a week, what they provided may not differ markedly from the social and emotional care provided by married fathers who reside full-time with their children.[3]

The implications of this call into question the purpose of marriage as it concerns the care and well-being of children, and the impact of divorce on relationships between fathers and offspring. It may be that having never-married parents and a "very involved father" is better for the emotional stability and well-being of children than having lived with married parents who subsequently divorce. Certainly, the question warrants investigation, given the rate of divorce and rising numbers of single-parenting homes in most demographic groups across the United States.

Ideally, mothers explained, fathers should be sufficient economic providers. However, mothers readily modified this ideal to better fit the financial situations of low-skill, low-income fathers. In so doing, mothers agreed with fathers that the paternal time spent with children was more significant than the receipt of child support, this did not mean they were completely satisfied with the extent of fathers' activities in this arena. Many expressed disappointment at what was, from their perspective, flaccid male parenting. Some mothers felt men could provide more time for their children than they actually did, particularly since they did not often provide substantial child support. Fathers did not disagree with this, but felt that pressures from work, multiple sets of children, and physical distance from children's homes strained their ability to be accessible and involved at an optimum level. Mothers acknowledged that black men in general were in a difficult position in today's contemporary social and economic spheres. However, they were often reluctant to accept men's excuses for not spending more time with their children. As one mother stated: "Women always have to make time for their kids, and we always do . . . Fathers shouldn't be able to get off from that." Mothers too, were stressed economically and would have liked more financial support from fathers. Again, there was general acknowledgment that men also were economically "strapped." Women generally felt that to castigate men and/or pursue them for more money may have a counter-effect. From their experiences, it would discourage men from visiting their children, and from contributing what little economic assistance they did provide.

LEGAL BONDS

Family policies and social institutions expect all fathers to provide their children with a legal bond to their ancestry and formal ties to paternal kin. In this study, none of the men indicated this was a primary element of their roles and functions as fathers. Fathers generally felt it was important for their children to know them as their "daddy." However, knowing paternity was not equated with a legal bond. Whether or not children carried their father's surnames seemed of little significance to live-away fathers or custodial mothers. The majority of these men's children did not have their fathers' respective surnames. As in times of slavery, children had access to both maternal and paternal kinship networks despite the absence of sanctioned bonds between father and child.

Traditionally, European American fathers have provided their offspring with paternal surnames so that children are legally recognized as their father's child. In this way, children were able to reap the benefits of significant financial support and inheritance that formal ties to their ancestry might bring. But this particular intent has little meaning for low-income black live-away fathers. In terms of material inheritance, property, wealth, and accompanying accouterments, these men have virtually nothing to pass on to their offspring. "All I can give him," said one father in reference to his three-year-old son, "is my bills."

PROVIDER

In U.S. society, how fathers function in their provider/breadwinner role is the basis for measuring their success or failure. Interviewed black live-away fathers consciously rejected this element as a defining feature of their success or failure as fathers. Furthermore, they considered it to be one of the least important functions of their fatherhood. Those that paid child support on a consistent basis expressed various reasons for doing so. For a few fathers, child support was a legal matter in which their nonpayment could result in legal action against them. One never-married father lived with his children and their mother for twelve years before separating from them. Without a court order, this father willingly provided consistent monthly economic support to his children. He explained:

> "I have always given them everything ... my constant love and attention ... as much of my time as possible ... and I make a good living so I give that, too. ... I don't need no judge coming between me and my kids ... I told her [the children's mother] as long as it stays between me and you then I'll take care of my own."

Still other fathers stated that they used child support as a means to make up for the lack of time they spent with their children. Yet, no father viewed the provider role as the most important aspect of his fathering. Nor did they use this as a criteria with which to rate their performance as fathers.

For these fathers, children were primarily cared for by their mothers or another maternal family member. In addition, various maternal and paternal kinfolk provided an array of new and "hand-me-down" goods—clothing, toys, shoes, linens, and furniture that in most cases neither parent could altogether afford to purchase. For most of these fathers at least one set of their children qualified for and received government welfare benefits at some point during their lives, regardless of fathers' economic situation. Welfare benefits addressed children's essential needs—health care, nutrition requirements, and housing; however, no welfare allowances alone were sufficient. Kin networks, social service organizations (food pantries, etc.) contributed to the survival of women and their children. Although such benefits and familial assistance did not guarantee a child the best quality of life, they nonetheless provided fathers and mothers with some sense of comfort.

Although fathers generally looked to others to assume the primary provider role for their children, they looked to themselves to "improve" their children's quality of life. They worked and sought higher education so that in the future they could help their children. In this respect, they expressed attitudes similar to those of custodial black fathers. Like their custodial counterparts, these fathers had great dreams for their offspring, and expected them to attain both academic and professional success (Robinson et al. 1985).

WHAT MOTHERS WANT FROM THEIR CHILDREN'S DADDIES

Despite their circumstances, fathers in this study well understood what policy makers and politicians expected of them as fathers. Recent welfare policies demand that states assign paternity to children and secure formal child support from fathers regardless of their economic circumstances. What was unclear to fathers in this study, was that the mothers of their children tended to harbor ideals and standards of fatherhood that were similar to those espoused through social policy. They reluctantly relinquish their right to demand child support for fear of what their children may lose in the long run.

For example, custodial mothers of children are compelled to reveal paternity information or face the potential penalties that include the loss of much-needed welfare benefits. However, many of the mothers in this study were reluctant about pursuing fathers for formal payments. Many receive some informal, though inconsistent, support from children's fathers. Consequently, they were concerned that formal pursuit of consistent financial support would not only discourage men from visiting their children but might possibly land fathers in jail if they are unable to meet payment terms. Mothers were also reluctant to pursue child support for another reason: when fathers provide child support through state agencies, the state benefits received for their children are reduced. Moreover, what low-income fathers are able to provide through state agencies does not significantly improve their living conditions.

Nevertheless, mothers often reported feelings of anger toward fathers for not doing more to provide for their children. Fathers, on the other hand, tended to feel they were doing the best they could economically, given the dire straits they often experienced. They felt that relative to their fathers, they were "pretty good" dads. They also felt that mothers had, at least, some support from state and other public and private agencies, which presumably made up for many of the things they could not give. Still, fathers recognized that even these sources did not provide enough, and maintained informal arrangements with the mothers of their children. Upon request, fathers attempted to help mothers and children with purchases of food, clothing, shoes, school supplies, and other needs. They also used various sources to get toys and other extra items for their children. At the time of their interviews, few of these fathers were paying child support through official means. They did, however, feel that there was often more they could do in terms of the social and emotional role they played in their children's lives.

"BUMPS IN THE ROAD"

Live-away parenting was not always easy. Fathers negotiated their paternal activities in the context of unfriendly attitudes and behaviors from some of the mothers of their children, the lack of support and guidance they received from their own parents, and employment and formal education schedules. Findings from past research on divorced live-away fathers suggest that such circumstances often serve as barriers, inhibiting men's ability to parent their children. Interviewed fathers perceived these elements as making it more difficult to perform fatherhood functions but not necessarily as "barriers" preventing them from doing what they desired to do for their children. One father referred to these "barriers" as "bumps in the road." They were considered small hurdles easily overcome by a determination to be a good father. In fact, these fathers perceived few if any permanent obstacles to their parenting. A "lack of time" and "physical proximity away from children" were the primary hurdles fathers felt that they were constantly leaping. Each was due primarily to fathers having multiple jobs, multiple families, and multiple sets of children. Mostly, these elements were considered quite simply as negative aspects of live-away fatherhood, of which fathers had little control.

Although fathers' relationships sometimes posed problems for their parenting, they were also a source of strength, providing support to their ability to perform the tasks of fatherhood. Assessing the gate-keeping activities of the mothers of their children was complex. Women generally felt their words and actions encouraged fathers' participation. From their perspective, it was often their encouragement that moved fathers to maintain involvement. From men's view, mothers were simultaneously encouraging and controlling. Women seemed to control when fathers could and could not visit with children, and enlisted the assistance of significant others (boyfriends, mothers, sisters, aunts, brothers, etc.) when fathers did not abide by their rules. Consequently, fathers expressed feelings of powerlessness. They sometimes felt like outsiders in their children's lives.

Nevertheless, most women encouraged fathers to spend time with their children, and fathers perceived that this was the most important expectation of them. Similar to the findings of Stack (1974, 1986) fathers tended to participate in their children's household as a close "friend" to the family. They ran errands, provided child care and transportation, performed yard work, and rendered various other services. In exchange, they sometimes were treated as one of the family. Mothers often provided fathers with meals, allowed them to relax around the house and watch television, and allowed them to spend time with the children in their home.

The mothers of fathers in this study also provided fathers a source of support and encouragement. Fathers' mothers encouraged their sons to spend time with their children, provided sons with comfort, and provided them with advice on childrearing and life in general. In times of disagreements, they also served as mediators between their sons and the mothers of their son's children. One woman recalled that out of anger and disappointment, she prevented her children's father from visiting with them for three months. She also refused to accept any gifts or money he offered the children. When his prodding to reconsider proved unsuccessful, the father simply took the items to his mother and the woman's mother. These women made certain the items reached their destination. "My children still needed to know I cared about them even though I did their mother wrong," the father explained. The mother agreed and relented. After some time, the two began communicating again.

THE DIFFERENCE BETWEEN FATHERS AND DADDIES

Fathers distinguished between two types of fathers—those that were "just" fathers and those that acted as "daddies." The former they described as "baby-makers," or those who demonstrated no care for their children. This type was presumed to have multiple children with different women; however, these relationships were rarely sustained for long periods of time. "Daddies" on the other hand, were those who expressed love, provided social support and companionship, and made their children a central part of their lives. No father in this study fit the "baby-maker" profile. It is important to note that at a glance some may have appeared to, particularly those who had no apparent contact with their children. Upon further exploration of their individual circumstances and decision making, even these relatively few men appeared to fall somewhere in between the definitions of "baby-maker" and "daddy." They expressed great love for their children, but felt overwhelmed and/or constricted by their circumstances. They also seemed to foresee few if any potential opportunities to change their situations. "Daddies" explained that they learned their father role through trial and error and from their own parents.

Mothers of fathers in particular, provided incentive and inspiration for sons "to do right" by their children—that is, spend time and be a "daddy" to them. Yet, the lack of interaction between men and their own fathers also inspired them to be good daddies. Similar to married fathers mentioned in Blankenhorn's *Fatherless America* (1995), these men were attempting to be better fathers to their children than they felt their fathers had been to them.

Not all fathers were able to negotiate the demands of parenting into their daily lives. Some fathers were quite literally absent from their children's lives. However, none fit the stereotype of the uncaring, selfish, absentee parent circulating in popular media. On the contrary, these fathers expressed deep concern for their children's well-being, and shared emotional accounts of how their disengagement from parenting occurred. Many reported their absence was in the best interests of their children. Their ability to parent was overwhelmingly impaired by what seemed to be overlapping experiences in two or more of the following life circumstances: substance abuse, illegal employment, incarceration, and contention between themselves and the mothers of their children. Additionally, some of these fathers appeared to have experienced acute poverty as children themselves and lacked significant sources of social support that may have strengthened their ability to co-parent. While involved fathers tussled with similar obstacles, they seemed to describe having access to various forms of social and economic support throughout their childhood, during pregnancy, and following the birth of their children. Several absent fathers generally felt confounded by their situations and/or felt that their ability to change their situation for their children would be a difficult and complicated task.

NEVER-MARRIED CO-PARENTING FAMILIES: AN INCOMPLETE INSTITUTION

Noncustodial fatherhood was a formal aspect of American slavery. Furthermore, from this period on, the nonresident father-custodial mother family form was sustained through social, economic, and political institutions. Never-married childbearing and co-parenting is historically established and persists in significant proportions in black communities. However, as an institution in U.S. society, it is quite incomplete. Despite its increasing prevalence among most demographic groups in the United States, it has yet to be accepted and instituted as a legitimate alternative to the nuclear family.[4]

Relative to laws and norms that protect and inform bonds within marital relationships, those that protect relationships and define appropriate behavior for never-married co-parents and partners are still evolving. The never-married live-away father, custodial mother, family has yet to embody a well-established structured pattern of paternal behavior that is a fundamental part of our American culture. What is more, the state's primary emphasis on paternal financial "responsibility" is complicated by the low and inconsistent earnings of many black fathers.

Low-income black fathers and the mothers of their children seem to be developing a definition of fatherhood and a pattern of behavior that best fits these economic circumstances. The mothers of their children, who are also economically deprived, often do their best to maintain paternal ties, even if it means relinquishing their right to child support. Thus, even the development of "child support payments" as a paternal norm for low-income men remains problematic. Custodial mothers and live-away fathers find themselves negotiating and defining their social roles, functions, and interactions with little institutional guidance or support. Consequently, fathers are often unclear about what mothers expect of them as parents. Mothers are constantly assessing and reassessing means to improve fathers' paternal sensibilities and behaviors. This is particularly difficult because there seems to exist so little general public understanding or verbal agreement on what fathers are supposed to do as live-away dads.

REDEFINING FATHERHOOD AND ADAPTING POLICIES TO FAMILIES

Fathers in this study seemed to discuss fatherhood in a way that best preserved their sense of accomplishment. Their definition of primary paternal roles and functions placed meaning in what they were best able to do for their children. To do otherwise would serve to inhibit their potential as parents and to set themselves up for possible failure as men and as fathers. Their definition of the most important aspects of fatherhood comes from their own interactions with significant others and from their understanding of life's options. It is also within these micro- and mesosystems that live-away fathers look for and find approval for their father functions. Theirs is a "bottom-up" perspective of live-away fatherhood that draws from the daily lives of those most affected by social policy decisions. It is unlike the "top-down" view of the world that characterizes the practices of many social scientists and social policy creators.

These groups tend to view the world and define the functions of black live-away fathers in terms of the values and norms of the dominant culture. Their definition of the most "desirable" father behavior—providing child support and a paternal surname—negates the values and behaviors of those who hold dissimilar views. At a minimum it places a lesser value on opposing perspectives. Thus, while black live-away fathers express a view of fatherhood that is based on their reality, theirs is a fatherhood that is provided little to no formal support or legitimacy. Social policies addressing child support and support for black fatherless families in general do not factor in the worldview of black live-away fathers. Overall, social policy efforts are far removed from the daily experiences of black men and women. For this reason, Christopher Jencks (1992) argues that many black men and women feel justified in carrying out alternative and adaptive means of survival to provide for themselves and the well-being of their children.

Critics might point out, perhaps correctly, that the evidence presented by fathers in this study is influenced by the tendency people have to present themselves in a favorable light. In fact, measuring the effects of mothers' and fathers' attitudes and behaviors on children's well-being were beyond the scope of this study. Consequently, conclusions drawn are suggestive rather than definitive. Nevertheless, it seems black live-away fathers are developing their own form of fatherhood despite a steady barrage of negative social messages, myths, and negative stereotypes. This attests to the importance black men place on their father/child bonds. Evaluating their fatherhood strictly in terms of the dominant Western paradigm undermines and disregards the subtle strength of what they do provide and can potentially provide for the well-being of their children.

MOVING FORWARD: IMPROVING CIRCUMSTANCES FOR PARENTS AND CHILDREN IN BLACK NONCUSTODIAL FATHER FAMILIES

Social policy attempting to address the emotional, social, and economic well-being of black children has—to date—been largely ineffective. Relative to other groups black children continue to have higher rates of poverty, juvenile delinquency, teenage pregnancies, death from homicide, drug use, school dropouts, and poor health. Social policies have attempted to combat such statistics by attempting to establish children's paternity, subsequently pursuing live-away fathers for formal payment of child support and by implementing various changes in welfare policy.

FATHERHOOD INITIATIVES

The final ten years of the twentieth century have witnessed strides forward in the quest to understand and define fatherhood for noncustodial parents and children. In 1995, President Clinton challenged federal agencies to develop strategies and initiatives to encourage increased positive father involvement with noncustodial children. His challenge was in direct response to rising numbers of single-parenting families, the disproportionate level of poverty in women-headed households, and the apparent lack of consistent, formal child support many families were receiving from noncustodial fathers. One year following, a conference, hosted by Vice

President Al Gore and sponsored by the U.S. Department of Health and Human Services (HHS), the Domestic Policy Council, and the National Partnership to Reinvent Government, brought relevant public agencies together to address innovative means of encouraging father involvement with children. In 1998, Gore authored the foreword to the Federal Interagency Forum on Child and Family Statistics report, "Nurturing Fatherhood: Improving Data and Research on Male Fertility, Family Formation and Fatherhood." The report was the culmination of a national effort. It summarized the presentations and recommendation of the Conference on Fathering and Male Fertility sponsored by the National Institute of Child Health and Human Development (NICHD), the Federal Interagency Forum on Child and Family Statistics, and NICHD Family and Child Well-being Research Network.

Federal agencies' work on improving fatherhood was based on research indicating that higher levels of paternal involvement are associated with increased well-being for children. Research findings suggest that father involvement produces fewer behavioral problems in youth, lower rates of adolescent pregnancy and childbirth, and higher academic performance among children and youth. Given these findings, HHS launched several initiatives, each expected to have a distinct and overlapping role in the national effort to promote responsible fatherhood. The initiatives were intended to do the following:

1. Increase family self-sufficiency by improving child support collection, promoting employment opportunities for low-income men, and partnering with the private sector initiative, Partners for Fragile Families, to help fathers and mothers share the legal, financial, and emotional responsibilities of fatherhood;
2. Strengthen parent-child bonds by emphasizing paternity establishment and, among other items, providing block grants to states to promote access and visitation programs for noncustodial parents, and to engage fathers in the early years of their children's development;
3. Prevent premature fatherhood by increasing reproductive health outreach and information on programs to male youth, and promoting family planning services for men.

The initiative also mandated federal dollars to promote fathers involvement in their children's health care, and to improve data collection, research on fathering, and evaluation of father-centered programs.

Not unexpectedly, father involvement initiatives and efforts have not been without difficulty. Father-centered programs focusing on low-income populations are often less than ten years old, are understaffed, lack technological support, and have clients whose needs are multifaceted and overwhelming. In African American communities, programs are also faced with low numbers of clientele. The Fathers' Center in St. Louis, Missouri is one example. Such low statistics, argued Halbert Sullivan, the center's executive director, make it difficult to secure continued and additional program funding. However, he said, even the low numbers are too high when one considers the individual time and commitment that each father-client requires to successfully make it through the program. The purpose of the St. Louis program is, first and foremost, to encourage never-married and divorced low-income black fathers between the ages of eighteen and thirty-five to become more involved in their children's daily lives. However, there appears to be some contrariety between the goals of centers such as these and federal and private granting agencies. According to another center director, funders are primarily interested in the "bottom-line." "Do the men get jobs . . . do they pay child support?" rather than the extent to which fathers have improved their relationships with their children and the children's mothers.[5]

WHAT ABOUT MARRIAGE?

The Fathers Count Act of 1999 (formerly H.R. 3073), which emerged from the House Ways and Means Committee in early November, may broaden the criteria for fathers center funding. Its intent is to provide funding for counseling and job training services directed toward nonchild-support-paying fathers. Additionally, its funding provisions will strongly encourage father-centered programs to promote marriage between poor mothers and the fathers of their children, based on the assumption that two incomes will boost children out of abject destitution. However, marriage between poor mothers and poor fathers will hardly raise these families out of relative poverty. The jobs most available to low-skilled, poorly educated black fathers and mothers pay minimum wage and are insufficient to meet the many daily needs of families with children. Moreover, high rates of divorce among those who marry young and experience financial difficulty may do more psychological and emotional harm to children than no marriage at all, particularly if divorce is bitter and hostile.

The promotion of marriage between black mothers and fathers may not be a realistic option for a different reason. William Darity Jr. and Samuel L.

Myers Jr., along with other researchers, argue that one of the primary causes for the decline in two-parent families is the limited supply of men suitable for traditional husband and father roles. The ratio of marriageable black men to black women is declining over time as poor and working-class black men are pushed to the economic margins of the market. Withdrawn from the productive labor market, these men are often pulled into criminal activity and substance abuse. Consequently, they are disproportionately institutionalized in jails, prisons, treatment centers and mental health facilities. High rates of black male homicide only add to the increasing excess of women over men at all ages over fifteen and further diminishes women's opportunity to marry.[6]

Equally important, evidence from mothers in this study suggest that they may not be interested in a male-dominated marriage or household. These mothers tended to play both expressive and instrumental roles in their households. They provided everyday care, and were primary breadwinners. Many expressed a desire for fathers to be more involved with their children. However, they did not equate this to marriage. Overall, mothers did not appear willing to give up control of their children. Nor did they want husbands who might turn out to be economic liabilities. Moreover, many fathers seemed to indicate that good parenting need not be associated with marriage. Additionally, they were hesitant about taking on the burdens they felt marriage might entail and giving up the social freedoms they associated with a single life. Thus, the promotion of marriage as a means to improve the well-being of African American children may be futile in cases where neither the fathers nor the mothers really want, given the conditions of their lives, to enter such commitments.

THE RIGHT TO MOTHER

A pantheon of social critics and researchers have questioned the traditional patriarchal paradigm of fatherhood, or at least have pushed for modification of its tenets. Within the past two decades a "Men's Movement" has called upon men to find a balance between work and family. Moreover, during this period there have been a countless number of men's groups who have attempted to redefine masculinity for men and for U.S. society as a whole. Such groups encourage men to expand what it is "to be a man" by adopting more expressive roles within their family and particularly in their relationships with their children. Recent studies indicate that the public is taking a more favorable view of men who participate in housekeeping, caregiving, and other traditionally feminine roles. The movement has primarily been directed toward middle-class white men and has received its most positive response from both men and women in this group. The struggle to redefine masculinity within a patriarchal society continues to be a strenuous uphill battle.[7]

What is most problematic about aspects of the Men's Movement and many father initiatives is that they continue to define the family and children's well-being in patriarchal terms, though it may be a kinder and gentler version. Missing from public discourse is a discussion about the rights of poor women to mother their children as unmarried parents. Many feminists may argue that federal funds directed toward father programs should more appropriately be provided for direct support of mothers and their children. Given trends in marriage, divorce, and out-of-wedlock births across race and class lines, one can expect a growing number of children will be raised in women-headed households. Given the types of occupations available to low-skilled men in all demographic groups, women must be able to support themselves and their children autonomously.

For low-skilled, low-income, single-parenting mothers in this study, the primary goals were to make enough money to live and support their children without any assistance from fathers, kin, or the state. Like the fathers of their children, poor single-parenting mothers face difficult economic circumstances. Generally earning median incomes lower than men, women of color tend to work in the lowest-paying and dirtiest occupations. While those below poverty may receive temporary assistance from the state, the amount and benefits remain insufficient to meet nutritional, medical, and other basic needs of their children. Simultaneously, the sexual division of labor places the daily care and nurturance of children squarely on the shoulders of women. Without time, awareness, or connections to the network of private agency shelters and food and clothing pantries, these women and their children are likely to suffer daily from poor shelter, clothing, and food. But even with the assistance of shelters, extended kin and child support from noncustodial fathers, their families still will likely live an impoverished life.

NONSUPPORTIVE WORK AND PAY

There are other perennial problems with attempts to connect black fathers to their children's lives based on traditional breadwinner ideals and assumptions of fatherhood. Low-income black fathers tend to be employed in work environments that inhibit fathers' ability to balance work and family. They tend to hold jobs that require long hours and hard labor. They generally receive few benefits such as family leave (paid or unpaid) and paid vacations; such benefits support parenting by contributing to the time men and women are able to provide to their children. In addition, these fathers tend to work at or about minimum wage. These minimal earnings barely afford them the money necessary to meet their own needs, let alone those of their children. Men who do not pay child support are subject to possible incarceration, garnishment of wages, loss of licenses, child support accrued arrearage interests plus back payments.

Recent federal welfare guidelines require mothers to name fathers on children's birth certificates and/or identify them in order to obtain and maintain government assistance. Consequently, more fathers are pushed and pulled into the judicial system. Here they may receive jail time or, at a judge's discretion, be assigned to one of the new and innovative father-centered programs. Programs like these are beginning to abound across the nation. The National Center for Fathering's Urban Fathering Initiative in Kansas City, Missouri, provides some alternatives. Among other goals, the initiative is intended to rescue fathers in the courts. It enables judges to sentence fathers, caught by the legal system, to a program intended to equip and inspire them to be better fathers for their children. The Father's Center in St. Louis has a similar strategy. Here fathers who remain in the program for a period of time and consistently meet program requirements are provided the opportunity to reduce court-awarded child support payments, sometimes to as little as $25 monthly. This provides some incentive for fathers to participate in the program, particularly if they are otherwise faced with judicial penalties. However, after two years, fathers are expected to begin full-payment of child support regardless of the pay they earn. The director explains men are expected to "at least get a minimum wage job . . . then once they have that they can move up to better paying jobs."

Realistically, rising educational demands, coupled with the decline in blue-collar employment offering living wages and benefits, means that few of these fathers will obtain anything more than subsistence wages. Moreover, the steady decline in real wages for all parents, regardless of income, make rearing children increasingly difficult. Yet, relative to those with higher incomes, poor mothers and fathers will likely have the most difficult time providing a decent standard of living for their children.

SUPPORTING NEVER-MARRIED CO-PARENTS
THROUGH SOCIAL POLICY AND COMMUNITY

American families are increasingly resembling the predominant African American noncustodial father-custodial mother family form. Furthermore, regardless of race and ethnicity, noncustodial fathers frequently do not provide for the financial security of their children, even when they can afford to do so. Addressing the experiences of low-income black fathers and their children may inevitably enable social policy makers and social work practitioners to better understand and assist other groups in similar circumstances.

Low-income live-away fathers must be guaranteed full employment at livable wages if they are expected to fulfill their parental financial obligations. At the macro level, local, state, and federal governments must legislate both for all working people if they hope for these parents to have the means to provide enough money to boost themselves and their children out of poverty. Under current conditions and policy emphases, women with children generally gain access to breadwinner's income solely through marriage. Black women are less likely than other demographic groups to marry and/or find mates that earn breadwinner wages. Unless livable wages are instituted, the problem of childhood poverty will remain unbounded in the United States, whether or not parents reside in the same household as their shared offspring (Orloff 1993).

But men's legitimate employment and higher wages alone will not sufficiently improve the well-being of black children. The nurturing and caring aspects of live-away parenting must be further defined and strengthened through institutional and community support. Government attempts to improve the well-being of poor black children and all children will continue to be ill-effective unless researchers and policy creators adapt their perspective of low-income black never-married parents to their reality. Social policy creators must recognize the primary elements of black live-away fatherhood as a "legitimate alternative" to the traditional patriarchal notions of fatherhood, particularly under current economic conditions. Additionally, the definition of fatherhood or the "good father" must be broadened to include the varying characteristics and experiences of low-income black families. Once a more inclusive definition is developed, policy creators can identify and more adequately support family members through legislation and public discourse.

To accomplish this task is complex. Researchers and policy creators must continue to seek to find a balance between the economic provider and nurturing roles. Current policies concerning child support continue to place primary emphasis on the economic support fathers are expected to provide for their children. The everyday nurturance and care for children continues to be gendered labor, and tends to fall most heavily on the shoulders of women. Relatively little importance is placed on the social or emotional relationship between fathers and their children. Yet, the well-being of poor children requires an investment in both time and money, and each element should be a calculated factor in the determination of child support (Klawitter 1994). Some live-away fathers can provide money and time; still others can provide more of one element than the other. Feminists have been arguing for decades that an economic formula should be applied to the caregiving and nurturant roles and functions of childrearing. So too should such a formula be calculated and applied to live-away father/child and mother/child relationships to insure that children are receiving at least a minimum of what they need for emotional, social, and economic well-being.

Presently, there is no adequate systematic means of accounting for the amount and type of care fathers provide to their children. Nor is their an adequate means of accounting for the informal economic support black live-away fathers seem to provide. Yet, while popular media, and politicians, and researchers continue to associate the presence of a father with positive well-being and quality of life outcomes for children, they have failed to adequately articulate what it is about fathers that directly links to this phenomenon. Is it for example, the financial support they provide to the household? Is it their physical presence in the household? Is it the amount and/or type of quality and interactive time they spend with children? Or, is it some or all of the above?

Is it possible to be a good father and not provide significant financial support to one's child? For some directors of father centers in black communities the answer is yes, especially if fathers are doing the most they can for their children. According to one director: "Men want to be fathers to their children and must learn how to do so despite their inconsistent and difficult financial state." He and other program facilitators also argue that men have increased self-esteem and self-confidence, and are more patient and willing to communicate with the mothers of their children, when they are working at legally well-paying jobs. This, they contend, enables them to feel a sense of power in daily parental decision making that affects their children's behavior and well-being. Thus, these programs find themselves attempting to strike a balance between nurturing and economic parenting activities that best fit the lives of their clients.

The goals of father-centered programs would be much easier if they were expressly aided by support from other community entities. In his foreword to Andrew Billingsley's recent work on the black church and social reform, *Mighty Like a River* (1999), C. Eric Lincoln argues that the church is a "vitalizing resource" for all Americans and a "defining reference" in the black community. Faith-based organizations in black communities have historically taken the lead toward social reform. Today they remain the most well-organized and entrenched networks within black America. Moreover, their leadership is often sought by politicians and policy makers for commentary and assessment of conditions for black families.

Yet, under current social and economic conditions, churches must become more ardent and vigilant social activists if they intend to continue as leaders for social change. Their leadership and membership must work as agents to address secular issues confronting black families. Moreover, dwindling resources among the poorest churches and black communities demands that faith-based organizations collaborate with other institutions and activist organizations to identify and address the needs of black mothers, fathers, and children.

Many churches have responded to the sustained secular crises among black families. Over two-thirds of 635 churches surveyed in Billingsley's study operated community outreach programs, a majority of which consisted of adult family support. However, effective support to custodial mothers and noncustodial fathers requires that church leadership and program coordinators think holistically and beyond traditional notions of family. Custodial mothers, live-away fathers, grandparents, aunts, uncles, and fictive kin all play a significant role in raising black children within the noncustodial father family form. Programs should seek to help family members to define the roles of family members and enhance positive communication and interaction, particularly between mothers and fathers.[8]

Although it exists separately from a church, the Lutheran Child and Family Services Fathers Center of East St. Louis, Illinois, attempts to do just that. Here, the Reverend Phoenix Barnes brings divorced, separated, and never-married fathers and mothers together to discuss their familial circumstances, their parental options and choices, and identify and define their appropriate roles as co-parents. The program also provides opportunities for fathers to seek employment and continued education. It also enables them to spend quality time with their children, and arranges familial outings that neither parent could otherwise afford.

Faith-based programs must also be prepared to address many of the problems that may further inhibit familial well-being, such as adult unemployment, substance abuse, incarceration, and low levels of education. Most importantly, as "vitalizing" agents, churches must take the lead in supporting and institutionalizing noncustodial father family forms by articulating their circumstances and needs to social service agencies, educational systems, and cultural media, institutions that can help legitimize this family form. But churches, social service agencies, and the educational system are only part of the solution. They cannot be wholly effective without further attention paid to living wages for poor and working-class people and women's economic ability to develop and maintain autonomous households.

Inevitably, what poor and working-class black live-away fathers actually do for their children rests with society's ability to provide them access to sufficient economic means. It is equally contingent on the legitimacy and support granted to their paternal status. It is also based on their ability to interact and communicate with those who assist in the co-parenting of their children. It is further influenced by black men's ability to define and voice their own vision of fatherhood in the context of their collective economic and social circumstances. For those men who have little else to offer, the provision of nurturance, love, and affection are priceless aspects of fatherhood. Said one father, "No matter what anybody else say, we black men have got to make fatherhood work for *us* . . . All our babies want is their daddies, and we have got to decide what that means."

NOTES

INTRODUCTION: FATHERS' LIVES IN CONTEXT

1. Walter Mosley is a contemporary African-American male, award-winning fiction writer. The character for which his work is best known is Easy Rawlins, a black male detective who becomes a father at various points in the author's series. See *Devil in a Blue Dress, A Red Death, White Butterfly, Black Betty, Gone Fishin'*, and *A Little Yellow Dog*. Also meet one of his latest male characters, Socrates Fortlow, in *Always Outnumbered, Always Outgunned*, which was also developed into an HBO movie.

2. The proportion of black children living below the poverty level was approximately the same in 1995 as it was in 1970. The percentage is almost two and a half times that experienced by white children in the United States in 1995. For Hispanics, the percentage was 39.3 percent in the same year. For a summary of these statistics and more on families, see Chadwick and Heaton, eds., 1998 (table H3–3, p. 252).

3. See Angel and Angel 1993, for a discussion of the health and well-being of African-American children and custodial mothers. Their experiences are compared to those of Latinos and European Americans; also see the U.S. Bureau of the Census 1992.

4. See Billingsley 1968, 1992; Herskovitz 1941; McDaniel 1994; Sudarkasa 1980, 1997; Wade Nobles 1974a, 1974b, 1978.

5. E. Franklin Frazier 1931, 1939; Daniel P. Moynihan 1965. For a brief and concise critique of Frazier's analysis, see Herbert G. Gutman 1975. And see Walter Allen 1995 for a concise critique of Frazier's work on black low-income families. Allen argues (and I agree) that some of the major problems of Frazier's analysis are that he (1) failed to specify the societal-level processes argued to determine black familial experiences, (2) denies the legitimacy of aspects of black familial problems that differ from normative white patters, and (3), which is referred to in this paragraph, implicitly attributes the economic deprivation of black families to cultural characteristics. Also see Walter Allen (1978), "The Search for Applicable Theories of Black Family Life"; Nathan Hare 1976, for a critique of Moynihan's "Temple of Pathology" thesis and its failure to adequately account for racial oppression. Allen also offers support for this critique. And see Oscar Lewis 1972.

6. Engerman 1977; Furstenberg, Hershberg, and Modell 1975; Scanzoni 1971; Ladner 1971. Also, again see Allen 1995.

7. John L. McAdoo (1993), "The Roles of African American Fathers: An Ecological Perspective," argues the logic of using this more holistic approach. For a full discussion of grounded theory, see B. Glazer and A. Strauss 1967; B. Glazer 1978; A. Strauss and J. Corbin 1998. When using grounded theory, one does not begin with a theory and then seek to prove it. Rather, the researcher begins with a topic of study, systematically and intensively collects and analyzes data on the subject, and then inductively derives categories and theories from the data that emerges and from which the theory is grounded.

8. Mothers of children were recruited in one of two ways: (1) twenty-one mothers provided the initial contacts arranging for me to meet the fathers of their children. They were recruited in a manner similar to that used for fathers. However, 10 of these women were contacted through child care centers and social service agencies that provided services to welfare recipients. And, (2) arrangements to meet the remaining twelve participating mothers were made through the fathers of their children.

Attempts were made to make contact with the mothers of each of these fathers' children's mothers. However, most initial contacts were made with the fathers themselves. Thus, they were the primary means by which I could make contact with the mothers of their children. Some fathers were reluctant to let mothers (or anyone) know that they were participating in the study. They expressed concern about the confidentiality of their identity and their responses. Another problem was a difficulty in making meeting arrangements that fit the potential female respondent's schedule and my own schedule and deadlines. A third problem was a difficulty developing trust with mothers with whom I did not have initial personal contact. Mothers were reluctant to be interviewed over the phone if they had not initially met me "in person." Those who agreed to meet or interview over the phone were not always extremely forthcoming with regard to responding to questions. Several seemed preoccupied with concerns about the nature of the study, the purpose of certain questions, how I came to meet their children's father, and the nature of that relationship.

Adult children of noncustodial fathers were recruited through word-of-mouth, snowball techniques, and other means similar to those used for fathers and mothers. These adult children were not the children of men in this study. Rather, they ranged in age from 76 to 93, and 17 of the 21 adult children were women. Interviews with elderly men seemed complicated by the following: those contacted tended to have very poor health and had difficulty participating in interviews, tended to live with relatives (often making it difficult to arrange interviews that satisfied the schedules of others in the household), and I had more success making contact with women than with men in this age group.

9. The term "distal" was initially used in my dissertation work on noncustodial African American fathers. However, some of my dissertation committee members had reservations about its use, suggesting that it sounded too negative, technical, and emotionally unappealing. I agreed with their perception of the term and found that "live-away" is better suited to describe the fathers of this study. However, I continue to search for a more appropriate and descriptive term.

1. "THERE'S NO SUCH THING AS A GOOD BLACK FATHER"

1. White and Cones 1999. The other conclusion that White and Cones draw from the March is that "race is an inescapable complication in American life that must be resolved" (p. 7). They argue that historical and contemporary racism have created economic and social obstacles that inhibit black men from an "optimal level of male functioning."

2. Harris, Torres, and Allender 1994; Kimmel and Messner 1989 also provide elaboration in paragraph by quoting findings directly. Also see Kimmel and Messner, eds., 1989.

3. The Million Man March 1995; Majors and Mancini Billson 1992; Wilson 1987, 1986.

4. Black women, too, have been subject to equally harsh stereotypes. They are generally represented as asexual mammies and/or whorish Jezebels. These images have historically inundated media and persist to the present and served to justify oppression and rape of black women during and since slavery. Similar to men, the images of African American women generally contrast sharply with those of European Americans. There exist ample research and analyses of this pattern of representation, see bell hooks (1992) for a contemporary analysis and Deborah White (1985) for a thorough historical analysis as two examples.

5. There are many works that offer excellent discussions of African American stereotypes. As a starting point, see Sterling Brown (1933) for a thorough description of black stereotypes and an analysis of how each served a particular function during slavery, reconstruction, and the several decades following. Also see Earl Ofari Hutchinson (1997). Though the work offers little new insight and lacks some objectivity, it does provide a description of past and present stereotypes that many students will find useful. Also, for classrooms, see the film *Ethnic Notions* (California Newsreel; San Francisco).

6. See Cheryl Johnson (1993). In this study Johnson analyzed eighteen hours of television programming from one of three national networks. The station and the day of the week were randomly selected. In general, articles appearing in popular

African American magazines seem to blame black men for many of the woes in the black community and simultaneously directing them to stand up and accept their responsibility. These responsibilities included obligations to family, to communities, and to themselves to pursue success in education and employment.

Messages suggest that good black men (those who are not breaking the law, who are legally employed, responsible, and financially independent) are difficult to find. In the feature article "Why Some Good Girls Prefer Bad Guys," *Ebony*, April 2000), the author argues that you can spot a "bad" black man as he walks across the room and his general manner. The author goes on to inform the reader that relationship experts have developed five general categories of common "bad boys." These are as follows: 1) The Player—suffers from low self-esteem and needs the companionship of many women to feel good about himself; he disappears after conquering a woman sexually. 2) The Scrub—is harmless but may need to be pampered and mothered; similar to a child, he throws tantrums when he does not get his way. 3) The Womanizer—"unlike the Player, who uses many women to boost his poor self-esteem; the womanizer gets his thrills from hurting women intentionally"; he has a biological need to attract women and be attracted to them; he also has a total lack of respect for the opposite sex. 4) the Hustler—the only job these men have is hustling hardworking women for their money; "when the money runs out, he's gone." Finally, 5) the Abuser—demonstrates his power or frustration by emotionally and/or physically abusing women.

Good men are also consistently portrayed as those who achieve great economic success, drive expensive cars, and have at least one beautiful woman at their side. For example, in his January 1998 monthly editorial, Bernard Bronner, founder of *Upscale* (subtitled "The Magazine for the Success-Oriented African American") advised blacks to choose their vehicles with care. After all he counseled, "the car not only serves as a means of transportation, but a symbol of success . . . style and profile in luxury with a Rolls Royce, Ferrari, Lamborghini. . . . or Lincoln Navigator." Overall, it appears that black popular literature provides primarily one of two images, the black male as a victim of racial oppression in need of spiritual, community, and familial motivation, and as a lazy brute who will not perform his responsibilities without such encouragement.

7. In 1998 President Clinton commissioned an advisory panel to study race relations in America. The panel was titled "Advisory Board to Race Initiative" and was chaired by John Hope Franklin, famed African American historian. After 15 months of research the panel provided a final report titled "One American in the 21st Century." The panel submitted the report to the president in September 1998. Kerner Commission 1968; Majors and Billson 1992.

8. The Franklin study also found that 63 percent of Latinos felt their demographic group was misrepresented on entertainment television. Consequently, in July of

1999, the NAACP announced the launching of the Television and Film Diversity Initiative to monitor the major television networks (ABC, CBS, NBC, and Fox). Their public strategy consisted of purchasing stocks in the major networks, publicly castigating the television industry, and threatening a boycott. La Raza, a Latino activist organization launched a similar initiative soon after.

9. Though empirical studies have found that children from single parenting households are economically disadvantaged compared to their counterparts in two-parent homes (see the work of Sara McLanahan in particular), there exist evidence that African American families' have historically provided meaningful social and emotional support and care for their children: Carol Stack 1974; Dorothy Roberts 1998; Cynthia R. Daniel 1998; Jacqueline Jones 1985; Andrew Billingsley 1969, 1992. For research suggesting that fathers have traditionally had a presence of some sort in black families, see Borchert 1980 and Stack 1974. Black single parenting mothers are less likely to receive child support payments than most other demographic groups—this is documented in various sources; however, see Edin and Lein 1997, for a discussion. For fathers' residence and involvement, see S. McLanahan 1999; Rivara, Sweeney, and Henderson 1986, for a longitudinal analysis of African American adolescent fathers, the majority of whom provided care and/or financial support for their children despite problems of unemployment.

2. SLAVERY, CIVIL WAR, AND RECONSTRUCTION

1. Genovese 1972; Gutman 1976; White 1985.

2. Genovese 1972; Gutman 1976; White 1985.

3. Also Genovese 1989; Fogel and Engerman 1974.

4. Genovese 1972:184–85; J. Jones 1985; D. White 1985.

5. *American Slave*, Georgia Narratives, 12:113. George P. Rawick, ed., *The American Slave: A Composite Autobiography*, is a 19-volume series of narratives collected primarily through the Works Progress Administration's Federal Writers Project during the years 1936–1938.

6. *American Slave*, Georgia Narratives, 12:60.

7. *Slave Narratives, Egypt, 1945*, 156–57.

8. Genovese 1972; J. Jones 1985; D. White 1983.

9. Berlin 1992; Genovese 1972.

10. Genovese 1972; J. Jones 1985; D. White 1985.

11. *American Slave*, Mississippi Narratives, 7:379–85 (Hannah Chapman).

12. *American Slave*, Mississippi Narratives, 7:61–62 (Nettie Henry).

13. Blassingame 1979; Escott 1979.

14. Higginson 1970; J. Jones 1985.

15. Higginson 1970; J. Jones 1985; Berlin et al. 1992.

16. *American Slave*, Texas Narratives, 4:174 (Martha Spence Bunton).

17. J. Jones 1985; Berlin and Rowland 1997; Escott 1979.

18. Berlin and Rowland 1997:203.

19. See J. H. Franklin 1997; R. Carnoy 1994; Takaki 1993.

20. Donna Franklin (1997), like Eric Foner, argues that the movement for black men to establish their patriarchy was strengthened by their participation in the Union Army because they, more than women, were more directly involved in the struggle for freedom. She and Eric Foner argue that black men during this period were attempting to "reassert" their leadership position in the family and ownership over wives, children, and labor. I argue that men could not possibly *reassert* rights that they never historically held as privilege. Also see John Hope Franklin and Alfred A. Moss Jr. 1998; Gutman 1976.

21. Billingsley 1969; Frazier 1939; Furstenberg, Hershberg, and Modell 1975.

22. Borchert 1980; Reed 1929. See the scholarly article by Virginia Young 1970. Also see Billingsley (1993) for a summary of trends in marriage among African Americans.

23. This is a study of the experiences of African American unwed mothers in New York City. It should be noted that in 59 percent of the unwed mother cases she studied, mothers resided with the fathers of their children.

3. "TIMES ARE JUST GOING TO GET WORSE . . ."

1. Robert Bullard 1989:28. Bullard summarizes the boom-and-bust period of the 1970s and 1980s and its effect on black Houstonians. In the years immediately following emancipation, blacks were able to acquire land, build businesses, and communities in several of the city's wards. While these wards remain predominantly black, property and businesses are no longer in the hands of those who reside there.

2. See U.S. Bureau of the Census 1990, General Populations and Housing Characteristics, and Labor Market data. See data at http://factfinder.census.gov.java.prod/da. . . . fac.Community FactsViewPage.

3. For an analysis and description of emotional labor, see Arlie Hochschild's work *The Managed Heart*. Although it is a qualitative study of the experiences of contemporary airline attendants, the concept readily applies to many service occupations held by African American men throughout the century.

4. Kasarda 1989, 1994; Ronald Taylor 1994:147–66.

5. In 1996, Congress passed and President Bill Clinton signed the *Personal Responsibility and Work Opportunity Reconciliation Act of 1996* (PRWORA). Prior to its passage, Aid to Families with Dependent Children (AFDC) was the essence of states'

monetary assistance to poor African American families with children. AFDC was an entitlement that the state was obligated to provide to all those who qualified. Most importantly, it provided an economic safety net to the nation's poorest citizens. Among other things, PRWORA replaced this safety net with Temporary Assistance to Needy Children (TANF). With TANF, the government is no longer obligated to provide for poor families or their children. The program places a five-year time limit on cash assistance and does not guarantee living wages or any type of job afterward. (Individual states have the power to enforce a shorter time limit if they choose.)

6. Pinkney 1984. For annual statistics about the conditions of black America, see also National Urban League (1998). Pinkney explains the difference between equality of principle and equality of practice. Legislative and judicial acts occurring between 1954 and 1968 elevated the citizenship status of black Americans. This provided them with "equality in principle." However, he argues, deep-rooted racial discrimination in employment, education, housing, etc. has maintained racial inequality. Thus, "equality in practice" has never been realized.

7. See also R. Taylor 1994; Crockett 1998; and U.S. Bureau of Labor Statistics, *Annual Average Tables from Jauary 2000 Issue of Employment Earnings* (www.bls.gov/cpsaatab.htm).

8. See U.S. Bureau of the Census, Current Population Reports, 1993: also see Jewell 1988; R. Taylor 1994; Gibbs 1988.

9. *The State of Black America* (National Urban League 1998) provides a general description and analysis of trends associated with black's experiences in education and the labor market. Additionally, Laura Horn and C. Carroll (1999) assess the characteristics of post-secondary students who depart school and either stay out permanently or stop and restart enrollment at varying times. Black men in general tend to have characteristics that fit stop outs and stay outs.

10. See also U.S. Bureau of the Census, census.gov/population/www/socdemo/educattn.html (table 8).

11. In *Savage Inequalities*, Jonathan Kozol (1992) describes the bleak academic environment of East St. Louis and other schools in low-income communities. Children in these poor schools are provided with an education that maintains their social and economic status. In contrast to their wealthier counterparts, they receive their education in schools that lack current books, labs, and other academic materials. Additionally, children often walk to school through neighborhoods teeming with pollution, empty burned-out, lead-filled buildings. Lack of air conditioning, inadequate plumbing, and poorly paid teachers create an inconducive learning environment.

12. The Sentencing Project maintains up-to-date data on incarceration by race and by gender. They may be contacted at: www.sentencingproject.org.

13. Some information on fathers in prison may be obtained from P.A.C.T., 2836 HempHill, Fort Worth, Texas, 76110, one of many organizations developed to address the needs and issues of incarcerated parents and their families. Missions, goals, and programs of such national and state organizations can be viewed on the Internet. Generally, contact phone numbers and addresses are provided on respective websites. Also see the Bureau of Justice Statistics, U.S. Dept. of Justice (ojp.usdoj.gov/bjs).

14. Staples (1990) attempts to theoretically link disproportionate substance abuse among blacks to racism and economic exploitation and marginality. By summarizing past research and statistics, he argues that a lack of employment and powerlessness among lower income black men have created the "opportunity for self-destruction through the use of alcohol and drugs, fratricidal violence and suicide." Their use and abuse of drugs is more public, which makes them more likely to experience an arrest and subsequent incarceration; also see Jewell 1988.

PART 2: EXPECTATIONS OF OTHERS

1. Kurdek's (1983) findings suggest that the relationship between custodial mothers and noncustodial fathers significantly impacts father's involvement. For more discussion on the mother's role as gatekeeper see Wallerstein and Kelly (1980), and Arendell (1986) for an examination of mothers' perception of fathers' involvement; also see Furstenberg (1995).

4. "JUST BE THERE FOR THE BABY"

1. Feldman 1987; Lowenthal and Chiriboga 1972.

2. Some fathers voiced uncertainty about how to characterize their relationships with the mothers of their children and/or reported no interest in mothers at all. Twelve fathers provided responses that fit this description. However, they tended to be fathers who were almost completely absent from the lives of their children and their children's mothers.

3. Kielcot and Fossett 1995; Lowenthal and Cheriboga 1972.

4. Parke and Brott 1999:191–93. Their list also includes the following suggestions: participate more in child care duties, take pride in the special way fathers father their children, be emotionally available, be a partner to your child's mother and not just a helper, show her respect and work to improve communication between yourself and the mother, know you legal rights with regard to your children and stay involved after separation and divorce. The author's also produced a list of "Seven Things Women Can Do to Get Fathers More Involved."

5. "BLACK MEN CAN DO BETTER"

1. National Urban League 1998; Shinagawa and Jang 1998. About 32 percent of black women were poor in 1994, compared to 11 percent of white women, 29 percent of Latinas, 15 percent of Asian women, and 23 percent of Native Americans. A similar pattern occurred for children: 46 percent of black children were poor, compared to 13.5 percent of whites, 41 percent of Latinos, 18 percent of Asian Americans, and 32 percent of Native Americans (see U.S. Bureau of the Census, Current Population Survey, 1994) and again see R. Albeda and C. Tilly (1997). Albeda and Tilly also discuss women's poverty and its relationship to geographical location. Those residing in the central cities make up 21 percent of all poor women, followed by rural areas (17.7) and the suburbs or small cities (9.9). Again, regardless of region, women and women of color are more likely to be poor.

2. Research findings by Hogan and Lichter (1995) suggest that relative to children of other demographic groups, childhood poverty among African Americans is highest regardless of their living arrangements. While parental marital relationships may reduce the rate of poverty for African American children, it will not eliminate it. Also note that women are more likely to be poor than are men, regardless of race, ethnicity, or region of the United States; see U.S. Bureau of the Census, Current Population Survey (1994); see also R. Albeda and C. Tilly (1997) for a thorough discussion of poverty statistics, how they are measured, and their limitations in providing an accurate description of poor America. See Wilson 1997; Anderson 1990, 1999; Edin and Lein 1997; J. Jones 1985; D. White 1985.

3. Arendell 1986; Furstenberg and Cherlin 1986; Geiger 1995; K. Edin and Lein 1997; Albeda and Tilly 1997.

4. Borchert 1980; Bell Kaplan 1997; Stack 1974, 1986; Edin and Lein 1997. Also see Elijah Anderson's discussion of "street families" in *Code of the Street* (1999). For a thorough study (and bibliography) addressing how women with children manage and survive in poverty, see Edin and Lein 1997; Edin 1991; Jencks 1993; Albeda and Tilly 1997.

5. Allen and Doherty 1996; Furstenberg and Nord 1985. Fathers' emphasis on social and emotional tasks were also reported in an article published from parts of this sample data (Hamer 1997).

6. See all of the following for detailed analyses and/or descriptions of women's use of various resources to sustain their economic well-being during slavery and beyond: J. Jones 1985; D. White (1985); Rainwater (1970); Sterling 1997; Schwalm 1997. See Edin and Lein (1997) for a contemporary analysis of poor women's means of utilizing surrounding resources.

7. See Luepnitz 1992.

8. Cherlin 1998; see also Kiecolt and Fossett 1995; Tucker and Mitchell-Kernan 1995.

6. WHAT FATHERS SAY THEY DO AS DADDIES

1. See Furstenberg and Nord 1985; Furstenberg et al., 1983; Hetherington, Cox, Cox 1982; Mott 1994; Seltzer and Bianchi. 1988; Arendell 1986; Furstenberg and Cherlin 1991.
2. Rivera, Sweeney, and Henderson 1986; Allen and Dohen 1996; Stack 1974, 1986.
3. Although Umberson and Williams attempted to recruit a racially diverse sample they were unsuccessful. Their sample consisted of mostly white, divorced men; also see 1999 article.
4. In chapter 5, mothers provide an analysis of fathers' disciplinarian practices. It should be noted that many felt that fathers did not know how to discipline their children appropriately. Many thought fathers were too strict, particularly with younger boys.
5. N. Williams et al. 1995; R. Taylor 1994; Jewell 1988; Patton 1981.
6. Horn made this comment during his appearance on the *Jim Lehrer News Hour*, June 17, 1996 (Horn 1997).

7. LIVE-AWAY, BUT ABSENT?

1. David Blankenhorn (1995), in *Fatherless America*, provides definitions for various live-away father formats. For example, the "deadbeat dad" is one who does not pay child support; the "visiting father" is one who, generally by way of divorce, is no longer the man of the house but someone who stops by for visits; and the "sperm father" is one who provide only the sperm to produce the child and no form of paternal care subsequent to the child's birth; also see *USA Today*, Thursday, June 17, 1999, p. 10D, "Crossing racial lines, coalition reaches to fathers." In this Health & Behavior section of the newspaper, three different articles appear about absent fatherhood. Most of the discussion emphasizes the absence of fathers in black America and discusses a recent coalition between Morehouse Research Institute and the Institute for American Values (founded by David Blankenhorn) to combat the problem of fatherlessness. In another part of the newspaper a brief summary of the findings reported by Sara McLanahan mentioned in this paragraph are also provided. Also see Valerie King (1994).
2. Fathers were asked to report how often they had contact with their children in the twelve months prior to the time of their interview.
3. See Kornfein-Rose (1992). While Kornfein's study suggests that some women who intentionally become mothers have not clearly defined the father role, her findings, for our purposes, must be read with caution. Her sample consisted of 17 well-educated, white women aged 20–30. Moreover, she provides little explanation for these

findings. Also see Elaine Bell Kaplan (1997) for an excellent ethnographic study of adolescent pregnancy among black mothers; Sara McLanahan (1999); Pamela Jordan (1995), for an exploratory analysis of mothers and fathers perceptions of one another's roles; and Allen and Doherty (1996).

4. See Chinhui Juhn (1992); Laseter (1997). Laseter provides an examination of black men's perspectives and explanations of declining labor market participation and thorough summaries of theoretical explanations of the subject.

5. Trina's living arrangements were "secret" because both she and her cousin were receiving government assistance. This required that they each be heads-of-household. However, both found that sharing an apartment made living expenses more affordable. Also, it was easier to manage the children and child care arrangements with two adults in the home.

6. Interviews with both Dwayne and Patricia were arranged by her Aunt Darlene.

7. "Single Fathers with Children Increase by 25%," New York Times, December 11, 1998; also see U.S. Bureau of the Census Special Report, Lyne Casper, Friday, December 11, 1998. Some attribute the rise in single-parenting fathers to the upsurge in men's interest in parenting (Wade Horn 1999), increasing social acceptance of men as fathers, and increase in supportive resources for fathers.

8. "AIN'T NOTHING LIKE TRYING TO BE A FATHER AND TRYING TO BE A MAN"

1. Mosley 1999. Mosley examines how changes in the economy have had consequences for the number of hours men and women with families work, the type of employment available, and the decline of real wages. He demonstrates that since the 1970s the average wage of a worker has declined by approximately 15 percent and that family incomes have remained steady due to more family members in the workforce and adults working more hours outside the home.

Parents also, because of a lack of time, experience conflict between work and family life, according to a nationwide survey conducted by the Families and Work Institute (Levine and Pittinsky 1993).

2. Teybor and Hoffman 1987; Seltzer and Brandreth 1994; Seltzer and Bianchi 1988; Loewen 1988.

3. Those with mental disorders are also overrepresented among the homeless. About 20 to 25 percent of the single adult homeless population suffers from a mental disorder (Koegel 1996). Also see National Coalition for the Homeless (1997) for information of the prevalence and history of homelessness among African American and other populations.

CONCLUSION: "GOT TO MAKE FATHERHOOD WORK FOR US"

1. The quote from Jones is used with caution here. Jones, or Amiri Baraka, is well known for his male chauvinism and this study's findings and conclusions offer little support for the patriarchal ideals about male and female relationships that he espouses. However, the issue of patriarchy as it relates to this is discussed in a later part of this chapter.

2. See Williams et al. 1995; Also see Jewell 1988; Majors and Billson 1992; Patton 1981; Taylor 1994.

3. See Rivera et al. 1986; Stack 1986; McClanahan 1999. Michael E. Lamb (1995) provides an excellent summary of the literature on what fathers do for their children. He also examines the influence of paternal involvement on child development. It appears that married fathers tend to provide about one-third of what mothers do regardless of whether both parents work 30 hours or more a week. One should note that the studies reviewed consist of primarily white samples. However, there are some indications that black fathers tend to do more in the household than their white counterparts. Yet, there is research that contradicts this as well. It is important to note that at least one study suggests that relative to middle-class and professional resident fathers, working-class fathers have increased their parental interaction with children more in recent decades. See Feree (1988), whose work suggests that part of the reason for this is that women in working class families are more likely to perceive themselves and be perceived by others as sharing the breadwinning role. Thus, she is in a better position than middle-class and professional women to demand an initiate greater participation in household activities and childcare. In middle-class families the need for women's wages is less apparent and more apt to be perceived as a privilege.

4. The term "noncustodial" is used to describe a live-away father status in slavery only for lack of a better term. There are definite qualitative differences between live-away status during slavery and present day circumstances. During the former, black men (and women) were bonded labor and had no control over where they lived and sometimes no say in the decision to partner with a particular woman. In contemporary times, blacks have a different relationship to the market. They are no longer bonded. However, their noncustodial status is influenced by (among other factors) their relationship to the free market, their inability to find meaningful employment, and their relationship to the mother of their children.

5. Several attempts were made to locate, contact, and telephone interview directors of father-centered programs with predominantly African American clientele. I developed a list which consisted of 38 organizations from various regions and cities in the United States. Of these programs, 9 were no longer in existence or at least had

only no-longer-in-service phone numbers. Eleven did not respond to repeated phone calls and letter surveys. Consequently, in the end, data was collected from 18 programs. This poor response may be a reflection of the small staff available to many centers. It appears that, in general, centers have part-time staff and are open for business less than forty hours a week.

6. Darity and Myers 1995; Kiecolt and Fossett 1995; Wilson 1987; Darity and Meyers 1990; Jackson 1978; Guttentag and Secord 1983.

7. Ballard 1995; D. Blankenhorn 1994; Griswold 1993. Quite recently, Wade C. Horn (1999) has argued that a "Fatherhood Movement," distinct from the men's movement, is emerging. It is distinct, he argues, because its focus is on the needs and well-being of children, rather than emphasizing the needs and feelings of fathers and men as is associated with the Men's and Father's Rights Movements.

8. Billingsley 1999. In the past decade, faith-based initiatives have increased across the nation. Federal grant availability and a general decline in the well-being of poor black communities have spurred the sharp increase in the development of non-profit programs housed within churches. Grant monies also encourage faith-based organizations to collaborate to provide services to their communities and minimize duplication.

BIBLIOGRAPHY

Albeda, Randy and Chris Tilly. 1997. *Glass Ceilings and Bottomless Pits.* Boston: South End Press.

Allen, Walter. 1995. "African American Family Life in Societal Context: Crises and Hope." *Sociological Forum* 10(4): 569—72.

———. 1978. "The Search for Applicable Theories of Black Family Life." *Journal of Marraige and the Family* 40 (February): 117–29.

Allen, William D. and William J. Doherty. 1996. "The Responsibilities of Fatherhood as Perceived by African American Teenage Fathers." *Families in Society* 77(3) (March): 142–55.

American Slave, The: A Composite Autobiography. [1941] 1972. George P. Rawick, ed. Series 1 and 2, 19 vols. Westport, Conn.: Greenwood. A series of narratives collected primarily through the Works Progress Administration's Federal Writers Project and compiled during the years 1936 to 1938

Anderson, Elijah. 1990. *Streetwise.* Chicago: University of Chicago Press.

———. 1999. *Code of the Street.* New York: Norton.

Angel, Ronald and Jacqueline L. Angel. 1993. *Painful Inheritance: Health and the New Generation of Fatherless Families.* Madison: University of Wisconsin Press.

Arendell, Terry. 1986. *Mothers and Divorce: Legal, Economic, and Social Dilemmas.* Los Angeles: University of California Press.

———. 1995. *Fathers and Divorce.* Thousand Oaks, Calif.: Sage.

Asch, Kim. 1998. "More Blacks Attend College: Greater Access Spurs Increase." *Washington Times,* December 3, p. A5.

Ballard, Charles. 1995. "Prodigal Dad: How We Bring Fathers Home to Their Children." *Policy Review* (Winter): 66–70.

Beach, Charles. 1988. "The Vanishing Middle Class? Evidence and Explanations." University of Wisconsin-Madison, Institute for Research on Poverty, Discussion Paper 864–88, July.

Bell Kaplan, Elaine. 1997. *Not Our Kind of Girl.* Berkeley: University of California Press.

Belton, Don, ed. 1995. *Speak My Name: Black Men on Masculinity and the American Dream.* Boston: Beacon Press.

Berlin, Ira, Barbara J. Fields, Steven F. Miller, Joseph P. Reidy, and Leslie S. Rowland. 1992. *Free at Last*. New York: New Press.

Berlin, Ira, Joseph P. Reidy, and Leslie S. Rowland. 1982. *The Black Miliary Experience*. New York: New Press.

Berlin, Ira and Leslie S. Rowland, eds. 1997. *Families and Freedom: A Documentary History of African American Kinship in the Civil War Era*. New York: New Press.

Bernard, Jessie. 1998. "The Good-Provider Role—Its Rise and Fall." In A. Cherlin, ed., *Public and Private Families*, pp. 64–82. Boston: McGraw Hill.

Billingsley, Andrew. 1968. *Black Families in White America*. Englewood Cliffs, N.J.: Prentice Hall.

——. 1992. *Climbing Jacob's Ladder: The Enduring Legacy of African-Amerian Families*. New York: Simon and Schuster.

——. 1999. *Mighty Like a River: The Black Church and Social Reform*. New York: Oxford University Press.

Blankenhorn, David. 1995. *Fatherless America: Confronting Our Most Urgent Social Problem*. New York: Basic Books.

Blassingame, J. W. 1979. *The Slave Community: Plantation LIfe in the Antebellum South*. New York: Oxford University Press.

Borchert, James. 1980. *Alley Life in Washington: Family, Community, Religion, and Folklife in the City, 1850–1970*. Urbana: University of Illinois Press.

Bowles, Samuel and Herbert Gintes. 1976. *Schooling in Capitalist America: Educational Reform and the Contradictions of Economic Life*. New York: Basic Books.

Bowman, Phillip. 1991. "Work Life." In James S. Jackson, ed., *Life in Black America*, pp. 124–55. Newbury Park, N.J.: Sage.

Bronfenbrenner, Urie. 1979. *The Ecology of Human Development: Experiments by Nature and Design*. Cambridge: Harvard University Press.

Brown, D. R. and L. E. Gary. 1987. "Stressful Life Events, Social Support Networks, and the Physical and Mental Health of Urban Black Adults." *Journal of Human Stress* 13: 165–74.

Brown, Sterling. 1933. "Negro Character as Seen by White Authors." *Journal of Negro Education* 2(1) (January): 179–203.

Bullard, Robert D. 1989. "Black in Heavenly Houston." In R. D. Bullard, ed., *In Search of the New South: The Black Urban Experience in the 1970s and 1980s*. Tuscaloosa: University of Alabama Press.

Cannon, L. W., E. Higginbotham, and M. L. A. Leung. 1988. "Race and Class Bias in Qualitative Research. *Gender and Society* 2(4): 449–62.

Carnoy, M. 1994. *Faded Dreams: The Politics and Economics of Race in America*. New York: Cambridge University Press.

Casper, Lyne. 1998. "U.S. Bureau of the Census: Special Report." U.S. Bureau of the Census, Washington D.C., December 11.

Cazenave, Noel A. 1979. "Middle-Income Black Fathers: An Analysis of the Provider Role." *Family Coordinator* (October): 583–92.

———. 1984. "Race, Socioeconomic Status, and Age: The Social Context of American Masculinity." *Sex Roles* 11: 639–56.

Chadwick, Bruce and Tim B. Heaton, eds. 1998. *Statistical Handbook on the American Family*. Phoenix: Oryx Press.

Cha-Jua, Sundiata and Clarence Lang. In press. "Strategies of Black Liberation in the Age of Globalization: 'Retronoveau' Civil Rights, Militant Black Conservatism, and Radicalism." *Black Radical Scholar*.

Cherlin, A. 1978. "Remarriage as an Incomplete Institution." *American Journal of Sociology* 84(3) (November): 634–50.

———. 1981. *Marriage, Divorce, Remarriage*. Cambridge: Harvard University Press.

———. 1998. "On the Flexibility of Fatherhood." In Alan Booth and Ann Crouter, eds., *Men in Families: When Do They Get Involved? What Difference Does It Make?* Mahwah, N.J.: Erlbaum.

Chinhui, Juhn. 1992. "Decline in Labor Market Participation: The Role of Declining Market Opportunities." *Quarterly Journal of Economics* 197 (February): 79–121

Cockerham, W. C. 1990. "A Test of the Relationship Between Race, Socioeconomic Status, and Psychological Distress." *Social Science and Medicine* 31(12): 1321–26.

Coontz, Stephanie. 1997. *The Way We Really Are*. New York: Basic Books.

Cowan, Carolyn Pape and Philip A. Cowan. 1988. "Who Does What When Partners Become Parents: Implications for Men, Women, and Marriage." *Marriage and Family Review* 12(3–4): 105–31.

Crockett, Dave. 1998. "United States' Current Politcal Economy and Its Impact on African Americans." Manuscript. School of Business, Marketing Department, Marquette University, Milwaukee.

Darity, W. A. and S. L. Meyers Jr. 1990. "Impacts of Violent Crime on Black Family Sturcture." *Contemporary Policy Issues* 8: 15–19.

——— 1995. "Family Structure and the Marginalization of Black Men: Policy Implications." In M. B. Tucker and C. Mitchell-Kernan, eds., *The Decline in Marriage Among African Americans*, pp. 263–308. New York: Russell Sage Foundation.

Davis, Richard. 1993. *The Black Family in a Changing Black Community*. New York: Garland.

Dickerson, Bette. 1995. *African American Single Mothers*. Thousand Oaks, Calif.: Sage

Du Bois, W. E. B. 1908. *The Negro American Family*. Cambridge: MIT Press.

———. 1978. *On Sociology and the Black Community*. Chicago: University of Chicago Press.

Edin, Kathryn. 1991. "Surviving the Welfare System: How AFDC Recipients Make Ends Meet in Chicago." *Social Problems* 38: 462–74.

Edin, Kathryn and Laura Lein. 1997. *Making Ends Meet*. New York: Russell Sage Foundation.

Ehrenreich, Barbara. 1986. "Two, Three, Many Husbands." *Mother Jones* (July–August): 8.

Engerman, Stanley. 1977. "Black Fertility and Family Structure in the U.S., 1880–1940." *Journal of Family History* 2(2) (Summer): 117–38.

Escott, Paul D. 1979. *Slavery Remembered: A Record of Twentieth-Century Slave Narratives*. Chapel Hill: University of North Carolina Press.

Farley, Reynolds, ed. 1995. *State of the Union: America in the 1990's*. New York: Russell Sage Foundation.

Felder, Henry. 1984. *The Changing Patterns of Black Family Income, 1960–1982*. Washington, D.C.: GPO.

Feldman, Shirley. 1987. "Predicting Strain in Mothers and Fathers of 6-Month-Old Infants." In Phyllis Berman and Frank Pedersen, eds., *Men's Transitions to Parenthood*. Hillsdale, N.J.: Erlbaum.

Feree, Myra Marx. 1988. "Negotiating Household Roles and Responsibilities: Resistance, Conflict, and Change." Paper presented at annual conference of the National Council on Family Relations, Philadelphia, November.

Fogel, Robert and Stanley Engerman. 1974. *Time on the Cross: The Economics of American Slavery*. Boston: Little, Brown.

Franklin, Donna. 1997. *Ensuring Inequality*. New York: Oxford University Press.

Franklin, John Hope and Alfred A. Moss, Jr. 1998. *From Slavery to Freedom*. 7th ed. New York: McGraw-Hill.

Frazier, E. Franklin. 1931. "Family Disorganization Among Negros." *Opportunity* (July): 204–207.

——— 1939. *The Negro Family in the United States*. Chicago: Chicago University Press.

Furstenberg, Frank F., Jr. 1995. "Fathering in the Inner City: Paternal Participation and Public Policy." In W. Marsiglio, ed., *Fatherhood: Contemporary Theory, Research, and Social Policy*, 119–47. Thousand Oaks, Calif.: Sage.

Furstenberg, Frank F., Jr. and C. W. Nord. 1985. "Parenting Apart: Patterns of Childrearing After Marital Disruption." *Journal of Marriage and Family* (November): 893–904.

Furstenberg, Frank F., Jr., C. W. Nord, J. L. Peterson, and N. Zill. 1983. "The Life Course of Children of Divorce: Marital Disruption and Parental Contact." *American Sociological Review* 48: 656–68.

Furstenberg, Frank, Jr. and J. Cherlin. 1991. *Divided Families: What Happens to Children When Parents Part*. Cambridge: Harvard University Press.

Furstenberg, Frank F., Jr., Theodore Hershberg, and John Modell. 1975. "The Origins of the Female-Headed Black fAmily: The Impact of the Urban Experience." *Journal of Interdisciplinary History* 6(2): 211–34.

Garfinkel, Irwin and Sara S. McLanahan. 1986. *Single Mothers and Their Children: Summary and Recommendations*. Institute for Research on Poverty, University of Wisconsin, Madison.

Geiger, S. M. 1995. "African American Single Mothers: Public Policies." In K. M. Vaz, ed., *Black Women in America*, pp. 244–60. Thousand Oaks, Calif: Sage.

Genovese, Eugene. 1972. *Roll Jordan, Roll*. New York: Vintage Books.

——. 1989. *The Political Economy of Slavery, Studies in the Economy and Society of the Slave South*. Hanover: University Press of New England.

Gibbs, J. T. 1988. "Young Black Males in America: Endangered, Embittered and Embattled." In J. T. Gibbs, ed., *Young, Black, and Male in America: An Endangered Species*. Dover, Mass.: Auburn House.

Glazer, B. 1978. *Theoretical Sensitivity*. Mill Valley, Calif.: Sociology Press.

Glazer, B. and A. Strauss. 1967. *The Discovery of Grounded Theory*. Chicago: Aldine.

Goffman, Erving. 1959. *The Presentation of Self in Everyday Life*. Garden City, N.Y.: Doubleday Anchor.

Gordon, Linda and Sara McLanahan. 1990. "Single Parenthood in 1900." University of Wisconsin-Madison: Institute for Research on Poverty, Discussion Paper 919-90, June.

Griswold, R. 1993. *Fatherhood in America: A History*. New York: Basic Books.

Gutman, Herbert G. 1976. *The Black Family in Slavery and Freedom, 1750–1925*. New York: Pantheon.

——. 1975. "Persistent Myths About the Afro-American Family." *Journal of Interdisciplinary History* 6(2): 181–210.

Guttentag, M. and P. F. Secord. 1983. *Too Many Women? The Sex Ratio Question*. Beverly Hills: Sage.

Hall, L. K. 1981. "Support Systems and Coping Patterns." In L. E. Gary, ed., *Black Men*. Beverly Hills: Sage.

Hare, Nathan. 1976. "What Black Intellectuals Misunderstand About the Black Family." *Black World* (March): 4–14.

Harris, Ian, José B. Torres, and Dale Allender. 1994. "The Responses of African American Men to Dominant Norms of Masculinity Within the United States." *Sex Roles* 31(11–12): 703–19.

Heald-More, St. John and Tamara Heald-More. 1995. "Fear of Black Strangers." *Social Science Research* 24: 262–80.

Heiss, Jerrold. 1971. *The Case of the Black Family: A Sociological Inquiry.* New York: Columbia University Press.

Hernandez, Donald. 1997. "Poverty Trends." In G. Duncan and J. Brooks-Gunn, eds., *Consequences of Growing Up Poor.* New York: Russell Sage Foundation.

Herskovitz, Melville. 1941. *The Myth of the Negro Past.* New York: Harper's.

Hetherington, E. Mavis, M. Cox, and R. Cox. 1982. "Effects of Divorce on Parents and Children." In M. W. Lamb, ed., *Nontraditional Families: Parenting and Child Development.* Hillsdale, N.J.: Erlbaum.

Higginson, Thomas Wentworth. 1970. *Army Life in a Black Regiment.* New York: Grosset and Dunlap.

Hill, Robert B. 1997. "Social Welfare Policies and African American Families." In H. P. McAdoo, ed., *Black Families,* pp. 349–64. Thousand Oaks, Calif.: Sage.

Hochschild, Arlie Russell. 1983. *The Managed Heart.* Los Angeles: University of California Press.

Hogan, D. P. and D. T. Lichter. 1995. "Children and Youth: Living Arrangements and Welfare." In R. Farley, ed., *State of the Union: America in the 1990s,* vol. 2: *Social Trends,* pp. 93–109. New York: Sage.

hooks, bell. 1992. *Race and Repression.* Boston: South End Press.

Horn, Laura and C. Carroll. 1998. *Stopouts or Stayouts? Undergraduates Who Leave College in Their First Year.* Washington, D.C.: Dept. of Education, NCS 1999087.

Horn, Wade F. 1999. "Did You Say Movement?" In W. F. Horn, D. Blankenhorn, and M. B. Pearlstein, eds., *The Fatherhood Movement: A Call to Action.* New York: Lexington Books.

Hutchinson, Earl Ofari. 1998. *The Assassinatin of the Black Male Image.* New York: Touchstone.

Jackson, J. 1978. "But Where are the Black Men?" In Robert Staples, ed., *The Black Family: Essays and Studies.* Belmont, Calif.: Wadsworth.

Jencks, Christopher. 1993. *Rethinking Social Policy: Race, Poverty, and the Underclass.* New York: HarperPerennial.

Jewell, K. Sue. 1988. *Survival of the Black Family: The Institutional Impact of U.S. Social Policy.* Wesport, Conn.: Praeger.

Johnson, Cheryl. 1993. "Television Commercial: The Social and Economic Implications for Men of Color." *Journal of African American Male Studies* 1(1): 47–55.

Jones, Dionne, ed. 1994. *African American Males: A Critical Link in the African American Family.* New Brunswick, N.J.: Transaction.

Jones, Jacqueline. 1985. *Labor of Love, Labor of Sorrow: Black Women, Work, and the Family from Slavery.* New York: Basic Books.

Jordan, Pamela. 1995. "The Mother's Role in Promoting Fathering Behavior." In S. Shapiro, M. Diamond, and M. Greenberg, eds., *Becoming a Father: Contemporary, Social, Developmental, and Clinical Perspectives*. New York: Springer.

Kasarda, John D. 1989. "Urban Industrial Transition and the Underclass." *Annals of the American Academy of Political and Social Science* 50 (January): 26–47.

Katzman, David. 1975. *Before the Ghetto: Black Detroit in the Nineteenth Century*. Urbana: University of Illinois Press.

Kerner Commission, United States. 1968. U. S. Congress Joint Economic Committee Hearings, 19th Congress, 2d sess. Washington, D.C.: GPO.

Kiecolt, K. J. and M. A. Fossett. 1995. "Mate Availability and Marriage Among African Americans: Aggregate- and Individual-Level Analyses." In M. B. Tucker and C. Mitchell-Kernan, eds., *The Decline in Marriage Among African Americans*. New York: Russell Sage Foundation.

Killens, John O. 1965. *Black Man's Burden*. New York: Trident Press.

Kimmel, Michael and Michael Messner, eds.. 1989. *Men's Lives*. New York: Macmillan.

King, James. 1997. *The Impact of Federal Housing Policy on Urban African-American Families, 1930–1966*. Bethesda, Md.: Austin and Winfield.

King, Valerie. 1994. "Nonresident Father Involvement and Child Well-Being." *Journal of Family Issues* 15: 78–96.

Klawitter, Marieka M. 1994. "Who Gains, Who Loses from Changing U.S. Child Support Policies?" *Policy Sciences* 27(2–3): 197–219.

Koegel, Paul. 1996. "The Causes of Homelessness." In *Homelessness in America*. Phoenix: Oryx Press.

Kornfein-Rose, Madeline. 1992. "Elective Single Mothers and Their Children: The Missing Fathers." *Child and Adolescent Social Work* 9(1): 211–33.

Kozol, Jonothan. 1992. *Savage Inequalities*. New York: HarperCollins.

Kurdek, L. 1983. "Custodial Mothers' Perceptions of Visitations and Payment of Child Support by Noncustodial Fathers in Families with Low and High Levels of Preseparation Interparent Conflict." *Journal of Applied Developmental Psychology* 7: 307—23.

Ladner, Joyce. 1971. *Tomorrow's Tomorrow: The Black Woman in Modern Society*. Garden City, N.Y..: Doubleday.

Lamb, Michael E. 1995. "The Changing Roles of Fathers." In Jerrold Shapiro, Michael Diamond, and Martin Greenberg, eds., *Becoming a Father*, pp. 18–35. New York: Springer.

Laseter, Robert L. 1997. "The Labor Force Participation of Young Black Men: A Qualitative Examination." *Social Service Review* (March): 72–87.

Lett, H. A. 1931. "Work: Negro Unemployed in Pittsburgh." *Journal of Negro Life* (March):79–81.

Levine, James and Todd Pittinsky. 1997. *Working Fathers: New Strategies Balancing Work and Family.* Reading, Mass: Addison-Wesley.

Lewis, Oscar. 1972. *The Children of Sanchez.* London: Penguin Books, reprint.

Liebow, E. 1967. *Tally's Corner.* Boston: Little, Brown.

Loewen, J. W. 1988. "Visitation Fatherhood." In P. Bronstein and C. P. Cowan, eds., *Fatherhood Today: Men's Changing Role in the Family,* pp. 195–213. New York: Wiley.

Lowenthal, M. F. and D. Chiraboga. 1972. "Transitions to an Empty Nest: Crisis, Change, or Relief?" *Archives of General Psychiatry* 26: 8–14.

Luepnitz, Deborah. 1992. *The Family Interpreted: Feminist Theory in Clinical Practice.* New York: Basic Books.

MacLeod, Jay. 1995. *Ain't No Makin' It: Aspiration and Attainment in a Low-Income Neighborhood.* Boulder, Colo.: Westview.

Majors, Richard and Janet Mancini Billson. 1992. *Cool Pose: The Dilemma of Black Manhood in American.* New York: Lexington.

Malveaux, Julianne. 1998. "Despite Education, Black Workers Still Face Challenges." *Black Issues in Higher Education* 15(16): 28.

Marsiglio, William, ed. 1995. *Fatherhood: Contemporary Theory, Research, and Social Policy.* Thousand Oaks, Calif.: Sage.

McAdoo, H. P., ed. 1997. *Black Families.* 3d ed. Thousand Oaks, Calif.: Sage.

McAdoo, John L. 1979. "Father-Child Interaction Patterns and Self-Esteem in Black Preschool Children." *Young Children* 34(2): 46–53.

——. 1993. "The Roles of African American Fathers: An Ecological Perspective." *Families in Society* 74(1): 28–35.

——. 1988. "Changing Perspectives on the Role of the Black Father." In P. Bronstein and C. Cowan, eds., *Fatherhood Today: Men's Changing Role in the Family.* New York: Wiley.

McDaniel, Antonio. 1994. "Historical Racial Differences in Living Arrangements of Children." *Journal of Family History* 19(1): 57–77.

McLanahan, Sara. 1999. "Dispelling Myths About Unwed Parents." National Summmit on Supporting Urban Fathers, National Fatherhood Initiative, Washington, D.C., June 14.

McLanahan, Sara and Gary Sandafur. 1994. *Growing Up with a Single Parent: What Hurts, What Helps.* Cambridge: Harvard University Press.

McLanahan, Sara, Irwin Garfinkel, and Dorothy Watson. 1987. "Family Structure, Poverty, and the Underclass." University of Wisconsin-Madison: Institute for Research on Poverty Poverty, Discussion Paper 823-87, March.

Million Man March Organizing Committee. 1995. The Million Man March, Day of Absence: Mission Statement. Washington D.C.

Mills, C. Wright. 1959. *The Sociological Imagination*. New York: Oxford University Press.

Morehouse Research Institute and Institute for American Values. 1999. "Turning the Corner on Father Absence in Black America." A statement from the Morehouse Conference on African American Fathers, Morehouse Research Institute, 830 Westview Drive SW, Atlanta, GA 30314. www.morehouse.edu/mri.htm.

Mosley, Fred. 1999. "The United States Economy at the Turn of the Century: Entering a New Era of Prosperity?" *Capital & Class* 67: 25–45.

Mott, F. L. 1994. "Sons, Daughters, and Fathers' Absence: Differential in Father-Leaving Probabilities and in Home Environments." *Journal of Family Issues* 15: 78–96.

Moynihan, Daniel P. 1965. *The Negro Family: The Case for National Action*. Washington, D.C.: U.S. Dept. of Labor, Office of Policy Planning and Research.

National Association for the Advancement of Colored People. 1999 (July). "NAACP Blasts TV Networks' Fall Season Whitewash" (press release). Washington, D.C.: NAACP.

National Coalition for the Homeless. 1997. "Homelessness in America: Unabated and Increasing." National Coalition for the Homeless, 1012 14th Street NW, Suite 600, Washington, D.C. 20005.

National Urban League. 1998. *The State of Black America*. New York: National Urban League.

Nichols, C. H. 1972. *Black Men in Chains: Narratives by Escaped Slaves*. New York: Hill.

Nobles, Wade W. 1974a. "Africanity: Its Role in Black Families." *Black Scholar* 5 (June): 10–17.

——. 1974b. "African Root and American Fruit: The Black Family." *Journal of Social and Behavioral Sciences* 20 (Spring): 66–77.

——. 1978. "Toward an Empirical and Theoretical Framework for Defining Black Families." *Journal of Marriage and the Family* 40(4): 679–90.

Orloff, Ann Shola. 1993. "Gender and Social Rights of Citizenship: The Comparative Analysiss of Gender Relations and Welfare States." *American Sociolgical Review* 58 (June): 303–28.

Osofsky, Gilbert. 1963. *Harlem: The Making of Ghetto, Negro New York, 1890–1930*. New Yori: Harper and Row.

Parke, Ross D. and Armin A. Brott. 1999. *Throwaway Dads: The Myths and Barriers That Keep Men from Being the Fathers They Want to Be*. Boston: Houghton Mifflin.

Pinkney, Alphonso. 1984. *The Myth of Black Progress*. Cambridge: Cambridge University Press.

Pomer, Marshall. 1986. "Labor Market Structure, Intragenerational Mobility, and Discrimination: Black Male Advancement Out of Low-Paying Occupations, 1962–1973." *American Sociological Review* 51(5): 650–59.

Popenoe, David. 1996. *Life Without Father.* Cambridge: Harvard University Press.

——. 1998."Life Without Father." In Cynthia R. Daniels, ed., *Lost Fathers: The Politics of Fatherlessness in America,* pp. 33–50. New York: St. Martin's.

President's Commission on Race Relations. 1998. *Advisory Board to the Initiative on Race,* Final Report, September 1998. Washington, D.C.: U.S. Office of the Press Secretary.

Quarles, Benjamin. 1953. *The Negro in the Civil War.* Boston: Little, Brown.

Rainwater, Lee. 1970. *Behind Ghetto Walls.* Chicago: Alsine.

Reed, Ruth. 1929. *Negro Illegitimacy in New York City.* New York: Columbia University Press.

Rivera, F., P. Sweeney, and B. Henderson. 1986. "Black Teenage Fathers: What Happens When the Child Is Born?" *Pediatrics* 78(1): 151–58.

Roberts, Dorothy. 1988. "The Absent Black Father." In C. Daniels, ed., *Lost Fathers: The Politics of Fatherlessness in America,* pp. 145–62. New York: St. Martin's.

Roberts, Sam. 1993. *Who We Are.* New York: Random House.

Robinson, Ira E., Wilfred Bailey, John Smith, and Bernice Bzrnett. 1985. "Self-Perception of the Husband/Father in the Intact Lower-Class Black Family." *Phylon* 46(2): 136–47.

Sandefur, Gary D. and Sara S. McLanahan. 1990. "Family Background, Race and Ethnicity, and Early Family Formation." University of Wisconsin-Madison, Institute for Research on Poverty, Discussion Paper 911-90, July.

Sanders, Cheryl, ed. 1995. *Living the Intersection: Womanism and Afrocentrism in Theology.* Minneapolis: Fortress Press.

Scanzoni, John. 1971. *Black Families in America.* Boston: Allyn and Bacon.

Schiele, Jerome H. 1997. "An Afrocentric Perspective on Social Welfare Philosophy and Policy." *Journal of Social Welfare* 24(2): 21–40.

Schwalm, Leslie A. 1997. *A Hard Fight for We: Women's Transition from Slavery to Freedom in South Carolina.* Urbana: University of Illinois Press.

Scott, Emmett J. 1969. *Negro Migration During the War.* New York: Arno Press.

Seltzer, Judith and S. Bianchi. 1988. "Children's Contact with Absent Parents." *Journal of Marriage and the Family* 50: 663–77.

Seltzer, J. and Y. Brandreth. 1994. "What Fathers Say About Involvement with Children After Separation." *Journal of Family Issues* 15(1): 49–77.

Shinagawa, Larry H. and Michael Jang. 1998. *Atlas of American Diversity.* London: Altamira Press.

Stack, Carol. 1974. *All Our Kin: Strategies for Survival in a Black Community.* New York: Harper and Row.

——. 1986. "Sex Roles and Survival Strategies in an Urban Black Community." In R. Staples, ed., *The Black Family: Essays and Studies.* 3d ed. New York: Harper and Row.

Staples, Robert. 1990. "Substance Abuse and the Black Family Crisis: An Overview." *Western Journal of Black Studies* 14(4): 196–204.

Stearn, P. N. 1990. "Fatherhood in Historical Perspective: The Role of Social Change." In F. Bozett and S. Hanson, eds., *Fatherhood and Families in Cultural Context.* New York: Springer.

Stier, H. and M. Tienda. 1993. "Are Men Marginal to the Family? Insights from Chicago's Inner City." In J. C. Hood, ed., *Men, Work, and Family,* 23–44. Newbury Park, N.J.: Sage.

Sterling, Dorothy, ed. 1997. *We Are Your Sisters.* New York: Norton.

Strauss, A. and J. Corbin. 1990. *Basics of Qualitiative Research.* Newbury Park: Sage.

Sudarkasa, Niara. 1980. "African and Afro-American Family Structure." *Black Scholar* 11(8): 37–60.

——. 1997. "African American Families and Family Values." In H. P. McAdoo, ed., *Black Families,* pp. 9–40. 3d ed. Thousand Oaks, Calif.: Sage.

Takaki, Ronald. 1993. *A Different Mirror: A History of Multicultural America.* Boston: Little, Brown.

Taylor, Ronald. 1994. "Black Males and Social Policy: Breaking the Cycle of Disadvantage." In R. G. Majors and J. U. Gordon, eds., *The Black Male: His Present and Future Status,* pp. 147–66. Chicago: Nelson-Hall.

Taylor, Sandra. 1992. "The Mental Health of Black Americans: An Overview." In R. Braithwaite and S. Taylor, eds., *Health Issues in the Black Community,* pp. 20–34. San Francisco: Jossey-Bass.

Teybor, E. and E. D. Hoffman. 1987. "Missing Fathers." *Psychology Today* (April): 36–69.

Toliver, Susan. 1998. *Black Families in Corporate America.* Thousand Oaks, Calif.: Sage.

Tripp-Reissman, T. and S. E. Wilson. 1990. "Cross-Cultural Perspectives on Fatherhood." In F. Bozett and S. Hanson, ed., *Fatherhood and Families in Cultural Context.* New York: Springer.

Trotter, Joe William, Jr. 1990. *Coal, Class, and Color: Black in Southern West Virginia, 1915–32.* Chicago: University of Illinois Press.

——. *River Jordan.* 1998. Lexington: University of Kentucky Press.

Trotter, Joe William, Jr., ed. 1991. *The Great Migration: In Historical Perspective.* Bloomington: University of Indiana Press.

Tucker, M. Belinda and Claudia Mitchell-Kernan. 1995. "Marital Behavior and Expectations: Ethnic Comparisons of Attitudinal and Structural Correlates." In

M. Tucker and C. Mitchell-Kernan, eds., *The Decline in Marriage Among African Americans.* New York: Russell Sage Foundation.

Umberson, Deborah and Christine Williams. 1991. *Noncustodial Parenting and Fathers' Mental Health.* Final Report to the Hogg Foundation for Mental Health, Austin, Texas.

USA Today. 1999. "Crossing Racial Lines, Coalition Reaches to Fathers." Thursday, June 17: 10D.

Wallerstein, J. and J. B. Kelly. 1980. *Surviving the Breakup: How Children and Parents Cope with Divorce.* New York: Basic Books.

White, Deborah. 1985. *Ar'n't I a Woman? Female Slaves in the Plantation South.* New York: Norton.

White, Joseph L. and James H. Cones III. 1999. *Black Men Emerging.* New York: Free-man.

Williams, Norma, Kelly Himmel, Andrea Sjoberg, and D. Torrez. 1995. "The Assim-ilation Model, Family Life, and Race and Ethnicity in the United States: The Case of Minority Welfare Mothers." *Journal of Family Issues* 16: 380–405.

Wilson, Willliam Junius. 1987. *The Truly Disadvantaged: The Inner City, the Under-class, and Public Policy.* Chicago: University of Chicago Press.

——. 1997. *When Work Disappears: The World of the Urban Poor.* New York: Knopf.

Young, Virginia. 1970. "Family and Childhood in a Southern Negro Community." *American Anthropologist* 72 (April): 269–88.

INDEX

abandonment by fathers, 84

"abroad" marriages, 37

absent fathers: attempts to reestablish bonds, 173–74; barriers to fatherhood, 160–61, 175, 208–209; contacts with children, 152, 230*n* (ch. 7); criminal activities, 162–63; current partner's attitudes affecting, 170–72; definitions, 12, 230*n* (ch. 7); description of, 152–54; effects of absence on children, 135–37; emotional isolation, 156–57; exclusion by mothers, 165–68; mothers' expectations of, 154–56; motivation for absence, 208–209; passive disengagement, 159–61; paternal roles, 154–56, 175; prevalence of, 151; stereotypes, 152; substance abuse by, 164–65; time factors in disengagement, 173. *See also* live-away fathers

active disengagement, 162–65

advertising, racial stereotypes in, 23

Advisory Board to the Initiative on Race, 28, 224*n*7

affirmative action, rulings against, 61

African Americans: competition with immigrants for jobs, 59; discrimination toward (*see* racial discrimination); education and labor market, 227*n*9; familial experiences, 2–5; granting of citizenship, 58; in Houston, TX, 55–56, 226*n*1; marriage rates, 123; mental disorders in, 196, 231*n*3; non-marital childbearing, 2, 32, 209–210; as second-class citizens, 58; stereotypes (*see* stereotypes, African American)

Aid to Families with Dependent Children (AFDC), 55, 148, 226*n*5

Albeda, Randy, 102, 123, 229*n*1, 229*n*2

alcoholism: impact on black families, 72. *See also* substance abuse

Allen, Thomas, 139

Allen, Walter, 221*n*5

Allen, William D., 106, 133, 134

American Film Institute, 22

Amos 'n' Andy (TV series), 22

Anderson, Elijah, 28, 229*n*4

Angel, Jacqueline L., 123

Angel, Ronald, 123

antagonism between parents, 88–91

Arendell, Terry, 105, 125, 228*n*1 (pt. 2)

Asch, Kim, 63

athletes, as fathers, 24–25

Atkins, Kevin, 140–141

Bailey, Dexter, 72

Bailey, Roland, 188

Ballard, Charles, 156

Banks, Justin, 53–55

Barnes, Phoenix, 219

Barnes, Victor, 172–73

Barry, Tony, 152–58

Bates, Kenneth, 85

Battle, Jasper, 37

Bell Kaplan, Elaine, 105, 229n*Æ*4, 230n3 (ch. 7)

Bennett, Derik, 27

Bennett, Scott, 135

Berlin, Ira, 42, 43

Billingsley, Andrew, 3, 219, 233n8

Billson, Janet Mancini, 21–22

Birch, Derek, 70–71

Birth of a Nation (film), 22

Black Codes, 47

black neighborhoods, 103

blacks. *See* African Americans

Blankenhorn, David, 12, 19–20, 25, 208, 230n1 (ch. 7)

blended families, 47–48

Bonner, Bernard, 224n6

Booth, Lilly, 45

Borchert, James, 48, 49, 105, 229n4

Boudry, Nancy, 36

Bowles, Samuel, 65

Bowman, Phillip, 62

Boys N the Hood (film), 24

Bradshaw, Dennis, 136

Brandreth, Y., 76, 192

breadwinners: African American women as, 229n6; fathers as, 17, 21, 146–50, 204–205; mothers as, 214

broad wives, 45

Bronfenbrenner, Urie, 5–6, 8, 14

Brott, Armin, 99, 228n4

Brown, D. R., 196

Brown, Sterling, 223n5

Bullard, Robert, 56, 226n1

Bunton, Martha Spence, 40

Bush, George: campaign ads, 22; veto of Civil Rights bill, 62

Campbell, Jeffrey, 169–70

Cannon, L. W., 9

caregivers: discipline provided by, 140; fathers as, 202–203, 218

Carnoy, M., 58

Carroll, C., 227n9

Carrolton, Jim, 143

Carter, Vernon, 140

Cazenave, Noel A., 21

Chadwick, Bruce A., 123

Cha-Jua, Sundiata, 71

Chambers, Theodore, 140

Chapman, Hannah, 39

Chapman, Wayne, 138

Cherlin, A., 18

Cherlin, Andrew, 123

Chicago Hope (TV series), 23

child care, availability of, 107

child custody, fathers seeking, 167–68

children: criminal activities, paternal reaction to, 99–100; expectations of fathers, 98–101; living in poverty, 2, 221n2, 229n1, 229n2; marriage impact on, 214; residing with stepfathers, 48; socioeconomic factors affecting, 211

child support: from absent fathers, 167, 168; in antagonistic parental relationship, 88; attempts to obtain, 121–23; automatic collection of, 146; availability of, 225n9; cultural values and, 127; financial vs. social support, 126; legal pursuit of, 105, 122–23, 125, 205–206, 216; from live-away fathers, 104, 105–106; misuse of, 147–48; motives for paying,

204–205; nurturing factored into, 218; payment of, 49, 50; as substitute for time with children, 205
churches, social activism of, 219–20
citizenship, 58
civil rights, 61, 62
Civil War (U.S.), 41–43
Clansman, The (play), 22
Clayton, Robert, 162–64
Clinton, Bill: on fatherhood initiatives, 211; race relations advisory panel, 224*n*7
coal miners, 60
Cockerham, W. C., 196
communication between parents, 92–94
Cones, James H. III, 21, 223*n*1
Conference on Fathering and Male Fertility, 212
cool pose, in fatherhood, 21
co-parenting: by never-married parents, 209–10; social support for, 217–20
Corbin, J., 222*n*7
Cosby Show, The (TV series), 23
criminal activities: of absent fathers, 162–63; attitudes toward, 71; black incarceration for, 71–72; black male involvement, 62, 69–72; of children, fathers' attitude toward, 99–100; hiding from children, 143–44; social mobility and, 71; as underground economy, 71
cultural values, child support and, 127

daddies, fathers as, 208–209
Darity, William, Jr., 213
daughters, fathers' influence on, 145–46
deadbeat dads, 12, 230*n*1 (ch. 7)

deindustrialization, 60–61
depression, economic, 60
discipline: administered by fathers, 139–41; administered by mothers, 140
discrimination. *See* racial discrimination
disenfranchisement, 46–47
disengagement of fathers: active, 162–65; current partner's attitudes in, 170–72; factors in, 168–72; geographic barriers, 169; other children affecting, 170; passive, 159–61; persistent, 172–75; resistant, 165–68; time factors in, 173
distal fathers, 12, 223*n*9
divorce: African-American, post-Reconstruction, 47; rates of, 213; in slave marriages, 37–38
Doherty, William J., 106, 133, 134
Domestic Policy Council, 212
Donnelly, Clyde, 174
drug abuse. *See* substance abuse
DuBois, W. E. B., 3

ecology of families, 5–8, 222*n*7
economic factors, in live-away fatherhood, 200–201, 204–205
Edin, Kathryn, 103, 105, 123, 229*n*4
education: barriers to college attendance, 157, 227*n*9; black college enrollment, 63–64; of black fathers, 64–66; black vs. white levels, 63; costs of, 74; high school completion, 63; increasing demand for, 57; in low-income communities, 227*n*11; social mobility and, 65; vocational, 65; of women in poverty, 102, 103
Ehrenreich, Barbara, 104

emancipation: impact on African American families, 43–44; noncustodial fathers following, 44–45; slave marriages, legitimization of, 46–47
emotional labor, 59, 226*n*3
emotional support, as paternal role, 137–39
employment: of African American men, 58–60, 62, 104; blue-collar jobs, decline in, 74, 216; conflict with family life, 231*n*1; educational demands, 216; impact on fatherhood, 177–78; inadequate income from, 215–16; job stress and parenting, 184–85; mobility in, 58–59; personal support vs. family support, 69; racial discrimination in, 55–56; relationships with employers, 177; relocation of jobs, 200–201; in service occupations, 59; shift work, 180–81; work schedule and parenting, 179–83
encouragement, as paternal role, 138
Engerman, Stanley, 4
environment, social. *See* social environment
equal rights, priority vs. practice, 227*n*6
ER (TV series), 23
Escott, Paul D., 35, 45
Evans, Carl, 66
Evans, Leonard, 162
exosystem, familial, 7

faith-based social programs, 220, 233*n*8
families: African cultural heritage, 3; children residing with stepfathers, 48; in Civil War, 41–43; ecological approach, 5–8; extended family and friends, 6–7; father-child microsystem, 6; fathers and self-sufficiency, 212; following emancipation, 43–44; matriarchal structure, 4, 102; mothers as custodial parent, 48, 102; multiple sets of children, 191–92; never-married co-parents, 209–210, 217–20; nuclear, 18–19; patriarchal perspective, 201; post-Reconstruction, 47; poverty and fatherlessness, 2–3; Race Relations Model, 4; racial discrimination and, 3; single-parent, 20, 48, 123, 215, 225*n*9; in slavery, 3, 39, 40–41; social networks, 219, 225*n*9; socioeconomic factors, 4, 221*n*5, 225*n*9; triangle of pathology, 4
Family and Child Well-being Research Network, NICHD, 212
Family Matters (TV series), 23
family planning services, for men, 212
Family Support Act, 105
father-centered social programs, 232*n*5
father-child bonding, by absent fathers, 173–74
fatherhood: after emancipation, 46–47, 226*n*20; barriers to, 120–21, 129, 168–69, 175–97, 206–208; ecological approach to, 5–8, 15; economic class and paternal attitudes, 21; economic instability as barrier, 188–90, 196; father-child microsystem, 6; fathers' concept of, 109–110; geographic barriers, 169, 178–79, 185–88; ideal image vs. reality of daily life, 125; ideal roles and functions, 17–18, 19–20, 32, 135t; legal bonds, 203–204; marginal nature of, 199–201; maternal involvement with other men, 89–90; meaning of, 199–220; media

stereotypes, 24; mothers' concept of, 106–111; multiple sets of children as barriers to parenting, 191–92; never-married parenthood as norm, 209–210; nurturing role, 218; paternal behavior, 26–31; paternal involvement and child welfare, 212; paternal role, 51–52, 106, 232*n*3; redefinition of, 210–11; in slavery, 33–34, 39; social and emotional roles, 125–26; social environment and, 13–14, 75–76; social expectations concerning, 75–126; social responsibilities and functions, 19; standards of, 17–32; stereotypes, 1, 26–32; traditional roles, 77; variance from mainstream norms, 201

Fatherhood Movement, 233*n*7

fathers: abandonment of families, 49; absent (*see* absent fathers); accompanied by children, societal attitude toward, 29–30; attitude toward parenting, 231*n*7; as breadwinners, 17, 21, 110–11, 125, 146–50; children's expectations of, 98–101; communication with children's mothers, 92–94; cool pose by, 21; current partnerships and paternal behavior, 76, 192–97; daughters' sexuality, attitude toward, 145–46; desire for personal freedom, 119; as disciplinarians, 139–41; education of, 64–66, 73–74; emotional isolation, 156–57; emotional support of children, 137–39, 229*n*5; good, defined, 99; initiatives for, 212–13; job training services, 213; lack of preparation for, 160–61; live-away (*see* live-away fathers); mothers' expectations of,

111–15; as natural nonconformists, 201, 231*n*1; noncustodial (*see* noncustodial fathers); in nuclear family, 19; paternity, identification of, 104, 105; as primary caregivers, 131–32; recruitment of research subjects, 8–10, 222*n*8; relationship with children, 100; relationship with children's mothers, 76, 78–91, 94; relationship with own father, 134; relationship with own mothers, 94–98, 208–209; responsible paternal behavior, encouragement of, 117–19, 119–21; as role models, 96–97, 142–44; role of, 105, 113–17; siding with children against mother, 137–38; socioeconomic factors, 10–11, 51–52; spending time with children, 135–37, 150, 178–79; support systems for, 156; vs. daddies, 208–209

Fathers' Center, East St. Louis, IL, 156, 219

Fathers' Center, St. Louis, MO, 213, 216

Fathers Count Act of 1999, 213

Father's Rights Movement, 233*n*7

Federal Interagency Forum on Child and Family Statistics, 212

femininity, fathers' influence on, 144–46

Feree, Myra Marx, 232*n*3

Fishburne, Laurence, 24

Foner, Eric, 226*n*20

food stamps, 148

Ford, Rolly, 97

Foster, Kyle, 173

Fragile Families Project, 151

Franklin, Donna, 46, 226*n*20

Franklin, John Hope, 224*n*7, 226*n*20

Franklin, Russell, 26–32
Franklin, Virgil, 146, 147
Frazier, E. Franklin, 3–4, 47, 221*n*5
Frederick D. Patterson Research Institute, 63, 64
Freedman's Bureau, 45, 46
freedom, paternal desire for, 119
friendship, between parents, 83–88
Furstenberg, Frank F., Jr., 4, 105, 106

Garfinkel, Irwin, 32, 133
Gary, L. E., 196
gatekeepers, mothers as, 76, 195, 207, 228*n*1 (pt. 2)
Gathers, Cal, 98
Geiger, S. M., 104
Genovese, Eugene, 37, 38, 40
geographic barriers: disengagement by fathers and, 169; in paternal behavior, 178–79, 185–88; transportation and, 186–87
Gibbs, J. T., 27
Gintes, Herbert, 65
Glazer, B., 222*n*7
Godfrey, Danny, 160–61
Good Times (TV series), 22–23
Gore, Al, 212
Graham, Oliver, 159
grandmothers, attitude toward grandsons as fathers, 96
grounded theories, 8, 222*n*7
Gutman, Herbert, 40, 226*n*20

Hall, L. K., 1
Hare, Nathan, 221*n*5
Harlem ghetto, 58
Harris, Theo, 27–28
Hayes, Dwayne, 165–68
Hayes, Roman, 64

Heaton, Tim B., 123
Henry, Carl, 136
Henry, Nettie, 39
Henson, Rosanna, 42
Hernandez, Donald, 104
Herskovitz, Melville, 3
Higginbotham, E., 9
Higginson, Thomas Wentworth, 45
Hill, Robert B., 126
Hill Street Blues (TV series), 23
Hispanics: living in poverty, 221*n*2; racial stereotypes in television, 224*n*8
Hochschild, Arlie, 59, 226*n*3
Hogan, D. P., 229*n*2
homelessness, increase in, 231*n*3
Homicide: Life on the Streets (TV series), 23
Horn, Laura, 227*n*9
Horn, Wade C., 150, 230*n*6, 233*n*7
Horton, Willie, 22
housing assistance, 148
housing segregation, 61
How Stella Got Her Groove Back (film), 23
Hughleys, The (TV series), 23
Hutchinson, Earl Ofari, 17–18, 223*n*5
Hutchinson (noncustodial father), 49

illegitimacy. *See* non-marital births
immigrants, 59
imprisonment, black rates of, 71–72
income: African American men, 62; African American women, 102; average wages, 231*n*1; childhood poverty and, 217; family members in workforce, 231*n*1; gap between blacks and whites, 62; impact on marriage and family, 217; nonsup-

portive work and pay, 215–16; racial
factors and, 56, 64
Institute for American Values, 32
intimate relationships: defined, 81;
paternal role in, 81–83, 192–97; termination of, 82
isolation, emotional, 156
I Spy (TV series), 23

James, Carter, 70
James, Daniel, 66–67
Jamie Foxx Show, The (TV series),
22–23
Jang, Michael, 20
jealousy, 193
Jeffersons, The (TV series), 23
Jencks, Christopher, 210
job stress, 184–85
job training, 213
Johnson, Cheryl, 23, 223*n*6
Johnson, Wesley, 56–57
Jones, Artie, 88, 89
Jones, Jacqueline, 43
Jones, Le Roi, 201, 232*n*1
Jones, Lewis, 45

Katzman, David, 59, 60, 75
Kelly, Calvin, 137
Kelly, J. B., 228*n*1 (pt. 2)
Killens, John Oliver, 15
King, Mark, 156
Klawitter, Marieka M., 218
Koegel, Paul, 231*n*3
Kornfein-Rose, Madeline, 155, 230*n*3
(ch. 7)
Kozol, Jonathan, 227*n*11
Kurdek, L., 76, 228*n*1 (pt. 2)

Ladner, John, 4

Lamb, Michael E., 232*n*3
Lang, Clarence, 71
Laseter, Robert L, 231*n*4
Law and Order (TV series), 23
Lee, Spike, 24
Lein, Laura, 103, 106, 123, 229*n*4
Lett, H. A., 60
Leung, M. L. A., 9
Levine, James, 231*n*1
Lichter, D. T., 229*n*2
Liebow, E., 133
Lincoln, Abraham, 42
Lincoln, C. Eric, 219
Little, Isaac, 85
live-away fathers: in "abroad" marriages, 37; aspirations of, 200–201;
attitude toward mothers, 142–43,
194–95; barriers to parenting,
206–208; bonding with children,
50–51; as breadwinners, 104, 146–50,
204–205, 217; as caregivers, 202–203;
child support provided by, 104; during Civil War, 41–43; current partnerships and paternal behavior,
192–97; dating relationships, 143;
defined, 11–13; economic limitations
of, 220; encouragement of participation by, 207; as familial form, 7;
following emancipation, 43–44;
generalizations, 25–26; ideal view of,
202; involvement in parenting, 49,
228*n*4; lack of commitment, 20;
legal bonds to children, 203–204; in
military services, 185–86; mothers'
expectations of, 205–209; multiple
sets of children, attention to, 191–92;
paternal behavior, 26–31, 50–51,
134–50; personal standards of
fatherhood, 131, 134, 135t; post-

emancipation, 48; prevalence of, 48–49; prisoners as, 71–72; relationships with mothers, 78–91, 228*n*2 (ch. 4); self-concept of, 31; in slavery, 33–34; social support for, 217; "sold away" separation from children, 38–39; support systems for, 156; time spent with children, 176, 179–83, 202–203; traditional fatherhood norms and, 77; transportation as parenting barrier, 186–87; as variant form of fatherhood, 211; vs. absent fathers, 151; work schedules and parenting, 179–83, 195–96. *See also* absent fathers; noncustodial fathers

liver cirrhosis, 73

Lutheran Child and Family Services, 219

Lutheran Child and Family Services Fathers' Center, 156

MacLeod, Jay, 68

macrosystem, familial, 7–8

Majors, Richard, 21–22

Malveaux, Julianne, 64

marriage: ceremonies, 46; child welfare in, 203; disconnected from childbearing, 124; economic factors in, 217; impact on children, 214; nuclear family structure, 18–19; options for, 91; rate among African Americans, 123; shortage of eligible men, 214; as social institution, 18–19

marriage in slavery: "abroad," 37; divorce and separation, 37–38; equality in, 35–36; following emancipation, 43–44, 46; legal sanction, lack of, 34; legitimization of, 46;

marital division of labor, 36; mother-child family unit, 39; nonlegal unions, 44–45; non-marital births in, 40; paternal role in, 40–41; slave owner attitudes toward, 34–35; "sold away" separation, 38–39; voluntary vs. involuntary, 35

Martin (TV series), 23

masculinity: fathers as role models, 144–46; redefinition of, 214–15

Masters, Fred, 100

Maxwell, Vernon, 25

McAdoo, John L., 14, 222*n*7

McDaniel, Antonio, 3

McLanahan, Sara, 32, 133, 151, 155, 225*n*9, 230*n*1 (ch. 7)

men, African American: attitude toward fathers accompanying children, 29–30; education, 63–69; family planning services, 212; imprisonment as rite of passage, 71; pessimism among, 67; prejudice toward, 27–28; service in Union army, 41–43; socioeconomic conditions, 2, 67; stereotypes, 1, 22–26; substance abuse, 72–73; unemployment among, 61

Men's Movement, 150, 214–15, 233*n*7

mental disorders, 196, 231*n*3

Merton, Robert K., 21–22

mesosystem, familial, 6–7

Mfume, Kweisi, 31

microsystem, familial, 6

military service, impact on parenting, 185–86

Million Man March, 21

Mills, C. Wright, 5

minimum wage employment, 216

Moore, Tilton, 66

Morehouse Conference on African American Fathers, 31
Morehouse Research Institute, 31
Mosley, Fred, 231*n*1
Mosley, Walter, 1, 221*n*1
Moss, Alfred A., Jr., 226*n*20
Moss, Gary, 159
mothers: attitudes toward marriage, 214; attitude toward sons as fathers, 94–98; bad, father's perception of, 90; as breadwinners, 214; child support actions, attitude toward, 122–23; encouragement of sons as parents, 207–208; expectations of fathers, 92–94, 106–115, 205–209; extended family support, 124–25; fatherhood defined by experience, 106–111; as gatekeepers, 76, 195, 207, 228*n*1 (pt. 2); good, father's perception of, 86; intentional pregnancies, 230*n*3 (ch. 7); involvement with other men, 89–90; irrelevance of men to, 124–25; living with fathers, 226*n*23; as primary caregivers, 77; relationships with fathers, 78–91, 228*n*1 (pt. 2); rights of single parents, 214–15; role of, 113–17; as study participants, 11, 222*n*8
motion pictures, stereotypes in, 22, 24
Moyers, Bill, 24
Moynihan, Daniel P., 4, 47, 221*n*5
Myers, Samuel L, Jr., 213–14

National Association for the Advancement of Colored People (NAACP), 31, 225*n*8
National Basketball Association (NBA), 24–25
National Center for Fathering, 216

National Coalition for the Homeless, 196, 231*n*3
National Institute of Child Health and Human Development (NICHD), 212
National Partnership to Reinvent Government, 212
Nettles, Michael, 64
New York Undercover (TV series), 23
NICHD Family and Child Well-being Research Network, 212
Nichols, C. H., 41
Nobles, Wade, 3
noncustodial fathers: ecological barrier to, 133–34; financial support of children, 217; following emancipation, 43–44; foundations in slavery, 33–34, 44–45; insufficient time spent with children, 105; participation in child rearing, 133; prevalence of, 49; redefinition of fatherhood, 211; relationships with mothers, 76; roles and functions of, 133, 135, 211; in slavery vs. present day, 232*n*4; socioeconomic factors, 53–57; spending time with children, 135–37; stereotypes concerning, 134. *See also* live-away fathers
non-marital births: acceptance in slavery, 40–41; acceptance post-emancipation, 48; among African Americans, 2, 32; expectation of fathers, 50; fatherless children, 49–50; increase in, 48; social support for, 50
nonresident fathers, defined, 11
Nord, C. W., 106
nuclear family, 18–19
NYPD Blue (TV series), 23

Orloff, Ann Shola, 215–16
Osofsky, Gilbert, 58
out-of-wedlock births. *See* non-marital
  births

parent-child bonding, 212
Park, Robert E., 4
Parke, Ross, 99, 228*n*4
passive disengagement, 159–61
persistent disengagement, 172–75
Personal Responsibility and Work
  Opportunity Reconciliation Act of
  1996 (PROWRA), 226*n*5
Pike, Evan, 68
Pinkney, Alphonso, 62, 227*n*6
Pittinsky, Todd, 231*n*1
Police Story (TV series), 23
Popenoe, David, 20
Porter, Glen, 139
poverty: children living in, 2, 221*n*2,
  229*n*1, 229*n*2; in fatherless homes,
  2–3; female-headed families, 102;
  geographical factors, 229*n*1; impact
  on absent fathers, 158; marriage
  impacts on, 104; paternal support
  and, 196; racial factors, 229*n*1; single-parent families in, 215; statistics,
  229*n*2; women in, 102
pregnancy, adolescent, 230*n*3 (ch. 7)
premarital sex, acceptance in slavery, 40
prisoners, 71–72, 162, 228*n*14
public assistance. *See* welfare benefits

quality of life, 67–69

racial discrimination: age factors in, 30;
  in employment, 55–56, 58–60;
  equality in principle vs. practice,
  227*n*6; family structure, impact on,

3–4; fathers accompanied by children, 28–29; in housing, 61; in
  media, 22–23; prevalence of, 201,
  223*n*1. *See also* stereotypes
Reconstruction: apprenticeship laws,
  47; black political role in, 46, 58;
  growth of caste system, 58
Reed, Ruth, 48, 49
relationship of parents: father's
  involvement with children and, 87;
  friendship, 83–88; impact on children, 101; intimate, 80–82; negotiation of, 92–94; respect for fathers
  and, 88
research subjects, recruitment of, 8–10,
  222*n*8, 230*n*3 (ch. 6)
resistant disengagement, 165–68
restraining orders, against fathers,
  167–68
Rhodes, Dante, 95–96
Rivera, F., 133
Robinson, Ira E., 205
role models, fathers as, 142–44
Roman, Randy, 173–74
Rose (slave), 35
Rowan, Paul, 137
Rowland, Leslie S., 42, 43
Rufus (slave), 35

Sanders, Tyler, 138
Sanford and Son (TV series), 22
Scanzoni, John, 4
Schiele, Jerome H., 127
schools, in low-income communities,
  227*n*11
Seltzer, J., 76, 192
Sentencing Project, 227*n*12
service occupations, 59
sex role, fathers' influence on, 144–46

shift work: impact on parenting, 180–81
Shinagawa, Larry H., 20
Singleton, John, 24
slavery: attitude of owners toward
marriage, 34–35; breeding of slaves,
45; child welfare in, 38; economic
basis of, 34; family structure,
impact on, 3; fatherhood in, 33–34,
39; marriage under (*see* marriage
in slavery); mother-child family
unit, 39; noncustodial fathers in,
232*n*4; out-of-wedlock births,
40–41; separation of children from
mother, 39
Smith, Harrison, 44
social environment, fatherhood and,
13–14, 75–76, 77
social mobility: criminal activities and,
71; education and, 65
social support: for never-married co-
parents, 217–20; for single-parent
families, 103, 107, 205
socioeconomic factors: affecting black
children, 211; in black advancement,
57, 62, 67, 227*n*6; in Depression, 60;
paternal attitude and, 21; in substance abuse, 228*n*14
spankings, 141
sperm father, 230*n*1 (ch. 7)
Stack, Carol, 105, 106, 207, 229*n*4
Stanley, Griffin, 164–65
Staples, Robert, 72–73, 228*n*14
stepfathers, children residing with, 48
Stephney, Bill, 25
stereotypes: absent fathers, 152; in
advertising, 23; African American,
22–26, 223*n*5, 223*n*6; in black popular journals, 23, 224*n*6; black
women, 223*n*4; Hispanics, 224*n*8;

ideal fathers, 17–20, 24; live-away
fathers, 26–32, 134; in media, 22–25.
See also racial discrimination
Sternhouse, Maggie, 45
Stier, H., 196
Stiles, Dimitri, 131–32
Stone, Abel, 92–93
Strauss, A.., 222*n*7
substance abuse: by absent fathers,
164–65; impact on fatherhood,
72–73; socioeconomic factors in,
228*n*14
Sudarkasa, Niara, 3
Sullivan, Halbert, 213
surname, in African American culture,
203–204, 210
system, socioeconomic, 67

Tate, Eldin, 85–86
Taylor, Ronald, 196
television: lack of diversity in, 31; nega-
tive image of black fathers, 24–25;
racial stereotypes in, 22–23, 223*n*6,
224*n*8
Television and Film Diversity Initiative,
225*n*8
Temporary Assistance to Needy Fami-
lies (TANF), 61, 107, 226*n*5
Terry, Raymond, 146
Thomas, Josephine, 113
Thompson, Richard, 171–72
Tienda, M., 196
Tilly, Chris, 102, 123, 229*n*1, 229*n*2
transportation, as parenting barrier,
186–87
Trimble, Dewey, 65
Tripp-Reissman, T., 19
Trotter, Joe William, Jr., 59
Turner, John, 42

Umberson, Deborah, 133, 230*n*3 (ch. 6)

unemployment: of African American men, 104; declining labor market participation, 231*n*4; increase among blacks, 158; paternal behavior and, 120–21, 188–90; rate of, 62

United Negro College Fund, 63, 64

Urban Fathering Initiative, Kansas City, Missouri, 216

U.S. Constitution, amendments to, 58

U.S. Department of Health and Human Services, 212

vagrancy laws, 47

visiting fathers, 12, 230*n*1 (ch. 7)

voting rights, 58

Waiting to Exhale (film), 23

Wallerstein, J., 228*n*1 (pt. 2)

Watson, Oliver, 69–70

Wayans Brothers, The (TV series), 23

Webster, Franklin, 64

welfare benefits: guidelines for, 216; limitations, 226*n*5; for single mothers, 103, 148–49, 205–206; vs. child support, 123

welfare programs, 226*n*5

Wells, Dwight, 168

White, Brian, 141, 145

White, Deborah, 37, 223*n*4

White, Joseph L., 21, 223*n*1

white supremacy, 46

Wilcox, Warren, 177–78

Williams, Christine, 133, 230*n*3 (ch. 6)

Williams, James, 83–84

Wilson, S. E., 19

Wilson, William Julius, 21–22, 61

Wilson, Woodrow, 22

women, African American: as breadwinners, 229*n*6; in poverty, 229*n*1, 229*n*4; stereotypes, 223*n*4

Woods, Junior, 72–73

work schedules: impact on parenting, 179–83